# A TIME TO DANCE

# A TIME TO DANCE

## American Country Dancing
## from Hornpipes to Hot Hash

## RICHARD NEVELL

*With drawings and wood engravings*
*by Randy Miller*

ST. MARTIN'S PRESS   NEW YORK

Library of Congress Catalog #77-76647
Manufactured in the United States of America

**Designed by Meri Shardin**


**Library of Congress Cataloging in Publication Data**

Nevell, Richard.
  A time to dance.

  Includes index.
  1. Country-dance—United States—History. 2. Square dancing. 3. United States—Social life and customs. I. Title.
GV1763.N48      793.3'1973      77-76647
ISBN 0-312-80522-5

PERMISSION CREDITS

New England Engraving by Randy Miller
    used by permission of William L. Bauhan Publishers, Dublin, N.H. from *More Than Land* by Heman Chase. Copyright © 1976.
"The Rumford" a dance by Dudley Laufman
    used by permission of Dudley Laufman. from *Okay, Let's Try A Contra, Men On The Right, Ladies On The Left, Up And Down The Hall* Copyright © 1973, Dudley Laufman.
Quote of Myles Horton on page 70
    from *Voices From The Mountains* by Guy and Candie Carawan, Alfred Knopf, New York © 1976 used by permission.
"Cross Country" a poem by Dorothy Stott Shaw
    from *The Selected Poems of Dorothy Stott Shaw* Copyright © Dorothy Scott Shaw. Used by permission.
"The Music Teacher" a poem by Billy Edd Wheeler
    from *Song of a Woods Colt* by Billy Edd Wheeler Droke House, Anderson, S.C. 1969. Used by permission.
Interviews in New England
    from *Country Corners* a film by Robert Fiore and Richard Nevell. Used by permission of Robert Fiore.
"Canadian Breakdown" a contra dance by Ralph Page
    used by permission of Ralph Page, Keene, N.H.
"Rip 'n Snort" and "Just Because" Two Square Dances
    from *The Basic Program of American Square Dancing* by The Sets In Order American Square Dance Society. Copyright © 1969, Los Angeles. Used by Permission.
Engravings "Irish Dancers" and "The Fiddler" by Randy Miller
    used by permission of R. Miller and J. Perron. From *Irish Traditional Fiddle Music Volumes I–III*, Copyright © 1974, 1975 Miller & Perron, Alstead, New Hampshire

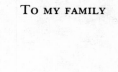

# Acknowledgments

Thanks to all these people who somehow contributed to this book: with friendship, words, food, beds, my nearly faultless Cortina, and endless inspiration. Special thanks to Loyce Stracener and Somer Hooker of Knoxville, Tennessee; Bob Fiore of Dublin, New Hampshire; Bob Osgood of Los Angeles, California; and my editor Paul De Angelis, without whom a large portion of this book would make little sense.

Dr. Otto Albrecht; The Appalshop people; Tom and Tootie Banks; John and Linda Bradford and family; Mary Ann Brosnan; Ethel Capps; Guy and Candie Carawan; "Calico & Boots" of Boulder, Colorado; Elizabeth and Sarah Cohn; The Colorado Historical Society; The Council of the Southern Mountains Bookstore; Cheshire Foreign Auto, Inc.; Bob and Kay Davis; Daron Douglas; Brad and Jane Donovan; Wilma Dykeman; Joe Dominick; Bill Eirich; Joe and Barbara Fadler; Hilary Feldstein; Buck, Nina and Tony Finney; Ralph and Sadie Ford; Kay Gilbert; Michael and Dixie Gurian; Doris Haddock; Frank and Carolyn Hamilton; John and Aleka Hankin; Sister Mary Hanssens and the Handmaids of the Sacred Heart of Jesus; Jane Henderson; Myles Horton; Ray and Ida Hull and The Ed Larkin Dancers; R.A. Jensen; Floyd and Aileen King and The Southern Appalachian Cloggers; Ken and Sharon Kernen; Jon, Nancy, Kaki and Molly Kinne; The Knoxville Country Dancers; Jody Kreider; Jill Lawler; Dudley Laufman; The Library Company of Philadelphia; Susan McKenna; Teri McLuhan; Bob McQuillen; Becky McQuillen; Trisha Minnemeyer; Rick Monahon; Rodney Miller; New York Public Library; Ray Orme; Ralph Page; John and Lyn Parker; Jack Perron; Barbara Piscitelli; Ralph Pierce and The Tennessee Mountain Cloggers; Martha Raymond and Lida Leino of Bookings Travel who tried to keep me off the DC-10's; Ruth Rising; "Rip 'n Snort"; Gertrude Larkin Roberts; Jean Schilling; Margaret Schweigert; Ken Segal; Dorothy Stott Shaw; Erika Shriner; Tina Staller; Bronson and Mary Shonk; Jon Sundell; Andy, Jane and Tracy Smith; Rose Smythe; Cami and Bill Tillson; Russ Thomas; Newton F. Tolman; Barry and Karen Tolman; Harvey Tolman; The University of Tennessee Special Collections Library; Tom Valovic; Tom Vinetz; The Vermont Historical Museum; Varney Watson; Jackie Ward; Walt Williams; Billy Edd Wheeler; Wayne and Mary Young . . . and to all the dancers, callers, and musicians too numerous to name, but all equally important, I am grateful to be one of you.

"To everything there is a season."

# CONTENTS

# INTRODUCTION

The first time I ever square danced was in gym class my first year in elementary school. I hated it. It was the only time you had to do anything with girls—girls with clammy hands; girls you always got into fights with on the playground; girls with unknown but deadly diseases transmittable only through gym class . . . and the worst girl was the teacher. She always picked someone to dance with to show the rest of us how to do it. The victim was forced to get up in front of all his fellow Girl Detesters and totally humiliate himself by swinging with the teacher, actually touching both hands at once. It was pure torture.

Dancing school came later but wasn't much better. Our teacher Miss Hallowell, one of the original Arthur Murray graduates and another ruthless embarrasser of boys, was determined to make ballroom wonders out of us. She played Guy Lombardo's rendition of Viennese Waltz hits of the Gay Nineties and kept time with a little metal cricket, a toy we often used to drive the teachers crazy in Sunday school. She used it to keep us in line, to call our attention, and just to remind us she was there.

No Man's Land was the middle of the dance floor. Flanked by the girls on one side of the room, the boys blended into the concrete wall on the other side, some of them camouflaged with clothes the color of the wall, hoping to remain unseen throughout the dance. Every week a different set of "volunteer" parents were the referees. Following the instructional part of the evening, there were usually some free choice dances, the most dreaded being the Ladies' Choice. Like a wave of wild cutthroats the girls moved across the basketball floor, trampling the chaperones, trampling Miss Hallowell, and causing many a comrade to faint with fear. Meanwhile my best friend Fossum and I cleverly beat a hasty retreat to the boys' room.

I suppose the first dancing I really enjoyed was down in Lynne Youngblood's basement. Lynne Youngblood was a knockout at twelve, out of my league unfortunately (she was too tall), and she had parents who had foolishly remodeled their damp old basement into a play room complete with ping pong, TV, even a refrigerator for Cokes and other soft drinks. But they were asking for trouble when, in addition to all the other threats, they added a big soft couch. The couch was like a shrine. Any boy who could talk a girl into sitting with him on that couch was considered nothing less than holy. The preliminary to the couch was a dance known as the Clutch. It started out simply cheek to cheek like what we saw on American Bandstand and later developed into the full embrace they dared not do on TV. There were almost never any lights on in the Youngbloods' basement. The parties would start with a few dim lights that were gradually extinguished one by one. A quiet hush mixed with giggles fell over us whenever the last light went out.

Later I danced with island girls in Maine in the summer, and throughout school days before college there were tea dances, pool parties, sock hops, and debutante balls. The debutante balls brought out the worst in me. The musicians were always third-rate Lester Lanin imitators trying to play Elvis Presley songs along with the usual fox trots and waltzes. The result was that nobody ever really danced at these dances. Boys only went to meet girls or to see who could wear the least formal clothes without getting thrown out: some of us wore blue jeans with shiny electrical tape down the side to pass as tuxedo trousers. But the dancing wasn't any more enjoyable than at dancing school. Except during the slow dances, the boys were mainly interested in acting cool, and so the girls ended up doing the Lindy with each other most of the time.

I wouldn't say I grew up hating dancing, but I would say that I grew up not really knowing what it is to dance because dancing was not something that boys did, at least not seriously. We never danced purely for the enjoyment of dancing but for some ulterior motive: it was a chore you had to perform if you wanted to hold a girl up close. Even so, we were brought up in such mortal terror of girls that the encounter was always tense. Dancing was a fearful part of growing up.

In college I heard about the Folk Dance Club and went to dance with Greeks at a picnic once. Everyone got drunk on Metaxa and we did a circle dance as in *Zorba the Greek,* where everybody holds the people on either side on their feet until the whole group falls down and never gets up.

After college I moved from Boston to New Hampshire and went to my first contra dance in Francestown.

Something about the Francestown hall is just right for a contra dance: maybe it's the spirit that still lingers in the hall, the memory of the feisty townspeople who in 1881 marched across the common and seized the hall from the dour Congregational Society who had taken it over. Or else it's simply the way the hall's blue dome looks on a sunny day or an icy night. I can't really pin it down, but when I went to Francestown for the first time, I knew something about the hall impressed me.

I had only been in New Hampshire for a few months, and this was one of the few trips I had taken out into the society that year, 1969. I remember thinking what a cornball scene it was going to be. I hadn't been to a square dance since grammar school. A friend had told me: "Yeah, but these are different," and I was prepared for almost anything.

The first thing I noticed when I entered the town hall in Francestown was the heterogeneity of the group. There were predictable kinds of people there: neatly dressed middle-aged couples who had been going to these dances all their lives, a few older folks, some teen-agers from town doing more sitting around than dancing. Then there were the ones who surprised me: the people who had left the city before me and gone to the country, "hip" people I had watched desert the Boston neighborhood I lived in. I remember that in Boston people talked about "so and so" who was living in a commune in Vermont—well, not all of these urban emigrants had gone to Vermont. A lot of them had made it only as far as New Hampshire, and as I looked across the floor of dancers in Francestown, I realized that many of them had discovered an old social function of New England: the contra dance.

Dudley Laufman was calling the dance that night in Francestown. He had been there long before the new people moved into the area; Dudley had been calling dances for years, ever since Ralph Page more or less quit. When droves of newcomers started coming to the dances, Dudley could have shut them out, not literally, but by making them feel unwelcome. He didn't. Instead he welcomed them, and conversely they welcomed the dance, and Dudley, and the musicians. To me the most amazing thing about this acceptance was that so many in the "counter-culture" held an anarchistic belief in freedom of the individual, especially the freedom of expression through the arts: yet here they were, obviously enjoying a dance which was clearly structured, almost regimental, and totally under the control of one person who told them what to do!

So here was my first impression of the contra dance—it had become a haven for young people like me who had left the city for a country life. Mistakenly I believed that the "new" contra dancers had given themselves totally to the dance, accepting the pure form. I later found that this was not true. In fact they were bringing something of their own to the contra dance, first a style that derived from their previous dancing experience in rock and roll, and later a desire to work within the old medium, to create new dances within the structure of the traditional dances. These dances, I later discovered, had historical roots going back hundreds of years. What I was seeing that night in Francestown was part of a chapter in the cyclical history of country dancing.

As for the dancing itself, my feelings were mixed: on one hand I had an irresistible desire to get involved; but I got a cold sweating fear when I thought someone might ask me to get out there on the floor.

Becky McQuillen took care of that. She paid no heed to my protests and excuses and dragged me out on the floor where I stood defenseless, flattered but scared. I don't remember what the dance was, but I remember when it was over I was still defenseless but also excited, exhausted, and dizzy. And I knew that during the process of that evening I shed an armor, a protective shield that had sheltered me from dancing for many years. The armor consisted primarily of a misinterpretation and miscalculation of what my body could do and enjoy. I became a dancer that night: for the moment unconcerned about losing some silly masculine image; unafraid of the innocent touching and communication built into country dancing. I welcomed the openness of the room, the eye-contact with dancers and the orchestra; people moving gracefully in a manner I had thought I could only see in the ballet; and music as interesting and exciting as anything I had ever heard. Best of all I had the secure feeling that I was learning something totally new but that I had really known all my life.

Six years after my initial experiences with contra dancing I met and began working with Bob Fiore, a filmmaker who had decided to make a documentary film about the contra dance in New England. After a year of work we finished a film called "Country Corners." In the process of its production I learned a great deal about filmmaking but even more so about dancing, not just contra dancing, but country dancing in general. What I learned first was that there was little available information about the historical and sociological aspects of the American country dance. There were plenty of dance manuals written by callers and dancing masters but little about the dancers, especially rural dancers, who relied on dancing for recreation and community contact. Present-day dancers often express a tremendous respect for the heritage and tradition of country dancing, yet few are able to tell very much about where it came from or who had maintained the tradition. In "Country Corners" we explored briefly the evolution of this traditional folk art in New England, but while we were making the film, we realized that the story of contra dancing in New England today is only a part of a story that includes all of America and many forms of country dancing.

In my research for this book, I immediately discovered that there was an enormous amount of country dancing going on in the United States: it seemed that every little community had its own favored dance, some of them old ritual dances done in costume and some just old social dances everybody had learned from their ancestors. Since I was particularly interested in the social kind of country dancing, I first decided to write about communities where country dancing is part of the normal recreational life of the general public. I was also particularly interested in the communities where the dancing had been going on for a long time, although I quickly discovered this to be a relative factor since "old" country dancing in New England and Los Angeles means two different kinds of dancing altogether. Yet the country dancing in these two parts of

America, and indeed other parts of this country, are closely tied; both in the historical, choreographic sense, and in the vaguer, but equally important spiritual sense. Beneath the similarities in the varieties of country dancing in America, there lies a bondage, the kind of unspoken understanding between people that comes only from having shared a mutual experience. Those who have not shared the experience are not bonded to those who have. They are not "in." They are not dancers.

My method of choosing communities to write about was as deliberate as making appointments all the way across the country in California and as chancy as knocking on doors and hanging around general stores in Tennessee. I traveled from dance halls to the homes of dancers from New England to California and into the South. The communities I ended up writing about are the ones where I could dance, play music, and feel at home with the people. When I didn't feel that bondage, that comfort, I moved on. But it shouldn't be assumed that these are the only places where people dance and have a good time. Wherever I traveled someone would come up to me and say: "You ought to go down to such and such a town—I hear they've got a great fiddler at the dance there!" There are many places I couldn't get to at the time, for many reasons, but when I start worrying about the places I missed I remember the words of a ninety-four-year-old dancer in North Carolina who told me: "I can't remember a lot of things now. I forget people's names. . . I'm gettin' where I can't talk plain, I can't see good, can't hear good, and I ain't no good; but I will get up and dance with anybody!"

Those words are the best expression of the spirit of country dancing I have ever heard, and I believe they are words anyone, dancers and nondancers alike, can understand. While this book includes many varied elements related to country dancing—historical, anecdotal and instructional material—to me the heart of the book lies in the words of dancers like ninety-four-year-old Rose Smythe; and it is my hope that people who read their words, even the nondancers, will find, like Rose, a time to dance.

# I

# HISTORY

dance was a success, the school would continue another week or so, and Natalie McClure announced for the third time that we had better get the hell out so she could go home. We walked through the steam-filled entrance hall out into the night. The rain had stopped. The departing dancers rolled down their windows shouting good-night as they drove off down the road.

Heading toward Dublin, I passed Child's Bog and eventually come into Harrisville, a brick village with a library that stands half in the upper pond. As I came around a corner, my headlights swept over someone's yard and I caught a glimpse of a garden with long rows of tomatoes. Oh God, I thought, not this again. My mind was overtaken by dancers and tomato plants, and I realized that this little fantasy might be turning into an obsession. Collecting myself, I decided that maybe it wasn't such a farflung idea after all, but at the same time decided to keep it to myself for the time being.

Unfortunately by the time I got to Barbara Piscitelli's house in Dublin, where I often stop for hot chocolate or wine after a dance, I could barely contain myself. I confessed that I had experienced a rather odd hallucination at the dance. "You're crazy Dick Nevell," said Barbara, sipping her wine and giggling, "but who's to say you're wrong?"

With that little bit of encouragement, my mind eased, and I decided to consult a friend of mine who's a dance therapist. Dance therapists, she said, have investigated the sources of human choreography, examining the earliest pictorial representations of dancers on the walls of prehistoric caves, and even the movements of primates who hold hands and circle around like dancing children. Knowing how certain movements indicate individual's psyche, or state of mind, dance therapists can apply a treatment program to help people overcome neurotic tendencies. She said if I wanted to learn more about the history of choreography, I should start out by reading *The World History of the Dance* by Curt Sachs.

In his book Sachs describes many dances of ancient tribes, showing how the choreography of these dances relates to other primitive peoples' dances around the world and also how these ancient dance patterns turn up in many of our modern folk dances today. He describes one Indo-Chinese tribe, the Naga, who dance as follows: " . . . their counter dances have six turns, exactly like the European double column dances: (1) crossing of the two columns (2) turning backwards (3) chain (4) snake line (5) large circle (6) two small circles and return to the original lines. This is the arrangement of a Spanish figure dance of the 17th century or of an English Country dance."[1] Well, I thought, this was really something. Still, it did not give me any rationale for my Nelson hallucination where I had seen long rows of dancers turn into long rows of tomato plants. Sachs had shown me that the contra dance, which I knew was born out of the English country dance, had roots in some ancient choreography, but he hadn't shown me why those primitive people chose those formations in the first place. I read on. Soon I found him saying this: ". . . The dance in which the men form one row, the women the other and dance opposite each other in a form of love play, is widely diffused and may be confidently assigned to a Protoneolithic culture level."[2] The Protoneolithic culture level, he says, ". . . is characterized by cultivation of the soil with picks, rectangular houses . . . matriarchy, skull cults, head hunting, cannabalism, fetishism and magic. As with the early planters the tendency in art is towards the geometric and ornamental: curves, spirals, and double spirals are preferred. To the old legacy of the dance is added the new motif of the head hunter and scalp dance. . . . Another addition is the arrangement of a line of men and a line of women opposite each other. The high leaping dances, which were to help the growth of the seed, seem also to belong here."[3] Now I was getting somewhere. If Sachs were right, there was reason to believe a connection existed between the way people danced and the way crops are planted, usually in rows or sometimes in circles. After all, dancers had to get their patterns somewhere, and why not from the most important geometric form in their community: the source of their food. But the evidence still seemed circumstantial to me, and I hoped to find a more specific example of an early dance of civilized, Anglo-Saxon history that would make all this information more pertinent to the contra dancing in New Hampshire.

The immediate forerunner of the contra dance as we know it was called Morris dancing; a ceremonial activity performed by men. Sachs offers this brief description of the Morris dance: "The classical form is still two rows of dancers of three dancers each. With innumerable variations these rows move to and fro. The circle is rarely used. Yet is is undoubtedly the older form, not only because line dancing in themselves are later, but because it still bears obvious traces of the old fertility ritual. One of the ring dances is called Bean Setting and requires rhythmical stamping and raising of the dance stick: the dibber or planting stick makes the holes in the ground to receive the seed."[4] And so it seemed to me, finally, that there was some validity in what I had originally thought was merely a fanciful image. Ritual dances were performed to dramatize and help insure the process of growing food that sustained life. I thought there must have been many dances similar to this that later became the contra dances of early England and eventually New England and America. Somewhere along the way these dances became more of a social function as people became more sophisticated and turned to nonpagan religion. But the basic patterns of our modern contra dances seemed to have definitely evolved from these very early ceremonial forms which were inspired and modeled after the dances of ancient people.

# EARLY DANCERS / FORMS

Early dancers in primitive tribes created their choreographic patterns based primarily on natural design. The two basic forms of nature are the circle, taken from the sun and the moon, and the column, or row, taken from primitive man's perception of the geometry in the growth of trees, mountain ranges, and their own crops of corn and other plants.

*Courtesy Dartmouth College Library.*

Hopi Indians "The Snake and Antelope Dance" by Edward S. Curtis

*Courtesy of the British Museum.*

An American Indian Circle dance. Drawing by John White in 1585.

This drawing by the English explorer depicts ". . . a solemne feaste, the green corn ritual." White's friend tells that the Indians danced around postes "carved with heads like to the faces of Nonnes covered with their vayles."
Description by Thomas Harriot, from *America,* part 1, 1590: *A briefe and true report of the new found land of Virginia*

# MORRIS DANCE

*Photograph by Nevell.*
The Phoenix Morris Minors led by Dudley Laufman perform a circle dance at the Fox Hollow Festival, 1976.

The history of country dancing is also the history of movements: the figures or components that make up each dance and the music that generally accompanies the dances. The basic formations that have dominated country dancing throughout history have been the circle, the double column (later known as longways, contra dance, string dances, or reels), and the square (later known as the quadrille). These geometric formations usually are the way we start and end each dance.

In the progress of the dance we perform certain *figures,* or movements, with our bodies, sometimes by ourselves but usually with a partner or a group of other dancers. Most figures in country and folk dances are simple and universally known but often reflect some local style or embellishment found nowhere else. For example, the swing is the best-known country-dance figure and is performed in many different ways, usually depending upon where you live or where you come from. I remember the first time I danced with someone in Denver, Colorado, and my partner, who didn't have any idea where I was from, said when we started to swing: "Oh, you must be from New England! You swing just like a New Englander!"

Different formations have been preferred by different communities. The contra dance is most popular and identified with New England, while the Big Circle dance is generally found most frequently in the southern highlands of Appalachia. And the square dance eventually found its home in the West, although it is now danced all over the United States and the world.

# THE BASIC FORMS OF THE COUNTRY DANCE

As we have seen, the choreography of country dancing has not changed very much since primitive tribesmen danced in circles and lines. These are still the basic forms used in country dancing in America today. The most modern of the three forms is the square, derived from the circle and the column dances, first introduced into America by French dancing masters in the late eighteenth century. Then it was known as the "quadrille," but as it became part of mainstream American country dancing, it became known as the "square" dance.

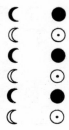

The Contra Dance

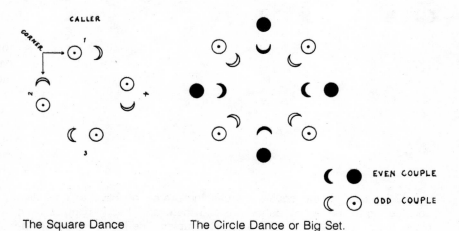

The Square Dance        The Circle Dance or Big Set.

*contra dances* In the contra dance some couples are active while others are inactive. This can occur in four different ways (see diagram below). In all contra dances the active couples progress toward the bottom of the set where they become inactive, and the inactive couples progress in the opposite fashion. The time it takes a couple to progress one place coincides with the progression of the tune, usually thirty-two measures long. The number of progressions it takes to get to the bottom of the set depends on how many couples there are in the set and what type of dance it is.

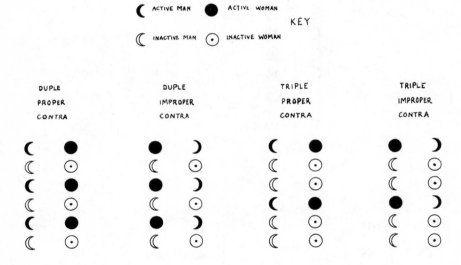

*square dances* In the square dances there are no active and inactive couples, as in the contra dance. Instead there are "head" couples (with backs to or facing the caller) and "side" couples. The New England quadrille is numbered differently than the Western square however.

QUADRILLE                                    SQUARE

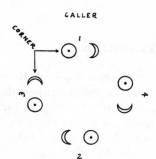
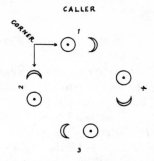

Square Dance / New England Style      Square Dance / Western Style

***the circle dances*** In the Big Circle or Big Set there is an active and an inactive couple who face each other in groups of four around the hall. Usually the couples are called, respectively, "odd" and "even" instead of active or inactive. Sometimes the basic form is changed to accommodate two couples facing two couples around the hall; and even more seldom, groups of three facing each other around the hall, two men and one woman or two women and one man.

CIRCLE

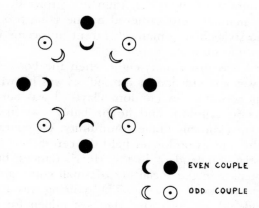

*Diagrams by Randy Miller.*

The Big Circle is progressive in the same way as the contra dance is progressive and also usually depends on the thirty-two measure tune for its structure. In fact the Big Circle formation is really identical to a contra dance, except that it has no beginning and no end.

## The English Tradition

Thirty years after the Pilgrims landed at Plymouth Rock in 1620, a man in the home country of England took an action that changed the course of country dancing forever. Barely two years after starting his business as a London bookseller John Playford, known to his friends as "Honest John," decided to publish a rather modest book with a long title: *The English Dancing Master, or Plaine and Easie Rules for the Dancing of Country Dances, with the Tune to Each Dance*. It was the first time that community dances, which were usually learned by being danced or watched, had been printed in a manual. The book contained 104 dances, all of them "country dances" such as rounds, squares, longs for four, and others. It contained the tunes for each dance and a very brief explanation of what figures to use for each dance but nothing actually describing the individual figures. In fact if you analyze the book, you can see that often different terminology is used for the same figure in different dances, indicating that Playford and his assistants who collected the dances were not accustomed to describing movements in any sort of uniform fashion.

The book also contained traditional tunes for the "treble violin," the same instrument known as a fiddle today and the lead instrument for country dances of all types, then and now. Presumably the tunes in Playford's manual were gathered by the same process as the dances and reflect the styles of the many different musicians who controlled dances in various communities.

Playford was just twenty-eight when the book was published. Apparently he was an avid dancer himself, as was his wife who taught dancing near their bookstore in London. Playford was born in Norwich, a small town outside London, and he probably was first exposed to the old country dances in his home community. Of course, by the seventeenth century the dances no longer held the ceremonial importance they did in pre-Christian England or in the Morris dances, but they still played an important part in the social life of small communities, where few other entertainments were available. The dancing was a wholesome activity for young and old and provided the best milieu for courtship and a good place for social visiting.

Besides being a publisher, Playford was a competent musician and wrote instruction books for many of the most popular instruments of the day: the cittern, the viol, and the flageolet, an instrument related to the penny whistle and fife, both of which are used widely in country-dance music today.

# TWO PAGES FROM JOHN PLAYFORD'S
## *THE ENGLISH DANCING MASTER*

Publisher John Playford's *The Dancing Master* was the first guidebook for dancing masters and country dancers. Published in 1650, it went through seventeen editions. Each edition expanded tremendously its repertoire of dances.

*Courtesy of the Dance Away Library.*

Frontispiece from *The Dancing Master.*

*Courtesy of the Dance Away Library.*

The "Roger of Coverly" a longways dance which later became known as "The Virginia Reel".

Publisher John Playford.
*Courtesy of the Dance Away Library.*

Playford's book was a tremendous success. It was published in seventeen successive editions over a period of seventy-eight years. It went through many revisions as each edition came out, and the book grew so that by the last edition, published over a seven-year period from 1721–1728, it contained 918 dances. It was a true best seller: probably few publishers have been as fortunate as Playford with their very first book. *The Dancing Master* brought income to the Playford family for the rest of his life and the lives of his sons, who took over the business after their father's death. The dancing public loved the dances in the book, and every dancing teacher in England and across the European continent had a copy and taught these lovely rustic dances to their students, who felt the need to be up on the latest fashionable dances of their times.

Needless to say Playford's book did more than introduce country dancing to the urban public. It changed the very nature of the country dance, by turning it into a commodity. For the first time in history this simple part of rural English folk life became salable.

As a result, the dances themselves were changed. As Playford and his assistants who produced *The Dancing Master* collected dances from the countryside or from dancing teachers already familiar with them, they often recorded different names for the same movement or figure. Cecil Sharp, the twentieth century English folklorist and best-known Playford analyst, points out that when a dance was performed in the country the person in charge, usually the fiddler, simply picked a tune he liked and then chose figures arbitrarily to go along with the tune—it was rare that

# EARLY COUNTRY DANCE MUSIC

Before the professionalization of country dancing, the local fiddler was more or less in charge of the recreational dancing. He knew the traditional tunes and so he naturally was the center of attention. Most early country dances were not standardized until Playford published them, except for the ceremonial dances which everybody knew. For general recreational dances, the fiddler might arbitrarily choose figures, or the dancers might pick them instinctively. Probably some tunes acquired figures that went with them fairly regularly in local areas, and this may have helped Playford and his assistants collect the dances.

"Itinerant Musicians" a painting by John Zoffany (English 1733-1810).

a particular collection of figures would become stereotyped and done the same way more than once. Unlike the dances, the tunes had convenient names and were played more or less uniformly from fiddler to fiddler. So that when Playford and his assistants put a specific dance together with a tune that was commonly played, the dances acquired names. (Of course, some dances were of old ceremonial origin and had been danced somewhat uniformly from generation to generation. An example is the old weaving dance which became "Sir Roger de Coverlay" and later in America "The Virginia Reel.") And so the first 104 country dances emerged with two new characteristics: uniformity and marketability. The die was cast for a new phase in the evolution of country dances.

Cecil Sharp has given us a very useful perspective on the effects of *The Dancing Master*. He explains that the country dance that previously was found only on village greens and in farmhouses slowly invaded the drawing rooms of the wealthy and challenged the popularity of the fancy dances of the day like the minuet, the gavotte, and the courante. At first, he says, this was not injurious to the country dances because they were merely viewed as a pleasant alternative to the more formal dances of polite society. However, eventually the following effect took place: ". . . as time went on it [the country dance] was challenged on its own merits . . . and subjected to an enervating influence which . . . ultimately led to its corruption . . . the decline hastened, as was inevitable, as it fell into the hands of the professional dancing master."[5] In Sharp's view, the dancing master was partly guilty of corrupting the dance. He points out that the success of Playford's *The Dancing Master* spurred the emergence of a whole series of dance manuals that clearly catered to polite society: the customers of the dancing masters.

Sharp was not the first dance scholar to scold the dancing masters who profited from the tremendous popularity of the country dances. In the very early nineteenth century, Thomas Wilson, himself a dancing master from London, included in his monumental *Analysis of Country Dancing* a scathing attack on Playford and his successive imitators.

Wilson claims to have resuced the "Old Figures from oblivion . . ." and ". . . the ridiculous antics . . . introduced by foolish persons, having no respect for the systematical principles of the Dance." Pointing his finger at the author of a book entitled *The Complete Country Dancing Master*—probably Playford—Wilson expresses his dismay at the inclusion of figures like "put hats over your eyes" and "cast up and kiss your partner," which he believed had destroyed the "pleasing sociability, beauty, and effect, which the original systematical construction of it no doubt was every way calculated to produce."[6] Wilson's book was designed to teach a system by which anyone could compose any number of figures to go with any given tune, a challenging and ambitious undertaking. The book was illustrated

# THOMAS WILSON'S
## *ANALYSIS OF COUNTRY DANCING*

In addition to mounting a scathing attack on the degraders of the country dance—the professional dancing masters of the late eighteenth century—Thomas Wilson believed he had devised a methodology for composing country dances in a natural and pleasing fashion. Here are two pages from Wilson's book.

Frontispiece from Wilson's *Companion to the Ballroom*. This engraving shows many interesting facets of early 19th century country dance. Note the different forms: the contra, circle and couple dances, as well as the assortment of intruments; fiddles, flutes, bagpipes, a harp and a French horn.

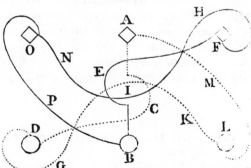

*Swing corners.*
The whole of the Figures as performed by the Lady and Gentleman.
FIG. VII.

*Photographs courtesy of the Dance Away Library.*

Thomas Wilson's diagram of the figure "Swing Corners", which later became "Country Corners" or "Contra Corners" in New England.

with beautiful, very carefully executed diagrams showing what he believed to be the basic movements of country dancing.

During the evolutionary process begun by the publication of dance manuals, many of the old dance forms, especially the rounds and the squares, fell out of use, while the longways—"for as many as will"—emerged as the most popular dance in England and even in Europe. We can see how this process took place by examining the successive editions of *The Dancing Master*. The first edition, published in 1650, contained only about thirty-five longways-type dances out of the 104 included in the book, but by the seventh edition, issued about 1700, more than half of the 208 dances were of this type. Finally the last edition came out in 1721–1728 and contained 918 dances in three volumes, of which 904 were longways dances.

It is clear why the longways dance, which later became the contra dance in New England, was the perfect dance of the time. During the eighteenth century the demand for country dancing rose astronomically, and the dancing masters logically had to cater to the greatest number of dancers they could. The dancers were taught the dances in schools so they could carry on without further instruction when the dancing master announced the name of the dance. And making the dances for "as many as will" allowed the dancing masters to fit in as many people as possible into each dance.

It was not only the dances that evolved. The commercialization also changed the people. According to Sharp: "Unhappily the injurious effects of its excursion into the drawing rooms of the upper classes reacted, to some extent, upon the dances in the country villages."[7]

John Playford and the other dancing masters of the seventeenth and eighteenth century probably had no idea of the side effects of publishing and standardizing the dances. Mass communication in the form of the printed book gained tremendous popularity for dancing as it got into the hands of the general public, but this expedient access also led the dances to become conventionalized, to lose their original spontaneity and characteristic joy and simplicity. Ironically, technology had at the same time both preserved and destroyed something meaningful to a community. It was not the first time this would happen in England and America.

### Colonial Dancers and Preachers

The first American settlers who arrived from Europe were not exactly the dancing types. Yet the stereotype of the Puritan as one who would sooner die than enjoy himself is unfair. The Puritans were not unified in their opposition to activities which, besides being acceptable in the eyes of God, were also pleasurable. According to Percy Scholes, historians have too often parroted anti-Puritan tracts of the seventeenth century as if they were wholly factual. Scholes explains that the Puritans, at least some of them, shared the attitudes of their favorite authors like Spenser, Milton, and the even stricter Bunyan in whose works "all good people dance, from the angels down." Even Oliver Cromwell, who was a famous lover of music, introduced "mixt dancing" at the wedding of his daughter Frances on November 11, 1657, and historians agree that they doubtlessly performed dances from Playford's book.

The Pilgrims of Plymouth plantation were probably too busy to entertain themselves with dancing and spent most of their time digging in for a winter in New England, but because they did not find time to dance does not mean that they were uniformly opposed to it.

As the New England colonies grew during the years following the landing at Plymouth Rock, the new settlers were becoming a more diverse group than the original Pilgrims, and some of these new settlers occasionally held dances in their communities. Barely thirty years after the colonies were first occupied by the English, Playford issued the first edition of *The Dancing Master*. It was published during Puritan rule in England.

Of course, not all Puritans were in favor of dancing. A Puritan writer, William Prynne, wrote a rather negative view of dancing. He said: "Dancing for the most part is attended with many amorous smiles, wanton compliments, unchaste kisses, scurrilous songs and sonnets, effeminate music, lust provoking attire, ridiculous love pranks, all of which savor only of sensuality, of raging fleshly lusts! Therefore it is wholly to be abandoned of all good Christians. Dancing serves no necessary use! No profitable laudable or pious end at all. . . . The way to heaven is too steep, too narrow for men to dance and keep revel rout. No way is large or smooth enough for capering roisters, for skipping, jumping, dancing dames but that broad, beaten pleasant road that leads to Hell. The Gate of Heaven is too narrow for whole rounds, whole troops of dancers to march in together!"[8]

It is impossible to know how most Christian Americans stood on the question of dancing. Clergymen were as divided on the issue as their parishioners. John Cotton of Boston approved of dancing, even that which involved mixed sexes, while the Mathers, Increase and Cotton, preferred to keep the dances unmixed. Controversies arose in Boston over dancing, especially when it occurred on the Sabbath. The most famous of these cases involved the confrontation among Judge Samuel Sewall and a local clergyman, Increase Mather, and a vagabond dancing master named Francis Stepney. On Monday, November 9, 1685, Judge

Sewall made the following entry in his diary: ". . . the Ministers of this town come to the Court and complain against a Dancing Master who seeks to set up here and hath mixt dances, and his time of Meeting is Lecture Day; and 'tis reported he should say that by one Play he could teach more Divinity than Mr. Willard or the Old Testament. Mr. Moodey said 'twas not a time for N.E. to dance. Mr. Mather struck at the Root, speaking against mixt Dances."[9]

Stepney probably stepped out of bounds for almost anyone in Puritan Boston when he boasted his dancing could do more good than attending church on a Sunday, and he paid for his arrogance when on December 17 Sewall ordered Stepney to end his career as a dancing master in Boston or face contempt charges. Two months after the ordeal with Stepney, Increase Mather mounted his attack on dancing in the Boston community, issuing his famous "Arrow against Profane and Promiscuous Dancing" for the second time, apparently as a direct result of the Step-

---

## EXCERPTS FROM *THE MAYPOLE OF MERRYMOUNT* BY NATHANIEL HAWTHORNE

The following passage demonstrates the kind of fictional accounts, mistaken for history, which portray the early Puritans as being totally against dancing and music, which they were not.

First Hawthorne describes the people of Merrymount as they are invoked by the "priest" of the maypole ceremony:

"Up with your nimble spirits, ye morrice dancers, green men, and glee maidens, bears, wolves, and horned gentlemen! Come, a Chorus now, rich with the old mirth of Merry England, and the wilder glee of youthful pair what life is made of, and how airily they should go through it! All ye that love the Maypole, lend your voices to the nuptial song of the Lord and Lady of the May!"

Then some Puritans break up the ceremony:

"Unfortunately, there were men in the new world of a sterner faith than these Maypole worshippers. Not far from Merry Mount was a settlement of Puritans, most dismal wretches, who said their prayers before daylight, and then wrought in the forest or the cornfield till evening made it prayer time again. Their weapons were always at hand, to shoot down the straggling savage. When they met in a conclave, it was never to keep up the old English mirth, but to hear sermons three hours long, or to proclaim bounties on the heads of wolves and the scalps of Indians. Their festivals were fast days and their chief pastime the singing of psalms. Woe to the youth or maiden who did but dream of a dance! The selectman nodded to the constable; and there sat the light heeled reprobate in the stocks: or if he danced, it was round the whipping post, which might be termed the Puritan Maypole."

ney case. Stepney's reputation must have been fairly well destroyed, for he apparently was forced to slip out of Boston quietly, heavily in debt and leaving behind a huge pile of unpaid bills. He went to New York where he again set up shop as a dancing master, but eventually his bad reputation caught up with him, and the New Yorkers threw him out as well. Judge Sewall was undoubtedly glad to hear of Stepney's departure but his troubles with dancers were far from over. One year after the Stepney incident, the judge ordered that a group of dancers in Charlestown cut down the maypole they had erected, who in turn erected a larger one in open defiance of the court.

Clearly, the battle lines were drawn. They were lines that would stay clear throughout American history. On one side were diehard Puritans who could not excuse dancing for any reason. On the other side were the less austere folk who enjoyed the old traditions from the home country. In the middle were the ones who probably thought dancing was fundamentally acceptable, so long as it did not interfere with one's work or religious life. Of course, the dancing taught by Stepney and other dance masters had probably changed considerably from the basic dances of the English rural areas. Sometimes silly, whimsical and even "decadent" additions had been tacked on to the old simple figures of the original country dances, and the Puritans were probably more disturbed by these "foolish" additions than by the dances themselves. The professional dancing masters, sophisticated and promoting the fashions of London society, cared little for Puritan values or folk customs, and it is no wonder that they often ran into difficulties in Puritan bastions.

But it was not only the Puritans of New England who kept the dancing masters alive. Increasing immigration to America brought people mainly interested in economic rather than religious freedom, and the trends set in London carried over among this relatively more secular, consuming public. This was especially true in urban areas such as New York, Philadelphia, and Williamsburg, and to a certain extent in rural areas as well. In Boston by 1716 two rival dancing masters were battling for students, and the competition became so heated that one of them had to move to New York. Dr. Alexander Hamilton visited Boston in 1744 and noted in his diary: "Assemblies of the gayer sort are frequent here . . . the gentlemen and ladys meet almost every week at consorts of musick and balls. I was present at two or three such and saw as fine a ring of ladys, as good dancing, and heard musick as I had been witness to anywhere. . . . I saw not one prude while I was here."[10]

In the Virginia colonies dancing masters also enjoyed acceptance. In 1716 the Board of Visitors of William and Mary College granted William Levingstone permission "to make use of the lower room at the south end of the college for teaching the scholars and others how to dance until his own dancing school in Williamsburg be finished."[11] Dancing occupied an important role in the social life of the early Virginians and was viewed as an essential part of the training of ladies and gentlemen. The Reverend Hugh Jones advised that William and Mary take a hand in this training who should be " . . . taught by such as the President and masters shall appoint,"[12] namely dancing masters.

Not all Virginians approved of such activity, however. Landon Carter, an older-generation Virginian of the eighteenth century, kept a diary in which he recorded the moral decline of two of his sons and a grandson who, he says, held an " . . . intemperate devotion to those 'bewitching' diversions; cards, dancing, liquor, horse racing etc."[13] Unfortunately for Carter, his viewpoint was not well supported by other Virginians. Historian Louis B. Wright explains that many of the Virginia planters desired to give their children the opportunity to learn the formality of genteel behavior and often sent them to England to be educated. "Nor is it strange," he says, "that skillful dancing masters should have been in demand in the colony. Throughout the colonial period dancing was the most popular of the social amusements, and not to know how to dance was to display one's lack of good breeding. To music furnished by servant fiddlers, the ladies and gentlemen of the colony danced the nights away."[14]

In 1759 the Reverend Andrew Burnaby traveled through Virginia and observed that the women there were "immoderately fond of dancing."[15] Burnaby also noted that the most graceful and formal dances enjoyed by the Virginians were the minuets, but that even the upper-class people danced the jigs and reels, which we can safely conclude were taken from Playford's book or one of the other imitations. One of those dancing Virginians was General George Washington who apparently enjoyed dancing to distraction. According to Washington Irving's *Life of George Washington,* the General not only enjoyed the minuet but particularly favored one of the dances from Playford's book, the "Sir Roger De Coverly," which later came to be known in America as the "Virginia Reel."

## Town and Country

Information on folk-life customs in rural colonial America is sparse, and it is ironic that we have to rely mainly on the history of the towns and cities to understand the course of country dancing in the early history of America. Outside of Boston, New York, and Philadelphia, American rural life was modeled after farming communities in England and other areas of the British Isles, notably Scotland and Ireland. As immigration into the New World increased, more people from the rural and highland areas of Britain came to America and naturally sought to settle in similar areas, particularly in the mountainous sections of New England and south all along the chain of Appalachian Mountains.

These highland settlers were of quite a different background from their countrymen who came from London and other urban areas. They brought with them a relatively unspoiled folk life which included many dances similar to those country dances published by Playford, but often uncorrupted by the professional dancing master who had not yet ventured far from his home turf. The Scotch and Irish settlers were mainly interested in maintaining their rural life-style, relying on their own ability to provide food and shelter for themselves. Some of them retreated deeper into the mountains than others, and so it would be wrong to generalize too much about the nature of the early mountain people in America.

The highland areas of New Hampshire and Vermont were organized relatively quickly and modeled after the towns in Britain's rural areas. Although the debate by clergymen over the propriety of dancing continued in New England in the eighteenth century, the staid attitudes of the abstainers were gradually overcome by the desire of the majority of people who wanted to retain their old customs and entertainments. As in England, many country folk followed the example of the trend-setting urban areas. The degree of their acceptance of urban styles depended largely on two factors: how close they were to the urban center geographically and whether or not they were visited by an itinerant dancing master.

The tradition of the itinerant craftsman in England carried over to early American culture. The traveling blacksmiths, tinkers, and other tradesmen took their services to community after community, following a basically habitual route which enabled them to establish themselves as reputable and trustworthy.

The dancing master essentially followed in that tradition: he went where he was wanted or allowed. In some cases this depended on the attitude of the local preacher. His operation was simple. Like the craftsmen, the dancing master would arrive in the community and make it known that he was available. He would be rented space in a home or possibly a town hall if one existed. He might stay in the town for just one night or longer depending on the size of the community.

Very few records of the itinerant dancing masters who traveled New England remain, but the best known of them was a John Griffith, whose career is partly traceable from newspaper accounts and from the dates and locations of his dancing manuals. He published at least eight known collections of dances, from Providence, Rhode Island to Walpole, New

Hampshire, but newspaper accounts find him having traveled as far
south as Charleston, South Carolina. Griffith seems to have followed the
habits of most dancing masters of the time, settling in different locations
for a season at a time, teaching in the immediate area and then traveling
out to neighboring villages. S. Foster Damon points out that Griffith's
dances were quite modern in nature, especially since most of the calls
and figures have names still in use today. Griffith taught dances which
were popular at the time but also made up many of his own in the idiom
of the day.

Typical of dancing masters of his day, Griffith probably placed adver-
tisements in local newspapers, somewhat like this announcement from
the *New Hampshire Spy,* in Portsmouth, New Hampshire, on March 20,
1789:

> "Dancing School. Mr. Flagg begs to inform those Ladies and Gentlemen
> who wish their children to acquire the knowledge of that polite Ac-
> complishment that he will again open a school, at the Assembly Room, on
> Wednesday the first of April next, and on the Saturday following, if a suf-
> ficient number of scholars offer. He will teach the mode of the English
> Minuets, Cotillions and the newest Contra Dances."

In the communities where the dancing master never visited, rural folk
enjoyed dancing and music more or less uninfluenced by the pretentious
gentility of the urban scene.

Town dancing became progressively more stylized as the American
colonies became increasingly sophisticated. By the time of the Revolution, everybody in both town and country was dancing "country" dances,
mostly contra dances, some of which were old traditional dances and
others composed to celebrate events of the war or the first American
heroes: "The Green Mountain Volunteers," "Jefferson and Liberty," and
the "Washington Quickstep." The contra dance was the idiom all composing dancing masters worked in, and whether or not they were sym-
pathetic to the cause of the Revolution they realized there was a market
for dances that celebrated the American struggle. It is likely that the
popularity of certain dances from the war years was a result of their
"Revolutionary" titles or lyrics. Some historians believe that contra
dancing was democratic in nature and in some way symbolized the battle
for independence—still, we should remember dancing was business for
the professionals, and it is unlikely that a dance that didn't "sell" was
kept alive for sentimental reasons.

After the Revolution ended, the new country began to build its future,
a future that held tremendous economic possibilities now that they were
free to trade directly with whomever they wished, especially France. The
wartime alliance with France had been significant not only because it
meant additional military muscle for the colonial army but also because it

brought the first "foreign" or non-British culture into American society. Even as the English country dances had skyrocketed in popularity across Europe during the eighteenth century, mainly among the upper classes, the French court had stayed aloof, unwilling to support anything too British. Typically, they renamed the country dance the *contredanse,* which later became contra dance in America, symbolic of the great influence the French were to have on American dancing in the nineteenth century.

The greatest propagators of the French influence were, naturally enough, French dancing masters who swarmed into the colonies during and after the Revolution, with sophisticated versions of country dances from the rural areas of England. After the French secured their own independence with a Revolution that was cultural as well as political, new dances quite different in style from the courtly ones popular with the ex-ruling class came into vogue. These dances were called "quadrilles," the French term for a square-dance formation of four couples. While this square formation was certainly not an invention of the French, it was their enthusiastic importation of the dance to America that sowed the seeds for great changes in dancing in America throughout the nineteenth century.

## THE FRENCH DANCING MASTERS

The alliance between the American colonies and France against the British in the Revolutionary War brought more than troops and guns to this country. Fashionable dancing masters from France, well acquainted with all the most contemporary dances including *les contredanses* or contra dances, opened schools all over the new nation, especially during the years following the war. The French dancing masters tended not to be as well traveled into rural areas as native men like John Griffith, but their repertoires were similar. The Frenchmen concentrated their efforts in areas of high society such as Newport, New York, and Philadelphia, but some were found as far north as Portsmouth, New Hampshire, the same town Mr. Flagg taught in, only five years later. This announcement appeared in the *New Hampshire Gazette* on September 23, 1794:

"Dancing school opened. Mr. St. Amand Most respectfully informs the Ladies and Gentlemen of the town of Portsmouth that he has opened his Dancing School at the Assembly House, where he will receive their children for tuition, and use utmost endeavor to instruct them in the very polite accomplishment of dancing.

*continued*

A French Dancing Master.

Days and hours for young Ladies,

Tuesday
Thursday   from 10 to 1 o'clock
     &
Saturday   from 2 to 5 o'clock, PM


For young gentlemen,

Tuesday
Thursday  from 6 to 9 o'clock P.M.
     &
Friday

The effects of the French dancing masters were long lasting. Gradually they introduced the dances of "society," infused with decorum, into the repertoire of all but the most remote areas of America; and, most importantly, they eventually introduced the quadrille, a dance for four couples, the forerunner of the American square dance.

Of course, these French dancing masters catered to a clientele of urban Americans who were becoming increasingly sophisticated in their taste for entertainment. One young lady, a Miss Sara N. Connell wrote in her diary, after attending a ball in Portsmouth:

November 28, 1805. Thanksgiving Day.
In the afternoon we attended a party of the Miss Vaughns. I accompanied Mr. Gleason to the hall. . . and several other gentlemen came in the evening. My favorite figure, "Chorus Jig" was called. I enjoyed the assembly highly. We came home at half past one. In vain did Morphus summon me to repose, for I never closed my eyes 'till daylight began to peep in my East window.

*Courtesy of the Dance Away Library.*
The Ladies Chain.

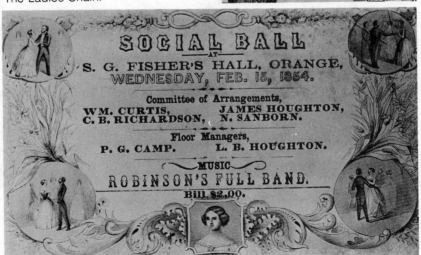

*Courtesy Vermont Historical Museum.*
An Invitation to a "fancy dance" in Orange, Vermont.

# RURAL DANCES / THE KITCHEN JUNKET

Much like the old community dances in Britain's countryside, the rural folk of New England gathered occasionally to dance, often in accordance with some kind of work activity: a husking bee, a quilting bee, or a wood gathering; perhaps a barn raising. Many customs grew out of these gatherings: such as placing a jug of homemade liquor at the bottom of the cornpile which gave extra incentive to the workers anxious to dance. It was also customary for anyone who found a red ear of corn to give a kiss to his or her sweetheart, or whoever might be close by!

The kitchen or the barn was the usual locale for such a dance, which often required the removal of kitchen furniture, even the wood stove on a cold winter night. The music was supplied by local fiddlers, who, until calling was introduced, simply announced the dances which everybody generally knew by rote. These junkets have continued to be a New England tradition but were commonplace in all rural areas of early America and were sometimes known as "barn dances," "square dances," or "kitchen rackets," depending on where they were held.

*Courtesy Library of Congress.*

Husking the Corn in New England.
During the husking if someone found a red ear of corn they were allowed to kiss the one next to them if they so desired. Later they danced.

The turn of the century marked a significant point in the country's dance history because it was at this time that the area began to develop more urban and less rural regions especially in New England. It was just before the War of 1812, and New England was well organized and thriving as both an agricultural and manufacturing region. The life-styles of the farmers and the manufacturers became more similar as sophisticated transport and communications reduced the distances between towns. After the War of 1812, which generated a great deal of anti-British sentiment, urban America refused to dance the English dances, thus securing even more strongly the popularity of the French "square" dances. Only in the back-country, rural areas of New England were the old English contra dances kept alive, largely because of the strong allegiance to the cultural traditions of the mother country.

These dances were held spontaneously in peoples' houses, sometimes in conjunction with some kind of work activity such as a barn raising or a husking bee and sometimes merely for fun and recreation. The nature of dancing in rural New England did not change very much or very fast, unlike the urban scene where new dances were constantly introduced, and old dances were dropped whimsically, and the whole program was controlled by the professional dancing masters. In the cities dancing became increasingly complicated, characterized by a refined style and adorned with the rules of etiquette adopted by the upper class, and naturally promoted by the dancing masters who catered to the tastes of the clients who were willing to pay the most for their services. Meanwhile the true country dance, which came to be called a "junket" or "barn dance," remained unadorned and basically unchanged. The contra dancing at a junket was vigorous, accompanied by music played by untrained fiddlers, while the quadrille dancing in the city became increasingly delicate and was often accompanied by music played by large, highly trained orchestras.

## The Southern Highland Tradition

Far away from the long, cold winters of New England, a different region of this country became the home of a group of people who also enjoyed the old country dances from Britain. Moving inland from the refined plantations of Virgina, settlers found refuge in the southern Appalachian Mountains of what is now Kentucky, West Virginia, Virginia, North Carolina, and Tennessee. Daniel Boone established the settlement known as Boonesborough around 1775, after some less significant explorations by colonists in the earlier part of the eighteenth century. Many of these early settlers came to the Shenandoah Valley by way of the Potomac Valley and even Boston, but many were originally from Scotland and Ireland, having fled those countries under siege because of their unpopular religious beliefs. They continued to spread out through the mountain areas of the southern Appalachian region, like the original settlers in New England, in search of a life free from persecution.

Like the Pilgrims and most colonial New Englanders, the settlers of southern Appalachia were determined to protect their independence from the very beginning, but they were not as prone to organizing as the New Englanders. In fact they moved farther and farther into the hills to get away from government interference in their lives, especially the tax-men who plagued them with outrageous demands. So intense was the hatred of the tax collectors that in 1771 nine resistors fought government troops at Almance Creek, and sentiment to gain complete freedom from the oppressive colonial government increased. This kind of organized effort on the part of the mountaineers was unusual since they were mainly interested in only the smallest form of community life, the family, a trend that still characterizes much southern Appalachian life today.

When the Revolution appeared to be an inevitability, the people of the southern mountains joined in. One of the leaders of a community in Tennessee was John Sevier, who headed the separatist colony of Watauga. Sevier was visited by the American revolutionary and frontiersman Issac Shelby, who had just heard from British Colonel Ferguson that if the mountain people failed to cease their opposition to colonial rule, there were going to be reprisals. Shelby traveled all the way from South Carolina to gain support from Sevier and found, much to his dismay, that the entire settlement was engaged in a three-day barbecue and dance. But Sevier was known to dance and fight with equal vigor, and so he gathered his ablest compatriots and went with Shelby to defeat the British at King's Mountain. From this point on, the mountain people made a significant contribution to the war effort, which they saw as essential in their fight to protect the independence they so badly desired.

After the Revolution life in the southern mountains more or less returned to normal; and, unlike New England, this region of America remained mostly rural, populated by people uninterested in the organized government. Writing in the magazine *Mountain Life and Work* (January 1936), historian Paul E. Doran said: "Since that early day of settlement comparatively few people have come into our mountains. . . . During the last 200 years we have been in a great measure a people apart. . . . In the beginning we were persecuted, then later we were forgotten, and when we were rediscovered we were looked down upon as inferior."[16]

Doran's observation illustrates well the noncorruption of the dance culture of the southern mountains. As other settlers moved through the mountains toward the Mississippi and westward, the mountain communities were relatively untouched by the sophisticated influences that so greatly changed the dancing in rural areas of New England and eastern Virginia, such as the French or the itinerant dancing masters. The music and dance of these communities came from essentially the same sources as New England dance and music, but in addition to the English influence, there was a strong Irish and Scottish element. The southern mountain people were not particularly enamored of contra dances. In fact they preferred dances which, as Cecil Sharp observed in the early twentieth century, originated in the rural communities of Britain, ones like those Playford had recorded in the first edition of *The Dancing Master*. These dances were performed in circle formation and sometimes in a four-couple square formation Sharp later named the Kentucky Running Set, a form of dance he believed to be the link between modern square dancing and the old pagan ceremonial dances of Britain. These older rounds and squares eventually developed into the Big Circle dances, still the most popular dances in the southern mountains, and the play-party dances for children which included singing old songs and rhymes while dancing.

One of the more interesting aspects of these mountain dances is that they were often done without any musical accompaniment, not because there weren't any musicians around, but because, as in early New England, the southern mountain dancers faced opposition from those who questioned the morality of dancing, and the fiddle was considered by many to be the instrument of the devil.

While the southern mountain communities were for the most part opposed to the kind of township organization that characterized New England communities, many people were conscious and serious about their religious beliefs. Immediately following the Revolution and on into the twentieth century, this area of the country was continually invaded by people wishing to aid the mountaineers who were uncommitted to the Christian life. One of these missionaries was Brother Martin Schneider who in 1783 reported hearing of a "frolick" at Colonel Shelby's (the same Shelby who visited John Sevier's barbecue), where there was shooting and fighting as well as dancing. Another of these missionaries was a young man named Peter Cartwright.

Cartwright was born in 1785 and made his home in Christian County, Kentucky. He was little interested in the missionary life until his sixteenth year, when he attended a wedding with his half brother and father. The year was 1801. Cartwright described the evening's events this way: " . . . there was a great deal of drinking and dancing, which was very common at marriages in those days. I drank little or nothing: my delight was in dancing . . . [Later at home] I began to reflect on the manner in which I had spent the day and evening. I felt guilty and condemned. It seemed to me, all of a sudden, my blood rushed to my head, my heart palpitated, in a few minutes I turned blind; an awful impression rested on my mind that death had come and I was unprepared to die . . . I fell on my knees and began to ask God to have mercy on me. . . . My mother sprang from her bed, and was soon on her knees by my side, praying for me, and exhorting me to look to Christ for mercy, and then and there I promised the Lord that if he would spare me, I would seek and serve him; and I never fully broke that promise. . ."[17]

And so the dancer Peter Cartwright was converted to missionary Cartwright, forever giving up his vices: cards and dancing. Instead Cartwright adopted the Christian way of life, traveling the southern mountain countryside looking for converts. Unfortunately he wasn't always successful at avoiding those who had sinned as he once had. Years after the conversion he encountered the following experience while traveling back to Kentucky: " . . . Saturday night came on, and found me in a strange region of country, and in the hills, knobs, and spurs of the Cumberland mountains. I greatly desired to stop on the approaching Sabbath and spend it with Christian people; but I was now in a region of country where there was no gospel minister for many miles around . . . and where the inhabitants knew no Sabbath, only to hunt and visit, drink and dance. . . . Thus lonesome and pensive, late in the evening, I hailed at a tolerably decent house, and the landlord kept entertainment. . . . The gentleman said I could stay, but he was afraid I would not enjoy myself very much as a traveler, inasmuch as they had a party meeting there that night to have a little dance. . . . He assured me I should be treated civilly [so] I dismounted and went in. The people collected, a large company. I saw there was not much drinking going on.

"I quietly took my seat in one corner of the house, and the dance commenced. I sat quietly musing, a total stranger, and greatly desired to preach to these people. Finally, I concluded to spend the next day [Sabbath] there, and ask the privilege to preach to them. I had hardly settled this point in my mind, when a beautiful, ruddy young lady walked very gracefully up to me, dropped a handsome courtsey, and pleasantly, with winning smiles, invited me out to take a dance with her. I can hardly describe my thoughts or feelings on that occasion. However, in a moment I resolved on a desperate experiment. I rose as gracefully as I could; I will not say with some emotion, but with many emotions. The young lady moved to my right side; I grasped her right hand with my right hand, while she leaned her left arm on mine. In this position we walked on the floor. The whole company seemed pleased at this act of politeness in the young lady, shown to a stranger. The colored man, who was the fiddler, began to put his fiddle in the best order. I then spoke to the fiddler to hold a moment, and added that for several years I had not undertaken any matter of importance without first asking the blessing of God upon it, and I desired now to ask the blessing of God upon this beautiful young lady and the whole company, that had shown such an act of politeness to a total stranger.

"Here I grasped the young lady's hand tightly, and said, 'Let us all kneel down and pray,' and then instantly dropped on my knees, and commenced praying with all the power of my soul and body that I could command. The young lady tried to get loose from me, but I held her tight. Presently she fell on her knees. Some of the company kneeled, some stood, some fled, some sat still, all looked curious. The fiddler ran off into the kitchen, saying 'Lord a marcy, what de matter? What is dat mean?'

"While I prayed some wept, and wept out aloud, and some cried for mercy. I rose from my knees and commenced an exhortation, after which I sang a hymn. The young lady who invited me on the floor lay prostrate, crying earnestly for mercy. I exhorted again, I sang and prayed nearly all night. About fifteen of that company professed religion, and our meeting lasted next day and next night, and as many more were powerfully converted."[18]

Thus missionary Peter Cartwright turned a rather low-key, innocent dance into a major religious event.

### White and Black on the Dance Floor

Cartwright's story is of special significance because it includes elements that characterize the evolution of dancing in the southern mountains during the first half of the nineteenth century, the time when that area was really the frontier of America.

The first element is the religious one. While post-Revolutionaries danced to their heart's content in Boston, New York, and Richmond without fear of reprisals from the local clergy, many of the diehard Puritans became missionaries and fled to the frontier in search of native folk who were heathens but as yet unspoiled by the influence of urban dancing masters, gamblers, and other decadent influences. The turn of the eighteenth century into the nineteenth century found these and many other Americans still experiencing the effects of the Great Awakening—the series of religious revivals which shook Colonial America before the Revolution. The newly enflamed missionaries and converts passed along their newly acquired salvation to others by way of preaching the gospel.

In New England strong relationships had been established between the town political and religious leaders, and these were not about to be changed radically by this new breed of zealot. But the southern mountains housed a multitude of people who, as Cartwright described them, held no firm religious beliefs and in some cases held such belief in contempt. Cartwright's host was obviously aware of his guest's beliefs and warned him fairly that he would be sharing the quarters that fateful night with people who danced to the music of a fiddle, considered to be the instrument of the devil. The issue seemed to be well known even in the back woods: you either danced or did not dance, and your choice would determine your everlasting destiny, at least according to men like Cartwright whose strict Puritanism entertained no rational excuses for activities that had no useful Christian purpose. Clearly this rural area of America was not free from controversies. While these southern mountaineers, who loved to dance, would have preferred to live in peace, hunting and farming, their mountains became a testing ground for the missionaries of America.

The various missionaries who traveled through the southern mountains brought with them as many varieties of Christian dogma as one could imagine. Preachers who were often unschooled and unsupported by an organized church flourished alongside the mainstream Baptists, Methodists, and Presbyterians. All of them held a common belief that the mountain people were fundamentally backward, sinful creatures in desperate need of salvation, an attitude that had usually been reserved for American Indians and for black slaves from Africa. But eventually all of these poor people, the "hillbillies," Indians, and blacks, were lumped together as those who were not "saved." These were also the people who generally still danced and held respect for their ancestral traditions, much to the dismay of the invading missionaries. These people became the object of pity and ridicule, an atittude that still carries on today. And their folk arts, part of their life-style both as art and work, slowly disappeared.

The Indians, especially the Cherokees, were systematically destroyed by Christian and non-Christian whites alike, until their culture and people were driven west on the Trail of Tears to virtual annihilation. In 1785 the Cherokees lost 43,000 acres to Revolutionary War veterans as punishment for aiding the British. By 1794 they had lost every bit of their homelands in Virginia and North Carolina and moved out to Tennessee where two missionaries, the Brethren A. Steiner and F. C. De Schweinitz, observed the Cherokees still performing their Green Corn Dances. They didn't last long in Tennessee. Eventually the white men's "treaties" formalized the complete extinction of the Cherokee and other Indian cultures. It seems evident that few of the Indian dance customs were appreciated by the white men, even those who favored dancing themselves.

But as the white settlers were ridding themselves of the Indian culture, they were at the same time introducing another one from Africa. As we see in Cartwright's story, the fiddler at the dance he attended was "colored," and as the dialect later indicates, this fiddler was not Indian but Negro, probably a slave of one of those attending the dance. The use of slaves at dances on the plantations in Virginia was common. They were trained to play the Scottish and Irish jigs and reels as well as the minuets; dressed up in fancy costume and put to work entertaining, they established early in American history the only place where the black man was able to work with respect.

All over the plantations of the South, slaves were allowed to dance, and some of them attended the whites' dances. Lynne Emery's work on black dance in the United States includes many interviews with ex-slaves who described the dances held in the South shortly before the Civil War.

One of these ex-slaves, Liza Mention, who worked on a plantation in McDuffie County, Georgia, compared the dancing then to modern ballroom dancing (she was interviewed in the thirties): "Dances in dem days warn't dese here huggin' kind of dances lak dey has now. Dere warn't no Big Apple nor no little Apple neither. . . . Dey had a string band wid a fiddle and a banjo, but dere warn't no guitars lak dey has dis day. One man called de sets and us danced de cardille [quadrille], de Virginia reel, and de 16 hand cortillion."[19] So it seems that the slaves had adopted many of the white peoples' dances. Another slave from Louisiana described some of the figures the dances included: "De prompter call, 'All get ready.' Den he holler, 'All balance,' and den he sing out 'swing your pardner,' and dey does it. Den he say, 'First man head off to de right, and dere dey goes. . . .' One thing dey calls, 'Bird in de Cage.' Three join hands round de gal in de middle, and dance round her, and den she get out and her pardner get in de center and dey dance dat way awhile."[20]

Like the Indians, the black slaves were a minority group under the control of the whites, but while the Indians were effectively prevented from maintaining any of their traditional culture, which was inextricably connected to the lands they were thrown off, the blacks held on to many of their native dances from Africa. These native dances were performed sometimes in their original form but later became meshed with the American and European dances popular at the time. The question is how much of the meshing was two-way, in other words, what effect did the slaves' dances have on the whites' dances? History has not treated this subject very well. My first encounter with the story of Peter Cartwright's attending a mountain dance was in the *Treasury of Southern Folklore,* published in 1949 and edited by the famous folklorist B. A.

Botkin. The version edited by Botkin fails to mention that the fiddler was "colored" as we were told by Cartwright in his autobiography (which by the way was Botkin's main source for the story). I do not wish to defame Botkin, but it seems suspicious to me that this fact was left out, especially since he describes the rest of Cartwright's story fairly completely. The exclusion of this fact indicates an attitude that poor people in the South, black and white, have suffered from since the time of slavery: the gross manipulation of their lives by the wealthy who feared that permitting the poor to mix and carry on their customs constituted a threat to the security of the feudal southern land owners. So that even the scholarly folklorists like Botkin have conveniently left the colored fiddlers out of southern folklore history because it was a kind of mixture the South was not yet prepared to recognize. This exclusionary process is the manifestation of an attitude started in the South by the missionaries and continued to this day by those who have looked upon the southern mountaineers as inferior, unenlightened ne'er-do-wells with no art at all.

The fact is that the slaves and the whites did trade folk dances to a certain extent. One ex-slave said: "My young master himself could shake a desperate foot at the fiddle; there was nobody that could face him at a 'Congo Minuet.' "[21] And another ex-slave, Isaac Stier, had this to say about the dances the blacks did: "Us danced plenty, too. Some o' de men clogged and pigeoned, but when us had the dances dey was real cotillions, lak de white folks had. . . . Long after the war was over de white folks would 'gage me to come 'round' wid de band an' call de figgers at all de big dances. Dey always paid me well."[22]

Here we have two examples of the exchange of steps between blacks and the whites. I am not sure what a "Congo Minuet" is but it's clear to me that the dance in some way must have combined formal white movements with African influence: perhaps in the rhythms of the dance. Stier's description of the men clogging and doing pigeon wings is another example of dancing carried on by both whites and blacks. In the urban areas of the United States, where the dancing had become increasingly genteel and formal, these steps were excluded from the quadrille, cotillions, and the Virginia Reels (the only surviving contra outside of New England by the mid-nineteenth century). They were considered absolutely taboo. The dancing teachers proclaimed "Doing one's steps" distasteful. One could walk lightly or glide, but any leaping or stamping of feet was considered vulgar. But in the country such steps were considered to be what separated a good dancer from a not-so-good one, and the people dancing in rural areas of the South and the North retained and encouraged the continuation of these steps, frowned upon by the urban fashion conscious.

## THE EXCHANGE OF STYLES AND ADORNMENTS
## BY BLACKS AND WHITES IN THE SOUTH

While clogging is found in some areas of New England, people in the southern mountains—blacks and whites—developed this ornament to the extent that it became the trademark of southern country dancing. Not to be ignored is the influence of Indians, especially the Cherokee, whose folk dances included similar footwork, the loud rythmic tapping of the feet to lightning fast fiddle tunes. The specialization around clogging caused individual dancers to become legends in their home towns or counties; they were known as "buckdancers"—a name of uncertain derivation, though some dancers speculate that it was derived from an Indian ceremonial dance where an individual warrior plays the role of the buck deer and dances in this fashion.

*Courtesy of Library of Congress*

"Contraband Children dancing the Breakdown"

*continued*

White Buckdancers.

Black dancers on a southern plantation.

Specialty dances such as clogging and jigs, while traceable to the step dances brought by settlers from Scotland and Ireland, were considerably altered by blacks and whites, who lived in the rural areas of the South, as were the fiddle tunes played at these dances. Specialty dances were most often performed by individuals or pairs, originally simply for fun. But eventually this activity took on competitive characteristics.

Slave owners often summoned their most talented dancing slave to perform for guests in the "big house," and eventually these owners began to pit their slaves against each other in dance contests, the most popular competitive dance being the jig. One slave described one of these jigging contests on a plantation in Texas: "One nigger in our place was de jigginest fellow ever was. Everyone round tries to git somebody to best him. He could put de glass of water on his head and make his feet go like trip-hammers and sound like a snaredrum. . . . He could whirl round and sich, all de movement from his hips down. Now it gits noised round a fellow been found to beat Tom and a contest am 'ranged for Saturday evenin'. There was a big crowd and money am bet, de master bets on Tom, of course. . . . So dey starts jiggin. . . . It looks like Tom done found his match, but there am one thing he ain't done yet—he ain't made de whirl. Now he does it. Everyone holds he breath, and de other fellow starts to make de whirl and he make it, but jus' a spoonful of water sloughs out his cup, so Tom am de winner."[23]

The slaves became renowned as the best jiggers in the South. The blacks' jig differed tremendously from the traditional Irish jig, especially as it seemed to involve making noises on the floor—like a snaredrum, according to the description above. This noisy stepping, called clogging in the mountains, was thought to be vulgar by rich whites but became quite popular in rural areas as an ornamentation used during figure dances. This is not to say definitively that the slaves invented what we now call clogging. Clogging has been done all over North America, in French Canada, Nova Scotia, and New England. But the southern blacks' special talent and the eventual use of this talent by profit-hungry plantation owners clearly helped to establish clogging as a strong element in southern country dancing.

After the Civil War, freed blacks often adopted these dances and used them to make money as free men in society. Some of them traveled around the countryside and danced on their own, others joined minstrel shows. In both situations they performed the old jigs, or sometimes the "Buck and Wing"—a dance which grew out of the "Pigeon Wing" and the "Buck Dance," both steps which crossed racial lines and became the showpieces of black professional dancers.

In rural areas of the South, poor people continued to include the buck dance, the pigeon wing, clogging and other adornments in their country dances; clogging especially became the trademark of dancers from the southern mountains. But this dancing was not restricted to whites or blacks, or southerners and northerners; rather it was continued by the nonwealthy, so-called "uncultured" people of rural America who continued country dancing in the country while the urbanites quickly left the "country" dances behind in favor of new dances more attuned to their life-style.

## Western Cotillion and Eastern Etiquette

As fancy ballroom dancing took over in the East, a new territory for continuing country customs was developing in the largest and certainly the most rural section of America, the West.

By 1849 occasional explorations by the brave were overshadowed by throngs of gold hungry fortune-hunters, and settlements began to spring up all over the West: oases for travelers all the way from the Mississippi to California. Naturally the new settlers brought their music and dances with them to these new frontier outposts and mining communities. Generally the miners were not the genteel type, and dancing in the West during its early days was vigorous and earthy. The favorite dances of the early frontiersmen were the "cotillion," a dance of French derivation that took the form of the fancy quadrille but retained the vigor of the old country dances and the traditional music; and the lively jigs and reels from Scotland and Ireland, now played in a unique American style. Unlike the quadrille, whose movements were memorized, the cotillion was more of a spontaneous dance consisting of figures made up on the spot by a "caller," the American version of the dancing master, oftentimes the fiddler who would just shout out directions to a dance at his discretion.

Calling soon became the trademark of American square dancing, a tradition that began with the cotillions and has carried on to the present day. Fiddlers and callers would make up dances on the spot to fit the old tunes, or sometimes new popular songs by Stephen Foster and other contemporary composers. Calling was not received very well in Europe, but on the western frontier of America it became the custom for fiddlers to tell the dancers what to do. These western callers were not in the least bit interested in the deportment and gentility of the city dances from back East.

Early western dances were vigorous, rowdy affairs where people took the opportunity to let off steam and get together with their usually distant neighbors. Before word got back to eastern farmers about the giant tracts of fertile land ready and waiting for their crops, setting off a tremendous migration of families to the West, the settlers were mostly men, and so often without partners. Indian women were then commissioned to dance with the men until white women began to populate the frontier.

The rough dancing style favored by these early frontiersmen included many of the embellishments favored by true country people back East such as the pigeon wing, but as the West became more civilized and way stations grew into towns, a newer class of people from the East made their way into places like Denver and brought with them the need for more fashionable and genteel dancing. In 1861 the *Rocky Mountain News* carried the following announcement about dances sponsored by the Masons of Denver: "A capital arrangement has been adopted for the dancing exercises at the Broadwell, on Friday night. The lower room will be set apart for the quadrilles, and the upper room for Fancy Dances. Both rooms are to be decorated in a magnificent style surpassing anything of the kind ever before seen in this region. . . . A large delegation of our mountain friends are expected to be present."[24] After the dance Saturday's edition of the News carried this item: "The festival last evening at the Broadwell House, given by the Masonic fraternity of this city, was by far the most brilliant affair ever witnessed in Denver. The attendance of ladies was very numerous, and the display of elegant and costly apparel equal to any seen on any similar occasion in the leading cities of the Western States."[25] Military balls were common in Denver at this time as the intensity of the Civil War grew but also because the frontier was even more immediately enmeshed in war with the Indian tribes. Military men were the real leaders of the early western territories and to a large degree set the style of entertainment available in the cities. It is interesting that the description of the dance at Broadwell's makes a point of mentioning how many ladies were present, indicating that either there weren't many ladies in Denver at that time, or that the dances were still a bit rowdy, perhaps because of the "mountain friends" who came.

Meanwhile western farms and ranches grew, and the dancing styles in these new rural communities reflected the backgrounds of the new settlers. Many of them came from New England where the contra dance was still the most popular in farming communities, and others came from the southern mountains where the square-dance formation was preferred. The cities of the West imitated the East however, and the dancing there began to reflect the influence of the new waves of immigrants from Europe who brought dances like the polka and the revolutionary waltz, the first of the great round dances to excite the dance halls of America. The waltz was initially looked upon by the moralistic public as an indecent dance because of the "lascivious" position the man and woman took, and the acceptance of this new dance caused heated debate

# ROUGH AND FANCY DANCING IN THE WEST

In the process of settling the West, easterners brought country dancing with them to the frontier. Especially during the gold rush days when men became rich overnight, the West demanded some of the refinements of eastern urban life—even amidst the wildness of the landscape.

*Courtesy of Calaveras County Historical Society.*

Californians dance on a Redwood.

*Photo courtesy of Library of Congress.*

Dance House. Cowboys whooped it up with square dancing in saloons.

among dancing teachers and clergymen for the remainder of the nineteenth century and onward.

The Centennial celebration came at a time when America was growing at a pace that seemed to outstrip any previous civilization. The celebration was wholly a celebration of progress: the industrialization of the East, the defeat and Reconstruction of the South, and the conquest of the West. The booming railroads, which had replaced the wagon trains, carried goods from factories in New England, where farming had been largely abandoned after the discovery of the great western plains. The plains and mountain areas were being cleared of the Indian "problem" through a process of incarceration and execution. Tall buildings appeared in New York. In the southern mountains men who wanted coal from the ground to make the steam engines move came with promises to the mountaineers and bogus Bills of Sale for their rich property. Progress meant everything. Resources were unlimited, thought the government, and little attention was paid to the survival of customs and traditions of the rural people in America. In fact, at the time of the Centennial celebration, there was nothing at all fashionable about country customs, nor much concern for the people who still held those customs dear. True, a handful of artists lamented the disappearance of the American country life and romanticized it in their work, but the majority of Americans chose to accept progress as inevitable and desirable, even if it meant the gradual extinction of the folk arts of their grandparents.

In 1875 William B. DeGarno's book *The Dance of Society* included three traditional dances, including the Virginia Reel, but warned that these dances were " . . . not considered fashionable, yet are more or less done all over the country." Meanwhile, waltzes and polkas were integrated into the popular quadrilles of the day, causing the clergy of the Episcopalian Church in America to consider banning all "square dancing," as it was now generally called, because it might promote sinful contacts between dancers.

Traditional dances continued to a certain extent in New England, where contras remained popular. An evening's program in the towns included the fashionable quadrilles and fancy dances found in the great halls of Boston and New York. On Thursday, December 23, 1875, a Mr. D. Tarbell advertised a "Social Dance" in East Greenville, Vermont, because he felt that "civil and innocent recreation" was "not only healthy, but moral, and tends to raise civilization to a more elevated standard . . ." The dance proposed to begin at 5 P.M. and end at 2 A.M. the next morning, including a supper. Adopting the formal customs of the balls in larger towns and cities, Mr. Tarbell's dance included floor and other managers, to keep order and prevent "riotous conduct and drunkenness."

Meanwhile, out in the truly rural communities of New England, the farming people continued to hold their junkets as they had since the region was settled by their forebears. These somewhat spontaneous affairs took place in someone's home, usually in the kitchen: all the furniture, including the stove, would be carried out of the room, and the dancing and music would carry on until everyone was satisfied they'd had enough. People brought pies and other good things to eat, and the food kept folks dancing late into the night.

The same kind of dances took place in the southern mountain communities located far from the towns and in back country settlements in the West. Anna Robison tells of the first social function in Mancos Valley, Colorado, " . . . a dance held in the John Brewer cabin in 1878. Manse Reid brought the fiddler from Dolores county, but his name is not known. Those present were the Misses Bradford, the Misses Clara and Callie Mitchell, Miss Ida Sheek, and all the cowboys in the country. They danced square dances."[26]

Cowboys, as it happened, were not always the most welcome guests at these small dances, as Jens Larsen explained later in the nineteenth century: "Dancing was enjoyed by all, and if the older folks did not dance, they went along to watch the younger ones have a good time. At one time the cowboys from 'Robber's Roost,' a big cattle ranch near the Arickaree River, greatly frightened the new homesteaders by appearing at a dance in boots and spurs and carrying guns. They rode up to the house with wild whoops, and the new comers did not know what was taking place. But when everyone got acquainted, they found the cowboys were a jolly bunch out for a good time."[27]

Meanwhile, as country people in various regions of the United States continued their rustic dances, city dwellers continued to adopt new dances and new styles. Still at the head of this culture was the professional dancing teacher, who had more than ever become the teacher not just of dances but of proper deportment and etiquette. Dance manuals, of which there were hundreds, were carried in their back pockets or purses in dancing schools all over the nation. Besides the dances, which were explained in detail, these handbooks contained long explanations of how people should prepare themselves, conduct themselves, and dispose of themselves at a gala ball, or for that matter any social situation. Throughout the nineteenth century these books appeared in many different editions, but all were essentially the same; they included less and less of the old dances, and, with the exception of the books published in New England, they became increasingly anti-British. Perhaps the most widely circulated of these manuals was *Dick's Quadrille Book,* published by Dick and Fitzgerald of New York in 1878. At the end of the book we find a short chapter on contra dances with the following explanation:

## ETIQUETTE IN COUNTRY DANCING

As America celebrated her first 100 years, proclaiming the virtues of unbridled growth, she began to suffer a severe deficit in her folk life, especially the customs of dancing and music of the plain folk. Even in outer areas of New England, manners and deportment shadowed the purity of the dances, and America turned to the fashions of Europe as if she were ashamed of herself.

*Courtesy of Dance Away Library*

The wrong way to dance, according to Allen Dodworth's *Dancing.*

*Courtesy of Dance Away Library*

Elias Howe's *Ball-Room Handbook,* featuring few traditional dances and a great deal of information on manners and rules.

"Dancing is essentially French in its derivation and nature; and the French names and technical phrases will continue to cling to the figures and movements used in dancing. The French Contre Danse became corrupted into the English Country Dance, with that characteristic facility that the English have of calling and spelling foreign words to suit themselves."[28] The book later explains that because so few contra dances are in use at that time, the chapter will include all the dances that are not quadrilles or round dances (round dances here meaning waltzes and other dances for solo couples).

Around this time the dancing masters found themselves at odds with two new additions to the dances which threatened the decorous nature of what they were trying to teach their customers: calling, which was becoming increasingly popular, and the swing.

S. Foster Damon tells of a dancer's first recollection of hearing a dance called in what was developing as a unique American style, in about 1870: "At this dance I heard, for the first time, the local professional fiddler, old Daddy Fairbanks. . . . His Queer 'Calls' and his 'York State' accent filled us all with delight. 'Ally man left' 'Chassay by your pardners' 'Dozy Do' were some of the phrases he used as he played 'Honest John' and 'Haste to the Wedding'. At times he sang his calls in high nasal chant, 'First lady lead to the right, deedle, deedle dum dum gent foller after dally deedle do do three hands around,' and everybody laughed with frank enjoyment of his word and action."[29] The dancing masters of the day were horrified by this low-class verbalization because it was felt to be unattractive, not to mention threatening to them since their purpose was to teach the dances until the dancers knew the movements by heart. The acceptance of calling by the public probably contributed more than any one factor to the decline of the professional dancing master.

The practice spread rapidly throughout the country. In New England fiddlers or callers would prompt the calls, or in some cases sing them along with the tunes, using nonsensical phrases to bridge the spaces between the actual figures, thus foreshadowing the patter calls used so widely in modern Western square dancing. Down in the southern mountains the same practice emerged and has remained, especially in the Big Circle dances where the caller makes up the dance spontaneously as the music progresses. And in the West the calling took on a special character as it reflected the new dialect of that region of America, the slang of the cowboy.

The swing, the other major contribution to dancing made at this time, was according to Damon, the invention of an anonymous New Englander. But whoever was responsible for this radical addition to the square dance, we can be sure it was not the dancing master. Unlike calling which threatened his livelihood, the dancing master objected to swinging as we know it today mostly on the grounds it was immoral. At first the man and woman joined left hands between them and the right hands were braced on opposite shoulders, a fairly innocent posture, but later the waltz position became the way to swing and that outraged the dancing teachers who contemptuously watched their students whirling away until they became too dizzy to stand.

The advent of swinging brought tremendous changes in dancing style and in the actual dances. Swinging was great exercise and great fun—dancers tended to include as much swinging as possible in the old

# THE SWING

A modern addition to country dancing in the later part of the nineteenth century was the swing. The standard position for the swing was the basic waltz position, but dancers invented a variety of styles of swinging, which they used to swirl themselves to exhaustion.

Swing/waltz position

Swing/ New England Buzz Step

Swing/ Hands on shoulders.

*Line Drawings by Randy Miller*

favorite dances. Some dances were actually changed by the addition. The old version of "Chorus Jig," a contra dance, ended with the figure "forward six and back," but later that last figure became "balance and swing," giving everyone the chance to spin around madly for a full eight measures of the tune. The dancing masters were doubly horrified as swinging invaded not only contra dances but their precious quadrilles as well. The quadrilles were the last bastions of etiquette in their view, and to corrupt them with swinging was the last straw. But they could not stop the tide.

In 1883 the dancing masters sought to organize themselves in order to effectively combat the corruption of their dances. Forming the American National Association of Masters of Dancing, they struck out at calling, especially those among their ranks who had sold out and joined the ever growing number of "big voice" prompters and callers. Their efforts were a classic exercise in futility. The dancing masters' last desperate attempt to hold on to their genteel dances faded fast in the latter part of the 1880's and 90's, so that by the turn of the century, very little of their etiquette made any difference to anyone. By this time people in American cities danced almost nothing but waltzes and two-steps, while out in the country the square dances continued, led by the singing callers and dominated by lots and lots of swinging.

# 1900: Land of the Future

America became, above all, a land of the future in the nineteenth century, not a land of the past, especially in industrialized areas where the emphasis was wholly on growth and moving forward. The Civil War itself reaffirmed this direction. The war had been the first test of federal strength, not only on a political plain, but on an economic and cultural plain as well. People found themselves being asked to clarify their identity as *Americans*. What it meant to be an American became increasingly clear after the war ended. For the northerner the war had been an affirmation of the undefeatable power of industry, while for the South the war clearly showed than an agrarian society simply could not stand up against that power. This realization established once and for all the priorities for urban industrialized society in America, even if that meant the sacrifice of weaker agrarian areas.

The rural frontiers of America were eliminated in a dialectical process throughout the first century of our nation's history, yet much of the folk life remains. The reason that any of this culture survived was because enough people through the years felt the importance of retaining some customs and made an effort to do so, even as pressure increased to reject old, out-of-fashion folk customs. Immigrants from Eastern Europe were particularly fervent about preserving their traditional folk dances even though they had left their home countries forever.

The Civil War and industrialization caused such a furor in America that every aspect of the folk culture was challenged or changed in some way, and when the dust had finally settled, it was only in the most rural areas that any folk life remained relatively intact. The evolution of the country dance in those remote places has taken different routes in the different regions of America. In New England the dancing more or less followed the example of England, and in rural areas the music and dance remained relatively unchanged by the effects of the dancing master. But gradually, as New England's economy shifted emphasis from agriculture to manufacturing, many rural areas disappeared and with them the older traditional dances and tunes—although there were enough sentimental feelings about British ancestry to keep the contra dances at least partially alive. The later part of the nineteenth century saw New England farming ebb rapidly as the migration West accelerated. The remaining rural New Englanders retained their traditional contra dances at their junkets although many of them enjoyed the new fashionable dances as well, at balls held in the town halls. The result of this combined interest was the partial formalization of dancing style, though the dancing was more profoundly changed by the advent of calling and prompting—which made the job of the dancing master virtually unnecessary—and the introduction of "buzz step" swinging.

In the southern mountains the Civil War caused an internal rift which touched off feuding between families and sometimes within families. These feuds kept this area of American at a cultural standstill for most of the nineteenth and on into the twentieth century. At the same time the tree and mineral resources of the area were being deviously acquired by large coal and paper companies. The mountain people found little to celebrate as they witnessed the gradual but steady annihilation of their land. Many of them had joined one of the local fundamentalist churches, their only real hope of salvation, which in general forbade any kind of dancing. A few "sinners" continued to dance, their style rough and still very reminiscent of early English dances and children's singing games. The southern country dance remained almost completely unchanged through the nineteenth century in the truly rural areas. The fiddler was the center of it all, playing the tunes based on the old Scottish and Irish reels but now bearing American frontier names like "Cumberland Gap" and "Cripple Creek." One of the dancers would call out the figures in no set pattern. Since there weren't very many different figures, the dancing was accessible to anyone inclined to get out on the floor. Essentially the dancers in the southern mountains were out for a good time with their neighbors; simple and unpretentious, unencumbered with urban "style." When the whole group wasn't dancing, someone was up buckdancing. This kind of dancing was practiced not only by white mountaineers in the South but by the blacks as well, who carried the dances with them from the plantations to their own settlements in the mountains.

By the end of the nineteenth century the dance in the southern mountain region of America had suffered different effects from that in New England, though the end results were basically the same: very few people were doing the old dances and those who were were thought to be destined to eternal damnation.

In the West there was an entirely different experience. Both the South and New England fed this new frontier with diverse dancing and musical styles. The first miners were a combination of city and country folks who brought a diversity of cultures. The only thing they had in common was a lust for gold. But as the West became increasingly civilized, this area began to show the typical signs of evolution: in urban areas the dancing was largely standardized in imitation of the fashionable trend-setters of Boston and New York. Out on the ranches and in the mountain mine areas, people tended to retain the old dances brought from their home region, mixing them together with a rough version of the dances they heard were popular in Denver and other western towns. This new frontier area was an area with a flavor all its own, different from any other part of the country, and the frontier people knew it. The result of this attitude was a new kind of dancing, based on a combination of the old country dances and the popular quadrilles and cotillions. This new dance became the Western square dance, and unlike its parent dances from the East, it was neither wholly rustic nor wholly sophisticated. It, in many ways, was like the oldest country dances of England before the publication of *The Dancing Master* because, like them, these early "cowboy" square dances were made up on the spot by the fiddler or the caller, unwritten and totally informal. There was such a mixture of people settling the West that these new dances infiltrated all different classes, eventually becoming the Western country dance. Like the rural areas of New England and the South, the ranch and farm areas of the West were less influenced by the fashions of the cities, but here the rural life was even stronger because the economic possibilities for agrarian activities were so much more promising. The great western plains would remain the agricultural food bowl, the provider to the increasingly populated East, and so ranch and farm life were relatively unscathed by industrialization. Of course, eastern sophistication did have a bearing on the western style of country dancing. The westerners were not totally cut off from the current fashionable dances and by no means completely opposed to some refinement of their dances. But, in general, the lack of communication and of sophisticated musicians simply did not allow for real "fancy" dancing in the West.

But in 1900 few people actually lived in the West, and the predominant trend in America was the decline of rural civilization. Gradually all true respect for the folk life of agrarian people was eroded, whether it be the Green Corn Dances of the Cherokee, the vigorous contra dances of New Englanders, or the clog dancing of the southern mountaineers. And even as the rural life disappeared, prints by Currier and Ives depicting country scenes were quickly consumed by city dwellers who tacked these romantic renderings onto their walls and lamented the passing of that golden life. When Currier made his first print in 1840 there were only 2 million Americans living in cities, but by the 1890's there were well over 22 million urbanites. By 1900 every seventh American lived in a city populated by more than 250,000 people. The Currier and Ives prints depicted a life-style in America that had already become mythical barely 100 years after the founding of the nation. Rural life, which at one point in American history had provided dances that entertained all classes, now was, for the vast majority of Americans, a vanishing curiosity idealized and yet forgotten.

The Gay Nineties saw the rise of the American emphasis on superficiality and outward, sometimes outlandish, displays of wealth: Stanford White's Madison Square Garden and his private parties where naked girls jumped out of cakes; Mrs. Vanderbilt's $11 million "cottage" in Newport; Lillian Russell's diamonds and bicycles. Coney Island, which had been a posh resort for the upper crust to moor their yachts, became accessible to the average New Yorker when the trolleys came, costing only a nickel. Freak shows, fried food, magicians, and the weird colored lights all over the Giant See Saw and the Canals of Venice, delighted them. And there *were* dance halls—smoke-filled and noisy—where clerks and secretaries danced two-steps to Sousa marches, the men wearing the ladies' hats and smoking cigars as they whirled around and around until they could only gaze with dizzied eyes at their equally giddy partners.

## Revival

When the nineteenth century turned into the twentieth, the only folk culture well known to the great masses of white Americans belonged to ex-slave blacks, who had given their music freely. Scott Joplin introduced ragtime to America with his tune "Maple Leaf Rag," and blacks in New Orleans were forming small bands that played music based on African rhythms they called "jazz."

Meanwhile, out in the country, old-style dancing wasn't quite dead. In England dance historian Cecil Sharp found a group of old men who still knew how to do the old Morris dances and brought them to London to perform. Sharp then began to collect the old country dances and interpret them, making them available to the public who he felt should be more aware and appreciative of the indigenous folk arts of his country. Sharp, an educator himself, started a trend among educators to include folk dancing in their physical education programs. The trend quickly spread to America, and in New York the school athletic director initiated a program to teach the students a variety of European folk dances. No American square dances were included in the program as yet—a result of the attitude still strong in American minds that our indigenous folk arts are generally unworthy and certainly have no place in any school-sponsored program. But for awhile these European dances enjoyed great popularity in the schools, even among the boys who were generally opposed to such activities.

Meanwhile dances like the "Bunny Hug" and the "Fox Trot" had replaced the waltzes and two-steps in urban ballrooms, but it was involvement in the First World War that began to convince Americans that their native arts might not be so bad after all. Curiously, the government's promotion of American spirit to boost the war effort was probably as responsible as any other factor in bringing back the old American folk dances into the mainstream of United States' culture, that is, into the cities.

In 1918 a book appeared in America called *Twenty Eight Contra Dances, Largely from the New England States,* which had been edited and selected by Elizabeth Burchenal. Ms. Burchenal had been involved with the folk-dance movement in the schools and had written other books on the values of the European folk dances, but this book of contras was the first one of its kind to point out the simple virtues of the old dances, not as artifacts of history, but as a worthwhile physical activity.

By the twenties the average American was listening to more jazz than anything else, and to the dismay of some, he danced to it in a fashion as vigorous as the old country dancers. The music was as fast paced as the fiddle music known at country dances. Like the early country dances, new music and dance were arts of the lowest classes and not yet controlled by the upper-class rich who had eventually dominated the folk arts in America since the Revolution.

Jazz and jazz dancing were the results of a long evolutionary process of the culture of America's working class. The roots of the music were in folk tunes and rhythms, primarily of southern blacks, but during the 1920's many jazz and folk musicians began to realize that their music and dance customs were related, founded in a simple life-style where music and dancing were an integral part of life. The style of that old music and dance was simple and spontaneous, sometimes raucous, and the new jazz was similarly characterized.

Henry Ford did not like jazz.[30] The inventor of the mass production of automobiles, Ford belonged to that group of men who more than anything sought to defend America against "revolutionary" changes. Dismayed at the success of a low-class art such as jazz, Ford searched for something to defeat it, and after visiting New England a few times, he became enamored of square dancing. Ford hired a man named Benjamin Lovett who knew something about the old dances and with his help set out to convince America to re-adopt the old dances of the past. Ford and his wife, with the help of Lovett, coauthored a book on dancing entitled *Good Morning: After a Sleep of Twenty-five Years, Old-fashioned Dancing Is Being Revived by Mr. and Mrs. Henry Ford.* Armed with this book, Ford initiated a publicity campaign that took him all over the United States on behalf of old-time dancing. In the introduction to *Good Morning* Ford severely denounces the "ultra modern dance" as being too "one and one" and lacking the group spirit of fun. He claims that the character of modern dancing is "determined by commercial considerations." The older form of dancing required room, he says, and urban cabarets are too small for square dances. Ford believed that " . . . a form of dancing has been encouraged that enables the largest number of paying couples to dance together in the smallest possible space. The result is that in the modern method the movement of the dance is mostly above the feet." Prophetically Ford claimed that "It is a revulsion from these conditions that the ultra modern dances are being abandoned, and the older dances widely renewed." Corruptive jazz was under attack.

But what was this dancing that Ford promoted? He claimed it was " . . . that style of dancing that best fits with the American temperament." But it should be understood that Mr. Ford's view of that temperament was limited. His return to the past only went as far back as the period when the "old" quadrilles and some contras were still danced in the ballrooms in cities and towns all over New England. Ford's book begins with thirty pages of lecturing on style, clearly modeled after the old dance manuals of the mid-nineteenth century, which emphasized etiquette above all else. The glossary of dance terms includes all the figures popular when "country" dances had been at their most genteel and stylized; but the glossary noticeably includes only a hidden explanation of swinging, and the illustrations of quadrilles show the swing only in its old form in which the partners simply join hands and do not engage in the waltz position. In the New England contras, however, Ford allowed that dancers might take the waltz position to swing—but only *once* around. Ford's partners, Lovett and his wife, are portrayed throughout

# HENRY FORD'S GOOD MORNING

A fierce opponent of jazz, Henry Ford sought to idolize the purity of the old New England country dancing and usurp the growing popularity of what he considered vulgar music. But, in truth, Ford really revived only the nineteenth-century version of the country dance, already largely stylized by Victorian propriety.

SWINGING PARTNER
Partners take waltz position, each with right foot forward, and turn with the toe of the left foot.

Position of the hands in balance four, chasse, and promenade as used in square and contra dancing.

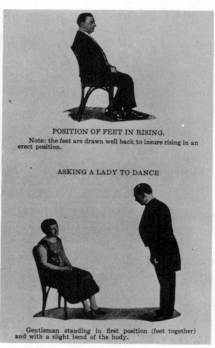

POSITION OF FEET IN RISING.
Note: the feet are drawn well back to insure rising in an erect position.

ASKING A LADY TO DANCE

Gentleman standing in first position (feet together) and with a slight bend of the body.

Ford's personal dancing master, Benjamin Lovett and wife, posed for the instructional photos in the book.

Henry Ford's version of country dancing included elements reminiscent of mid-19th century concern with deportment.

the book dressed in formal attire, demonstrating not only different dance positions but also such important dancing skills as the correct "position of the feet when rising" from a chair.

Ford's reverence for New England was unsurpassed only by his reverence for propriety and decency. His revival of the old square dances was certainly a major contribution to the history of contra dances, the minuet (which was included in the book), and some of the early ballroom round dances such as the polka and the varsovienne. But Ford's sources were clearly not the original folk dances of this country but rather the updated, sophisticated versions of the country dances that really emphasized morality and manners more than exercise and community spirit. Ford's revival really did little to restore respect for the folk life of rural Americans because he failed to understand that the nature of the dancing he liked so well was originally far more spontaneous and free than he allowed.

In addition to visiting New England, Ford traveled to the southern mountains, specifically Lincoln Memorial College, where he danced some of the old mountain dances. However, Ford apparently did not think that these dances, which had never become genteel or refined in any way, belonged in the ballroom with the dances from New England.

Ford's rejection of the southern mountain dances was typical of the attitude toward mountain culture during the late twenties and thirties when this "revival" of square dancing began. In an article from *The Etude,* a music magazine published in Philadelphia, author Arthur Smith had this to say about "Hillbilly Music": "What could be more absurd than this patter [Hillbilly folk songs]. Only one thing: the existence of hundreds of thousands of native Americans who love and buy typical "Hillbilly" songs . . . What songs do the lowly native white folks of the South sing anyway? They are popularly supposed to sing the old, sweet Stephen Foster folk songs, but do they? No. A great, unnumbered, inarticulate multitude of them live in a sort of subterranean musical world of their own, singing, rather, about Annie Wagner 'who did not fear the chair,' about Billy the Kid, 'who at the age of twelve, killed his first man,' about Floyd Collins, Mary Phagan, Jesse James, and Frank Dupree. . . . These folk are interested, like children . . . in trains, wrecks, disasters, and crimes. . . . While none of these songs could be called religious, there is a homely moralization tacked on every one . . . the singers . . . are generally blind, wandering minstrels. I never knew one of these backwoods bards to be in any sense educated. . . . The universal favorites all spring from unlettered founts."[31] Mr. Smith, it turns out, was a dealer of sound-reproducing machines who also sold records he despised "daily to farmers, laborers and mechanics, to young and old, rich and poor, yes, even to bankers, contractors, salesmen and merchants."[32] His attitude toward the "hillbilly" in 1933, when this article was published, represents the educated class' attitude toward folk culture, but it is interesting that even Smith admits that interest in this music was crossing normal class barriers.

But the truth is that in spite of the attitudes of educated men like Smith and Henry Ford's desire to keep the old dances as proper as they were during the Victorian era, the old dances were enjoying a revival on a much wider scale than they liked to admit.

In 1935 a little magazine called *Yankee,* published in Dublin, New Hampshire, began a series of articles devoted to country dancing, authored by a staff member, Beth Tolman, and a local caller, Ralph Page, from neighboring Nelson. *Yankee* was and still is devoted to stories and customs of New England, and in the first year of publication the magazine devoted a great deal of attention to country dancing. The articles by Tolman and Page appeared in every issue of *Yankee* through 1936 and into 1937. Later they were collected into *The Country Dance Book* published in 1937 and reissued in 1976. In addition, *Yankee* published a calendar of events around the New England area which included announcements of the country dances called by Ralph Page in southern New Hampshire.

Page started out as a fiddler, but as he said: "I wasn't too good. I could get along, but I wasn't the good fiddler. . . . In Nelson we used to get together every two or three weeks to play these old dances just for the hell of it, just because we liked to play them. So we thought for goodness sake let's hire the Stoddard town hall and have a dance. There'll be friends enough, maybe we can make some money to buy a couple of loaves of bread or something." This was in 1930, the middle of the Depression, and a lot of people were out of work. So Page and Harry Frazer, who was going to be the caller at the dance in Stoddard, cooked up the idea to make a little money having old-time dances. Page's uncle had been a fine caller, but Ralph was content to play the fiddle and dance. Unfortunately, the night of the dance Harry Frazer developed a quick and serious case of laryngitis. He looked at Page and told him he'd have to call the dance. Page said, "What do you mean? I never opened my mouth to call a dance. I never even said 'Down the Center' to myself out loud," and Frazer said "your father was a pretty good fiddler, and your mother was a wonderful dancer, and your uncle was a caller, and your grandfather was a dancing master. You can be a caller." Page replied, "Harry, what you say is true, but they might have been horse thieves but that wouldn't make me one." But the rest of them said: "go ahead and call." ". . . I was just thrown into the wolves . . . I want to tell you we did contras that night . . . and the first thing I called was the Virginia Reel . . . I had them marching when they should have been reeling, and reeling when they should have been do-si-doing! . . . Oh, what a disaster!"

Later, the Sunday after a dance down at the Munsonville Community Hall on Christmas night, Page's uncle, Wallace Dunn, who had been a caller, invited Ralph over to his house for some "help." Page did not take up the invitation at once, but finally one Sunday he went over to see what kind of help his uncle had to offer: "I went up and after the usual palaverin' (cause with an old Yankee you don't get into the thing right off, you hedge into the subject; we talked a little about the weather, a little bit of gossip, what happened to the minister's daughter and the village idiot) and finally he says: 'Well, I suppose you want me to tell you what you're doing right, about the calling?' 'Well,' I said, 'it would be nice.' He said: 'You weren't doing anything right. You were doing everything wrong. You've got to lead the dancers. You've got a good voice because you can sing. But if you're going to be a caller, you're going to be a good one or you ain't going to be one! You ain't going to bring shame to the family'!" Page's uncle then offered to help him learn the art to insure against family shame. Armed with J. A. French's caller's handbook, which contained quadrilles and contras, Page began his lessons. "Before the winter was over we went through the whole book and I memorized the whole thing and I called them while he played the fiddle and my aunt played the pump organ. And he made me sit right next to him. I know why. When I called on the wrong time or the wrong beat he wouldn't hardly stop, he'd just keep fiddling, but he'd flip his bow around and hit me on the ear! Wow, by gosh, you get hit on the ear and you'll learn how to call!"

By 1938 Page and his orchestra were busy four and five nights a week working in the Monadnock region of southern New Hampshire. He was quickly building a reputation as the best caller of the old contra dances, as well as quadrilles and squares. "We had a full orchestra, ten full men. . . . You always had to have a cornet and a clarinet, and the fiddle, base viol, piano, drums. We had saxophones. We were playing in big dance halls for this area . . . accomodating five or six hundred people, sometimes a thousand people . . . and you take five hundred people walking across a floor you've got to have more than just one fiddle or you ain't going to be heard!" The dance revival was in full swing by this time and had spread to the cities of the Northeast as well, but Page recalls that the square-dance revival was not all roses. The biggest problem was alcohol. "There's certain things which you cannot allow at a good square dance, you cannot have a lot of drinking . . . you can't have people drunk on the floor [and] I didn't hesitate to throw them out of the hall . . . "

Since Prohibition was lifted, Americans had accepted alcohol as their national tranquilizer. "Booze" invaded all social functions, including square dancing—a fact that was to cause concern and dancing problems not unlike those that confronted dancers back in Puritan New England. A lot of people thought Page might be able to deal with the difficult issue. He described his start as a caller in Nelson this way: "When the selectmen [of Nelson] asked me to run dances in the town hall we had a man there running dances and fights had developed on the floor and everything else, and so they got disgusted and wouldn't let the

# RALPH PAGE

Generally considered the most successful modern contra dance caller, Ralph Page got his start in Nelson, New Hampshire, a community then and now a center of contra dance activity. Page was brought in by the town fathers of Nelson to "clean up" the dances, which had become rowdy affairs.

*Photo courtesy of Barry & Karen Tolman*

Ralph Page calling in the Nelson New Hampshire town hall.

Nelson artist F.W.P. Tolman's "Portland Fancy" depicts the old-time spirit of the country dance.

hall . . . and they came to me and said 'would you run the dances? and clean them up?' And I said sure I'll clean up the dances but I've got to have some backing. Will you people back me? And they said they would and they did." Page's get-tough policy worked quite well and soon the people more interested in drinking than dancing stopped coming to his dances.

Page, with coauthor Beth Tolman, explained why the dancing had become popular again in Nelson: "We villagers and visitors, young and old, dance the country dances every Saturday night in the old town hall. Why? Because we've always danced them, for one hundred and seventy years; because there are plenty of available musicians who have grown up in the purple of the country dance tradition. . . . We'd rather shake down a Hull's Victory, or pot a large specimen through to the measures of 'Pop Goes the Weasel,' than do all your slithery Four Hundreds in all your dancing dives in the United States."[33]

Nelson, New Hampshire, wasn't the only place in New England where the dancing had caught on again. Page and Tolman describe dancing they found in Vermont, Massachusetts, and Maine, but they are quick to point out that the interest in the old dances was not universal but peculiar to communities like Nelson, where people had ancestors known for their musical or dancing abilities. There were, in fact, many people in New England who did not approve of dancing, ostensibly for religious reasons, but largely because drinking had begun to give the country dances a bad name. Others just didn't know anything about it, or if they did, they didn't care; but Ralph Page and Beth Tolman felt strongly about the goodness of square dancing. They thought it provided once and for all a chance for anyone to get close to his roots, to get close to his neighbors—no matter what their racial background, and most of all get away from the social activity dominated by useless drinking. It is interesting that their message really differs little from the message of the original Puritan philosophers like John Locke. Page and Tolman, along with other proponents of the country dance, saw the value of dancing for its simplest virtues, unencumbered with affected courtesies added to the dances during the nineteenth century. They understood the importance of the dances, not as historical artifacts but as the activity that helped early Americans express their allegiance to a community spirit. They also understood that the dances and music were as worthwhile as any other form of art offered by the more sophisticated part of society. But most importantly, they recognized the need for change in the dancing to meet the needs of the changing society of dancers; tradition was in their minds but was not to stand in the way of the reasonable evolution of a folk activity, which by its nature should remain spontaneous and free.

Throughout the thirties American folk life began to gain the respect of more and more Americans. Projects like the Federal Writers Project helped the country gain insight into the customs of rural folk who previously had been ignored, forgotten, or looked down upon as inferior. Working-class people had initiated a battle for a decent life years before, which came to a head during and after the Depression. Implicit in this fight was a demand for fairness not only on economic grounds but cultural ones as well. "Hillbilly" music became the idiom for songwriters like Woody Guthrie and others involved in the labor movement, who expressed the virtues of a class of Americans previously thought of as having no art at all. And in addition to this new and prolific production of folk songs, the folk dances of America were able to gain the respect they deserved, not only in New England but in the South and West as well.

Myles Horton, the well-known former director of the Highlander Center in Tennessee, recalls some events that occurred during the first fierce and dangerous days of the labor movement, a time when resistance to management unfairness was met with guns instead of promises: "one of the strange things about a situation like that is not just the terror, but that people manage to keep some sense of humanity. I remember being up in Harlan County [during a strike] around that period, people scared to death all the time, and yet they decided to have a square dance. . . . There was no public place to have a square dance, so everybody would go in and take the furniture out of somebody's front room, take down the stove, move the furniture, move everything out, and have a square dance. Dance until about two or three o'clock in the A.M., then put up the stove again, bring the furniture back in, and the next day shoot it out with the gun thugs."[34]

I don't mean to imply that people who wanted to have a square dance in the southern mountains in the thirties had to worry about getting shot. Puritan morality wasn't that strong. But Horton's story is a perfect digest of the twentieth-century history of southern Appalachian folk life.

In the last part of the nineteenth century and through the first three decades of the twentieth, Appalachia was either ignored or looked down upon by the rest of the country. Mountaineers were stereotyped as illiterate, drunken hillbillies who had no time for work or any other worthwhile effort. Their crafts were considered crude and barely utilitarian by modern standards, and their music and dance were thought to be "childish." Luckily, a few of the more sensitive visitors to the southern mountains found a great deal more than a bunch of barefooted simpletons. One of them was Cecil Sharp, who came to find folk songs he could trace back to English origin, but went home having seen the Kentuckians dance beautiful dances he thought had been preserved from the early seventeenth century. Others, like John C. Campbell, the southern folklorist, saw a different folk life—one of tremendous value, but that had been buried by forces outside Appalachia. Others who lived in the area realized the truth: that their folk life and, indeed, basic cultural identity had been nearly wiped out. So too had their forests been leveled by lumber companies and their men had died in company mines—100 a month from accidents and uncounted more from black lung disease. There was little cause for celebrating in the southern mountains, but some natives recognized that the arts themselves weren't actually dead but that the will of the people almost was. And it was this handful of people who sought to help their neighbors and themselves recognize the worthiness and meaning of their traditions.

In the 1930s two of these native mountaineers, Myles Horton and Don West, founded the Highlander Folk School in the Cumberland Mountains of Tennessee. Modeled after the Danish folk schools Horton had visited, Highlander was founded to meet a vital need of the southern mountain people: a need to reject the prejudicial attitudes of disapproving outsiders and build a new self-respect for their lives and their traditions—which, of course, included music and dancing.

Horton and West had quickly become involved in the struggle of working-class mountaineers to gain fair wages and working conditions in the mines and the cotton mills. Naturally resistance was heavy and often deadly, but perhaps even more threatening to the success of the workers was the ability of the mine and mill owners to wait it out longer. It was the perseverance needed to last through the long strikes that would make or break the movement, and Horton and West realized that, in addition to the counsel they gave on political tactics, they had to somehow help the workers gain the confidence they needed to carry on in the worst circumstances. It was this need that brought music and dance to Highlander. Music soon became an integral part of every program for it was clear to Horton and West that the songs, fiddle tunes, and dances could help build the mountaineers' pride in every aspect of themselves, including their history and arts.

Perhaps the greatest virtue of the music and dancing program at Highlander was its relationship to the people. It was seen not as a precious historical artifact but, rather, as an expression of the community that gave birth to the arts. This expression was living, so that it changed and grew continually to fit the needs of the people. At Highlander people were encouraged to sing new songs along with the traditional, to dance new dances along with the old ones, to express their individual spirits through their singular versions of buckdancing.

It should be noted that Highlander wasn't the only place where dancing and music got a new start in the mountains. Where resistance from the fundamentalist churches wasn't too strong and where some of the

## ROSE SMYTHE / DANCER

Rose Smythe is ninety-four years old and lives in Canton, North Carolina, a small town in the Smoky Mountains west of Asheville. She remembers the local attitude of the church toward dancing when she was just a teenager living in the mountains:

"I was born in Macon County and I lived in Oak Grove where our church was. Now the Baptist people didn't like for their children to dance, but the Methodists didn't care. But because me and my friends went to the dances, they wanted to turn us out of the church. Well they tried me and my friends for dancing the next morning at church, after we'd been dancin' the night before. When it came around to my boyfriend they said 'What do you have to say?' and he says: 'I've not got anything to say, I'll dance when I get ready!' and then they asked me the same thing and I told them 'I've got no apologies to make,' and so they decide to exclude us from the church, and we were, but my name's still on the book'!"

Generally the dances Rose Smythe went to were at "workin's":

"We called it buckdancin' out there. We just danced at different places around the community, like if they throw a cornshuckin' or something, and then we'd shuck that corn out every bit before they'd let us dance, and then they'd give us a supper and then they'd take the beds out of the room and we'd have a square dance till 12 o'clock, but we had to stop for Sunday.
"Some people was real heavy, you know, with their feet on the floor, but I wasn't. I didn't dance like the rest of them. You couldn't hear me dance, you just had to look at my feet. . . . And there was a man in Asheville. He was the best caller, the head man, and I never heard nobody in my life could call as good as he did. He just sung a song with it. He called them dances and it was just singin'. There ain't many people can call a dance good."

One of the most interesting dances Rose went to was in Cullowhee, North Carolina:

"After the time of slavery there came a few in there, niggers, you know after the North and the South quit fightin', and they had their own dances, and my husband used to make the music for them, with Alda Smathers, who was a fiddler and my huband was a banjo picker. The niggers danced just like we did, with the same figures, but a nigger can outdance a white person anytime, especially buckdancin', all by themselves, you know. They didn't pay my husband to play. We just went to play for 'em. And I danced with one of them one time.
"I can't remember a lot of things, now. I forget peoples' names. . . I'm gettin' where I can't talk plain . . . I can't see good . . . can't hear good . . . and I ain't no good! . . . but I will get up and dance with anybody!"

more progressive churches bowed to change, other communities regained interest in the old dances. The dances were mostly learned from people in the remotest "hollers" and coves, where dancing had never stopped being part of the community, where preachers either didn't go or didn't care.

Where Fundamentalist preachers did have control over the morality of their parishioners, dancing and music were opposed and damned as sinful. A big part of the problem was, again, alcohol. Part of the stereotype of the mountaineer Horton and others had to contend with was that of the "moonshiner." True, a great deal of distilling went on in the woods and, like their Scottish forebears, many mountaineers enjoyed a taste of their whiskey; but not all mountaineers were alcoholics. Unfortunately, many mountaineers came to believe in the stereotype of themselves. This, coupled with the effects of a generally puritanical clergy who made the most of any incident involving whiskey and dancing, helped to promote a general belief among many that it was impossible to separate the two activities.

I do not want to leave the impression that in the thirties everyone in the southern mountains suddenly started dancing again. In fact the movement met with tremendous resistance: from the clergy who saw it as sinful; from conservatives who saw it as an expression of "revolutionary" forces behind the labor movement; and from "the educated" who were ashamed of their background and kinsmen who lived in the mountains. But people like Myles Horton, Don West, and countless dancers and musicians gradually gained strength, and interest in the mountain folk life spread steadily.

"Way up here in the mountains, there's a lot of little old schoolhouses, deserted now, and every one of them has a tradition of square dance. How you could ever find it, I don't know, but that was the recreation of those people up there. I know a woman who taught up there and she told me about a mother who tied her son to a horse, and the horse knew the way to the school. They'd get there half-frozen and when it was time to go the teacher would tie him back on and send the horse home. That's the kind of country it was and in all of those little schoolhouses they danced."

This is Dorothy Shaw talking about the mountains near where she lives in Colorado Springs, Colorado. She and her late husband Lloyd came to Colorado Springs in 1914 to teach at the high school there. He taught at the high school for two years until an opening for the principalship at the nearby Cheyenne School came up and he took it. Shaw held a tremendous interest and love for the mountains, and as principal of the Cheyenne School he encouraged the students to make the best of the great opportunities available in their community for mountaineering, skiing, and other indigenous activities including square dancing. Shaw wrote in 1943: "In my first years at Cheyenne School I found a strong community prejudice against dancing. I began to experiment with the European folk dance as a social adjunct to our athletic program. When I had won my football team to it the whole school accepted it and we had great fun."[35] Inspired by Elizabeth Burchenal, the author of many dance manuals, whom he lured to his school from Denver, Shaw indeed developed a dancing program which became so well known around the country that he began to take his students out to exhibit what they knew. They were performing all European dances at this time. They traveled to Los Angeles, Boston, New York, and New Orleans, and as Shaw told it: "We soon after that first trip added early American dances to our repertoire. And then I found that we had hidden away, almost lost to sight, fragments of the old authentic cowboy dances. The old callers were cagey at first and their memories had gone pretty rusty."[36]

Shaw kept digging though and began to collect dances from old folks who remembered them. Meanwhile, word spread that the Cheyenne School group, who had entertained people all over America with their European dances, were now doing American dances as well. Shaw had taken many of his American dances from Henry Ford's *Good Morning,* but soon he had enough authentic western dances to fill his own book, which he entitled *Cowboy Dances.* These were square dances, closely related to the southern mountain running sets, but were always restricted to the four couples. But, most importantly, they expressed uniquely the folk life of the West, primarily through the patter calls laced with cowboy slang and the new figures with names that symbolized the West: the Texas Star and Wagonwheel. Soon the Cheyenne Mountain Dancers had done away with the European dances altogether and were performing a complete program of Western square dances. "They were doing the old American Square Dance pure and simple, with figures executed as called, and with a great deal of laughter, and fervor and joy. . . . There's one place where they'd flap those girls and flap like thunder! because that was one of the old calls. It was action, action of the body, and the soul inside the body just gets up and shouts with joy! The cerebrum was at peace . . . the caller told you what to do and you did it," says Dorothy Shaw.

Lloyd Shaw published *Cowboy Dances* in 1939, and by the summer of 1940 educators from all over the country were coming to learn about the "American Folk Dance" as Shaw called it. One summer he had over five hundred people in attendance at one of his workshops. It didn't take long for the Western square dance to gain an identity all across the country. These summer sessions continued throughout the World War II

# THE CHEYENNE MOUNTAIN DANCERS

Caller and leader Lloyd "Pappy" Shaw.

*Photo courtesy Caxton Printers,
Caldwell, Idaho.*

*Photo courtesy Sets in Order American Square Dance Society.*

The Cheyenne Mountain Dancers
"The soul inside the body just gets up and shouts with joy!"—Dorothy Shaw

years and western dancing grew at a steady rate. Meanwhile, the Cheyenne Mountain Dancers continued to perform exhibitions all across the country, and in 1948 the group returned to Los Angeles.

One of the people most impressed with the Cheyenne Mountain Dancers at the Los Angeles exhibition was Bob Osgood, who had met Lloyd Shaw three years before the group came to California. Osgood had been working for a soft-drink company in the public relations department, and in the course of traveling across the country he discovered that his hobby of square dancing was enjoyed by people all over America. "There were all these bodies moving around after the War and nobody knew anybody, but it seemed to be the thing and I suddenly found myself in the middle of something that was about to explode. It was amazing how different it was everywhere." The differences in the regional dancing styles caused Osgood to think that some kind of communication was needed among dancers across the country, so in 1948, with the inspiration of Lloyd Shaw on his side, he issued the first issue of *Sets in Order,* a magazine devoted to Western square dancing. "We put out 5,000 copies in November '48 and the magazine immediately grew. It became a sort of communication center, not trying to set policy, but a place to exchange ideas that in time became policy themselves. One of the things that sort of established us was that as the square dancing grew it appeared that something like standardization might be appropriate, so that people could avoid promenading four different ways in the same area. The magazine served other purposes such as showing costuming, which was no big deal really, except that some people came to dance in dirty sweat shirts, which helped keep the barn dance idea alive, and we felt we needed to get away from it. So as the magazine grew we came to a place where we were really serving as more than a magazine."

In addition to publishing the magazine, Bob Osgood's involvement in square dancing included becoming a caller and teacher for the thousands of Californians anxious to learn this new activity. A lot of callers went to learn from Lloyd Shaw, including Osgood, and by 1948 with all these callers and the magazine, southern California became the hot spot of square dancing. "We had regular television shows, and the newspapers carried what amounted to a picture strip on How to Dance every day. Myself and another caller started teaching classes at the Beverly Hills High School, one of us in the boys' gym and the other in the girls' gym. The class was supposed to start at 7 P.M., but by 5:30 the lines would already be around the block, and by the time we opened the doors, both classes, 25 squares in each, would be sold out! It was the thing to do. We had a lot of outstanding callers here, almost all the recording companies were here; the television center was here. We made five movies for major studios."

# THE SQUARE DANCE BOOM

*Photo courtesy of Sets In Order American Square Dance Society*

In the late 1940's modern square dance came alive and grew astronomically. This huge dance took place in Seattle.

The square dance boom was on. Clubs, associations of clubs, and callers sprang up everywhere, not only in southern California, but across the entire country. Still, southern California was the center. On a warm Thursday night in July, 1950, the city of Santa Monica celebrated its seventy-fifth anniversary with a square dance. City officials allowed a long section of Wilshire Boulevard to be blocked to traffic so that there could be dancing in the streets. There were beautiful lights in the palm trees that swayed in the breeze off the Pacific. Bob Osgood and Lloyd "Pappy" Shaw shared the duties as masters of ceremonies and thirty-five callers from southern California were there with musicians. By the time that evening of dancing was in full swing 15,200 dancers had turned the evening into the world's largest square dance.

## Notes

1. Curt Sachs, *World History of the Dance* (W. W. Norton), pp. 158–159.
2. Ibid., p. 159.
3. Ibid., p. 214.

4. Ibid., p. 336.
5. Cecil Sharp, *The Country Dance Book* vol. 5 (Novello & Co.), p. 9.
6. Thomas Wilson, *Analysis of Country Dancing* 1811, p. 305.
7. Cecil Sharp, *The Country Dance Book* vol. 6 (Novello & Co.), p. 12.
8. William Prynne, *Histriomatrix.*
9. Samuel Sewall, *The Diary of Samuel Sewall* (G.P.Putnam's Sons), p. 39.
10. S. Foster Damon, *The History of Square Dancing* p. 5.
11. Louis B. Wright, *The First Gentlemen of Virginia* (Dominion, 1964), p. 83.
12. Ibid.
13. Jack P. Greene, *Landon Carter* (Dominion, 1965), pp. 23–24.
14. Louis B. Wright, *The First Gentlemen of Virginia* p. 82.
15. S. Foster Damon, *The History of Square Dancing* pp. 12–13.
16. Paul E. Doran, "The Backgrounds of the Mountain People" from *Mountain Life and Work,* January 1936.
17. Peter Cartwright, *The Autobiography of Peter Cartwright* p. 34.
18. Ibid., pp. 207–208.
19. Lynne F. Emery, *Black Dance in the United States 1619–1970* (National Press Books) p. 100.
20. Ibid.
21. Ibid., p. 26.
22. Ibid., p. 100.
23. Ibid., p. 91.
24. From *Rocky Mountain News* vol. 2, no. 44, February 20, 1861.
25. Ibid.
26. Interview on file in Colorado Historical Society, 1934.
27. Ibid., undated.
28. Dick and Fitzgerald *Dick's Quadrille Book* p. 92.
29. S. Foster Damon, *The History of Square Dancing* p. 40.
30. Cecil Sharp didn't like jazz either. Of jazz dancing he had this to say:
"These dances, popularly and collectively known as the Jazz, came to us heavily charged with negroid characteristics, presumably contracted in the Southern States of North America, and associated with a very distinctive type of syncopated, or rag-time music. The sawing movements of the arms, the restless, vibratory shakings of the shoulders and the close embrace, the merciless tom-tom rhythm and clatter of the music, all of which may be traced to negro influence, have since been considerably modified, and dancers now affect a far more restrained and dignified style than that which characterised the dance in its earlier form. Had it not been for the unsettlement of mind, manners and habits, which followed in the train of the Great War [WW I], and the fact that at the moment this was the only available dance with which to satisfy the craze for dancing, which set in after the Armistice, it is permissible to doubt whether a dance of so inferior, and in its earlier forms so objectionable, a type, would have gained a foothold in this country [England]. Truth to tell, there is little to be advanced in its favour and much that can be charged against it."
From *The Dance: An Historical Survey of Dancing in Europe* by Cecil Sharp and A.P. Oppé (London, New York 1924) pp. 31–32.
31. Arthur Smith, "Hillybilly Folk Music" from *The Etude,* March 1933, p. 154.
32. Ibid.
33. Beth Tolman and Ralph Page, *The Country Dance Book* (Countryman Press), pp. 7–8.
34. Guy and Candie Carawan, *Voices from the Mountains* (Alfred Knopf), p. 123.
35. *Current Biography* 1943, p. 689.
36. Ibid., p. 690.

# II

# BASIC FIGURES

Country dances can be most easily understood if you think of them as either choral dances—dances that require a group of people to do them; or solo dances—dances for one person or a couple. The couple dances are also called "round dances," the waltz and polka for example.

As we have seen, the choral country dances are usually danced in one of three forms: the double column or contra formation; the circle formation, and the square formation. All three of these forms are figure dances; that is, they are made up of figures that are performed according to the structure of a tune. The most common structure is provided by the traditional fiddle tunes, primarily jigs and reels. Usually these tunes have two parts that are repeated, very similar to old folk songs that have a verse and a chorus. In the case of dance tunes one part, say the verse part, is called the "A" part, and the second, or chorus part, is called the "B" part. Depending on what type of country dance you're doing, these two parts are used to structure each dance.

Round dances—dances for couples such as the waltz and the polka—became popular among American dancers during the nineteenth century. During an evening of country dancing, polkas, waltzes, and other traditional rounds are commonly interspersed with the regular figure dances: more so in New England and western dances than in the South where the dancing has been less affected by the influence of these more sophisticated ballroom-type dances. It is worth noting that the round dances enjoyed by Western square dancers have become as complicated as some of their figure dancing. Some of them are so elaborate that they require someone to cue the movements.

It is worth noting that the round dances enjoyed by Western square dancers have become as complicated as some of their figure dancing. Some of them are so elaborate that they require someone to cue the movements.

The waltz, in its original form, and as a basis for the more complex round dances, is the most common of the rounds. The basic 1–2–3, 1–2–3, 1–2–3 is well known, and in this instructional section of this book I will not go into any detail about how to waltz. Suffice it to say that the waltz step is very easy to learn, and yet "good" waltzing requires an undefinable input of personal expression and style. The same holds true for the polka, which is more or less a very fast waltz step, and the schottische, a kind of skipping dance.

Waltzing

So now let us look at some of the figures used to compose the simple choral country dances of America. This section of the book will introduce twelve basic country dance movements or figures common to all three major types of American country dancing: Contra dancing, Big Circle dancing, and Square dancing. In addition to these figures, each regional type of dance has added special figures which characterize that type of dance. The most important of these special figures are explained in the specific dance example listed at the end of each regional section.

It is worth mentioning that dancing style ultimately determines how these figures are performed. What I am giving here is a basic explanation of the figures. But individual dancers have often modified the figures radically to suit their momentary mood. Often these modifications become fashionable. For example, it is fashionable among young New England contra dancers to spin like tops as they execute a do-si-do: and some very imaginative Western square dancer added Flip Wilson's elaborate greeting to the allemande. A fundamental problem with every instructional dancing book since *The Dancing Master* is that the style of dancing is always changing—usually as a result of the enthusiasm of the dancers. I can't think of any better reason to admit that what I describe here will be out of date tomorrow; for, after all, it is the dancer who makes the dance, and the most valuable contribution he gives to the dance is his imagination, his most free and graceful body movements, his respect for his fellow dancers, and his joy for dancing.

This glossary of Basic Figures by no means provides a comprehensive instructional manual for country dancing, but it will make it possible for the novice dancer to get started, which is the whole point!

## The Figures

1. *The Allemande:*   This figure may be performed with any number of other people in the dance: a partner, a corner, the "one below" or the "one above." The caller should make it clear who you are to Allemande, and with which hand, left or right. When the figure is called, the two dancers designated for the Allemande join hands as "arm wrestlers" do and turn once around. In an "Allemande Right" the right feet meet to make the axis, and the left feet move around the axis like the pencil in a compass. The enjoyment of the Allemande is enhanced when the two dancers lean back away from each other as they turn.

2. *The Balance:* One of the more simple yet mysterious figures, the Balance, is done alone, with one other dancer, or sometimes in a line of three or more dancers. The simplest Balance is done by gently kicking the right foot forward or to the side while hopping on the left foot, and then repeating that movement kicking the left foot and hopping on the right. In New England a couple holds right hands when balancing, but in the Western square dancing very often hands are not held. I never saw any body balance in the South, but the basic step is similar to the basic step of the buckdancing done there.

3. *Circle:*   Probably the easiest figure of all, Circling, is done by any number of people joining hands and moving in a circle to the left or to the right. A very basic figure of primitive dancers, Circling often begins or ends a dance. It may symbolize the sun or the moon or in modern times the earth; its effect is to unify the dancers.

4. *Do-Si-Do:*   Like Allemande, the "Do-Si-Do" is a figure with a French name, derived from *dos à dos* that is, back to back. And that is essentially what the figure consists of. Two dancers dance toward and past each other, passing right shoulders and then, without turning, return to the place dancing backwards, passing left shoulders. The Do-Si-Do can be embellished in any number of ways. In New England it is currently

fashionable for each partner to spin like a top as they Do-Si-Do. Some
people flap their arms like pigeon wings or stamp their feet in a clog
step while they do it.

5. *Forward and Back:*   A dancer can go Forward and Back with one
other dancer, or with another couple, or with a whole line of dancers. It
simply means dancing forward toward the other dancer(s), almost close
enough to touch, and then dancing back to place. Sometimes in a circle
dance the caller will have the circle "all go to the Center and Back,"
which is simply a variation on the Forward and Back. Lots of dancers
like to give a whoop when they do this, which is fun—the louder the
better.

6. *Grand Right and Left:*   For some reason this figure confuses people to
no end. It's really very simple. On the call each dancer simply turns to
his right and faces the person opposite him; extends his right hand just
as if to shake hands, then passes that person's right shoulder and extends the left hand to the next oncoming dancer, shakes left hands, passes left shoulders, and then proceeds around the ring "right, left, right,
left, etc." until the caller thinks of something else to do. Callers like this
figure a lot. It gives them time to think. (In the south this figure is
sometimes called "Rights and Lefts," not to be confused with Figure 12,
"Right and Left.")

7. *Ladies Chain:*  Also known as "Ladies Change," this is a figure performed by two couples standing opposite each other. As in a Grand
Right and Left, the ladies dance toward each other extending and joining right hands, then pass right shoulders as they extend their left hands
to the opposite men waiting their arrival. As they join left hands with the
men, they are guided around by the man in a U turn. The man sends
them back to meet each other in the center again to join right hands,
passing right shoulders, taking the left hand of the awaiting partner who
U turns them again, back to place. Sometimes a dance calls for a
Half-ladies Chain, in which case the dancer simply goes halfway, stop-
ping after the first U turn.

8. *The Promenade:*   Undoubtedly the easiest figure, I've always felt the Promenade was also the most romantic. I always think of some handsome couple "promenading" right off the floor out on to some starlit balcony. Anyway everybody always knows how to promenade. It's just dancing along side by side with your partner in any number of different ways (see illustrations). Promenades last as long as you want them to unless the caller tells you to stop. People promenading with their sweethearts always take a few extra steps.

9. *Sashay:*   Also known as "Chassez," the French word, this is a figure slightly less common than the others described here. To do it, a couple joins hands facing each other and simply slides to the left or the right depending on what the caller has directed. You extend the foot that's closest to the direction you're going to go out, simultaneously with your partner who is extending the opposite foot but in the same direction. Then, simultaneously, the other foot is brought up to meet the other foot. This procedure is repeated in one direction until the caller tells you to stop or come back to place. What makes the Sashay hard is doing it with someone who's a lot bigger or smaller than you are and consequently takes a different size step.

10. *The Star:*   Like the Promenade, the Star has many different regional styles (see illustrations). Essentially "to Star" means to make a four-pointed formation with another couple and to circle around to the left or right depending on the call. The hand formation varies: hands may be crossed, or hands may grasp wrists. In the "Texas Star," used in the Western square dance, hands are held up, palms in. My personal feeling is that the Star is one of the more mystical figures; that its form is kin to that of the flower, and consequently, like the Circle, directly inspired by a form in nature.

Two Star Formations

Swing/waltz position

Swing/ New England Buzz Step

Swing/ Hands on shoulders.

11. *The Swing:*   Not surprisingly, the best figure in country dancing is the most difficult; not only to explain in words but to do! Our illustrations show three of the popular positions to take while Swinging. Like the Allemande, the success of the Swing depends upon the tension and weight created by the two dancers leaning away from each other just enough to increase speed, momentum, and balance, most importantly balance. But the success of Swinging also depends largely upon other less technical factors: such as whom you are swinging with, how much room there is to move in, and the mood of the dancers. Also, it can be safely said that you can't Swing with just anybody. Some people are better at it than others. Why this is so remains a mystery to me, a mystery I don't care to solve, but suffice it to say that the joining of two matched swingers brings the greatest joy to country dancers.

RIGHT AND LEFT THROUGH

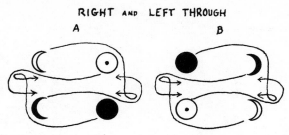

12. *Right and Left:*   Also known as "Right and Left Through," this figure resembles the Ladies Chain. It is done with two opposite couples
(partners face each other) who dance toward each other, passing right
shoulders with your partner. Change places with the person you danced
over with, turning back to face the opposite way. Dance back passing
right shoulders again on the return trip and change places. Couples
should end up where they started.

In the following section of this book, dancers express their particular af-
fection for different dances, which are made up primarily of the figures
described above. It is hoped that readers who are inclined to do so will
try these dances out sometime, hopefully under the direction of a good
caller. I should add that a caller will also give many literal calls which
have not been described here because they are self-explanatory: calls like
"All Clap Hands," or "Cross Over and Cross Back to Place." Finally,
there are, of course, thousands of other figures in country dancing
which have been described over and over in dance manuals throughout
history. These manuals have been listed in a catalogue section at the end
of the book, along with a listing of materials which give access to the
music appropriate for dances of this type. But the figures listed here will
get you through the dances in this book (plus the special figures in particular dances), and make for a good basic foundation for any dance.
   I suppose if I had to think of the most important piece of advice to
give to a beginning dancer, it would be this: be a good listener. If the
caller knows what he's doing and you listen to him and no one else, these
figures will make absolute sense to you.

# III

# NEW ENGLAND
# CONTRA DANCING

I

I learned how to do a two-step the other night, and I learned how to do a schottische. I hope I can remember how to do them, but if I don't, then I'll probably get another chance next time I go up to Ray and Ida's. The thing about the schottische is the hop, or the bounce, or whatever you want to call it. But in the two-step the important thing's the two; two together, gliding around. Ray and Ida, they can really two-step, and Wayne Young fiddles just right for the dance.

Ray and Ida Hull live in Royalton, Vermont, just off the interstate. Royalton has one law school, one inn, one fire station, one railroad station, and one tavern, where the locals hang out to drink beer and listen to loud music. Sometimes at night when the Amtrak train roars through the town, the law school, fire station, railroad station, and tavern all tremble and the music disappears. Ray and Ida live up on a hill, on the second floor of an old woodframe house. The last time I'd been up in Ray and Ida's kitchen was in the dead of winter. We drank whiskey and talked about contra dancing, and Ida kept bringing out food: pizza and potato chips and dips. Ray's the caller for a group of dancers who give exhibitions of old-time contra dances in New England. The group was founded in 1934 by caller Ed Larkin.

Larkin remembered some of the old contra dances from dances he went to in peoples' homes. His daughter, Gertrude Roberts, tells how her father first discovered the dancing:

"He went to this dance they called a 'kitchen junket.' A whole neighborhood would gather in someone's kitchen, and that's how they got the name of the kitchen junket. They'd have them in different people's houses and they'd dance until about midnight; and then at midnight they'd put on a baked-bean supper, or people would bring pies and doughnuts and things like that and they'd have a regular feed. And then after the supper they'd clear off the table and go to dancing again! And sometimes it would even get along time for some of them to do chores and be on a Saturday night, and they'd go home and do the chores and come back, and they might well be dancing through Sunday forenoon! . . . I can remember the first kitchen junket I ever went to and that one was at my uncle's. Of course they all gathered around and danced in the kitchen. They used to have the old organs then. It wasn't pianos and someone would play the chords on the organ and then there'd be the fiddler. And usually that's all the music there'd be, the fiddle and the organ . . . I was probably about ten years old and I just couldn't imagine what was happening, because normally, you see, I was supposed to be sent to bed before it got to be daylight . . . but one time I went and looked out the window and it was getting to be daylight and I hadn't been to bed yet!

"Back then it was all horse and buggies . . . and Dad used to like to have me go along to the dances. He had a small farm and a sawmill and he sugared and all, and he got tired after the dance and he'd want to sleep on the way home so he'd like to have me go to kind of drive the horse along—course that was OK with me too! One time we started out to a dance over in North Randolph in winter time and there was deep snow and it was drifted . . . and you had to keep warm to get there. So we had the old-fashioned freestones, heated up on the stove so they were nice and hot . . . and you wrapped them in newspaper and you had one to put in your lap to keep your hands warm and one to put down at your feet. And then when you got into the sleigh you had this big old laprobe you put over your lap. And then you had the kerosene lantern, and you lit that, and we put it right down between the two of us and its heat helped to keep us warm. Anyway we started out to East Randolph and it was very drifted in the road so we had to go around out into the field. Well we got out there in the field going along and the runners caught into a drift and out we went! Sleigh tipped right over and we went right out with it into the snow. But we picked ourselves up and got our things back together and went on. We got over to the dance and decided not to go back home on that same road. So we took another one after the dance and headed out towards home. Dad was asleep. Down one bank of the road was quite steep and he was leaning one way and I had to hold him, the reins and the horse! He used to wear this big fur coat, and he was leaning way over and so I'd grab that coat. He looked like he was going out over the bank and I just kept pulling him back in! Anyway we got home at seven in the morning and one of the neighbors was out milking when we went by. I went to bed and I didn't get up till four the next afternoon. . . . That was just a winter experience.

"Dances were usually in the local neighborhood. There were those that didn't approve of course. For some it was against their religion to dance and some of them didn't care for dancing so they stayed home. It was just a common thing. 'Course they always used to have their old homemade cider down in the cellar and they'd have their cider pitchers too which made it a little jolly in the crowd!"

Ed Larkin started out as a fiddler for public dances but soon fell into directing the dance troupe. He directed the demonstration group until his death in 1954 at the age of eighty-six. Mrs. Roberts recalls how he first came to start calling for exhibition:

"He started the dance troupe, what we now call the Ed Larkin Dance Troupe, because of a fellow in Tunbridge by the name of Edward Flint. He had a place called Antique Hill, where he had an old log cabin, an old cider press and that kind of thing, for people to come and see the old crafts. This was down at the Fairgrounds in Tunbridge, and one year he thought it would be nice to have a group down there to demonstrate some of the old-time contra dances. So he asked my father to get a group together, which he did, and we danced at the Tunbridge fair just about every year since then.

"But before that he just played at public dances around the area. So when he started the troupe he went around to all the different towns where he had noticed a particularly good dancer, and he'd ask them to dance in the troupe, and that's how he got them together originally. He didn't insist on having precise steps all the time, because he wanted it more or less natural, but he wanted people who were good demonstrators to be on the team, people who could keep to the time of the changes.

"Dad liked to pick dances that had the best changes in them, not the ones where you just sashay and promenade all the time. He had an old Howe's violin and dance instruction book that had the bars of music and the dance changes underneath. He liked the intricate dances, like 'Chorus Jig,' where you've got 'contra corners' to turn. He played the fiddle, he managed the floor, and he called the changes. And he didn't have a microphone . . . he had a voice that carried right out the whole length of the hall. I realized that once when I did a change too quick. I sashayed the center a little bit before I should have and my name was rung right out, right down through the hall! It didn't make any difference who it was . . . you were in place where you were supposed to be or you got spoken to!"

During Ed Larkin's years as director of the troupe, one of the most memorable events was when he took his dancers to New York for the World's Fair of 1940. Henry Ford was there with his dance team from Dearborn, Michigan, and the Larkin Dancers competed in a contest against the Ford team which the Larkin team won. After Larkin's death the group returned to New York for the World's Fair of 1960, but there was no competition this time; they went simply to demonstrate the old dances. Now under the direction of Ray Hull, the Ed Larkin Dancers perform all over New England. Many of the dancers were on the original team Ed Larkin started. They are local people: farmers, housewives, factory workers; and they dance beautifully, with care but with much freedom and spirit.

The second time we went over to Ray and Ida's was on a late summer night. Ray went out to the woodshed and brought in a jug of something and we all drank it: it was a mixture of corn whiskey and apple cider laced with some fermented maple syrup. Fiddler Wayne Young and his wife Mary snickered when Jack Perron took a big swig and said how smooth it was, and Bob Fiore, the true Italian gourmet, used it to wash down his pizza. Wayne and Jack and I argued about who would play the next tune, graciously deferring to one another, until finally somebody said, "By Jesus I'll play one" and everybody said "Great! great tune." Then after that tune, the argument would start all over again, we'd go round and round deferring to one another like three graduates of diplomacy school until we'd end up with a standard tune like "Fisher's Hornpipe" because we all knew it, to one degree or another. Jack Perron played smooth and intricately; Wayne Young played "danceably," in the French Canadian style; and me—well, I call it percentage fiddling: 50 percent of this tune, 80 percent of that one, and sometimes the whole 100 percent.

"Great Jesus," said Ray, "we need the piano. . . . Ida let's go downstairs, down to Pop's . . . he's got a piano down there." So we gathered up our fiddles, the pizza and the beer, and headed down the stairs to Pop's. We went through a narrow crooked stairwell into a kitchen with a floor that was frost-heaved and an old tin ceiling, and then on into the living room filled with a collection of postcards and shoeboxes that buried the center of our attention, the piano, an upright, totally out of tune with itself but perfect for the occasion. Wayne started in playing a tune, and Jack took the piano while I tuned my mandolin. Ray and Ida started dancing . . . gallops and schottisches and waltzes and two-steps. We rolled up the rug and all took our share of maple-syrup apple cider. Bob Fiore the filmmaker was taking it down on the camera, whirring away on his head. The tunes kept coming out of Wayne, and Ray and Ida waltzed and two-stepped appropriately. Midnight, one, two o'clock. "Jesus," said Ray, "got to work tomorrow, I mean, this morning." But he and Ida kept on dancing. Fiore fell asleep, Perron could hardly keep on the piano stool, and Wayne became a human fiddle jukebox, an extension of his bow, a piston of horsehair.

*Ray:* "I'm not that much up on music. I can keep time with it, but I never could play. I've tried to when I was young, but maybe I didn't work on it enough . . . but I've danced all my life. My folks used to take me when I was a baby and put me to sleep in the corner somewhere and they'd play. I had a brother that started playing at dances when he was nine years old on fiddle . . . he was tremendous. The first time he ever had a fiddle in his hand he could play it. If I could only have been that way I'd be playing today. But the prompter is important. His timing has

got to be right. It helps the music, it helps the dancers if the prompting
is right. . . . The prompter can slow the music a little bit, not too much, if
he sees the dancers are getting a little bit ahead of it . . . but with this
fiddler I just give him a look, or I'll hesitate before I make the next call,
and he knows. . . . I make mistakes, I don't intend to, and our dancers
make mistakes. We don't pretend to be perfect, but I do try to have my
timing down."

*Ida:* "Sometimes he gives a wrong call and some of us, we'll follow it
anyway, even though we know it's wrong, and everybody says: 'Well, he
said it!' But you're supposed to know them well enough to do it right no
matter what he says!"

*Ray:* "Well, they're supposed to listen to the prompter. They got to
be pretty well on the up-and-up if they're listening to the prompter and
he makes a bad call, and anybody can . . . 'cause we're not professionals.
Like I say, when we go out on exhibition we try to bring it back like it
was a hundred years ago and they weren't perfect!"

Something about a waltz always makes for a good ending to a dance,
large or small. So we waltzed. Jack waltzed with the piano. Wayne waltzed
with his fiddle and bow. Bob Fiore waltzed with some character in a
dream. I waltzed with my mandolin. Mary waltzed alone, and Ray and
Ida waltzed, balanced and spinning together, connected like maple seeds.

*Ray:* "And what's so nice about these dances is that you can go on the
floor with your partner and you can meet a dozen people or more during that dance . . . she's going down one way and you're going down
another and you're mixing in and you get to meet all the people in your
set, and like in 'Portland Fancy' you can meet pretty near everybody in
the hall! 'Cause you keep going . . . that's what's so nice about this
old-type dancing is you get to meet everybody. It's the whole hall dancing together."

Leaving for home after this dance was an event. We lingered outside at
Ray and Ida's, star gazing, speculating about the weather, and trying to
start the car. We stood in the summer predawn light half in the car;
half-dazed but full of energy. Wayne and Mary left first, and then Jack,
Bob, and I got into my car. Ray and Ida said: "Now don't forget us.
Don't forget us."

By the time I turned on to the interstate in Sharon, after passing the
law school, the train station, and the bar in Royalton, the others were out
cold. I drove home alone, passing a truck somewhere around Windsor.
"Don't forget us," they'd said. I remembered that they had said that to
us the last time we were there.

Every so often Fiore woke up and asked if I were still awake. Then he
fell out again. I passed a deer crossing and wondered when I would ever

# THE ED LARKIN DANCERS

Wayne Young, fiddler.

*Nevell*

The Ed Larkin Dance Troupe

*Nevell*

*Courtesy of Gertrude Larkin Roberts*
Ed Larkin

Ray and Ida Hull

*Randy Miller.*

see a deer cross at a deer crossing. Whenever I drive late at night and it suddenly becomes dawn, I try to pretend that it's really dusk and I am traveling backwards through the day. But it doesn't work: the milk trucks, the empty town roads at sunrise with the streetlights still on, the piles of undelivered newspapers stacked up on sidewalks dispel my fantasy. Passing by a dairy farm, a farmer was out starting up his milking machines. The new tin roof on his barn shined like chrome. I thought of the poem by Roethke: "I wake to sleep, and take my waking slow. I learn by going where I have to go," and I remembered another thing Ray Hull said:

"You know, fifteen years ago the young people didn't want to have anything to do with us, but today they're filling the hall when we have open house. It's coming back. I believe it. We've tried to keep this thing going and we've done our best . . . of course now I enjoy going to see other types of dancing, too. Like over in New Hampshire you've got Dudley Laufman. Now he calls a little different, and those kids dance a little different, they kind of whoop it up more, but I think he's done a great job."

## II

Dudley Laufman is one of those people who's always moving. I guess that's what makes him a dancer's dancer. When we filmed him up at his house in Canterbury, we had him sitting at a desk piled high with old pictures and letters, a good scene for an interview but somehow inappropriate for Dudley because he seemed stiff and unnatural. Behind him birds flew in and out of a feeder. His wife Patty and daughter Windy were bustling around the house, but Dudley sat there, immobilized under the hot lights, crammed into a corner with a cameraman and soundman hovering around, and two interviewers firing questions at him. We talked for a long time and Dudley told us how he was first exposed to the country dancing:

"The very first time I heard the music I was working on a dairy farm over in Freemont, and we used to have corn roasts on Sunday night. We'd have a hymn sing and then we'd end up doing the Virginia Reel in the living room. Jonathon played the fiddle and his wife played piano, and that was the first time I heard the music, responded to it and could identify with it. . . . But the first time I ever heard any really good country dance music was at the New England Folk Festival, back in the forties, and I went into the hall and I heard McQuillen playing his accordion with about five old fiddlers and I was pretty excited about it. Then I started going to dances with Ralph Page's Boston orchestra. Then I got dragged up to a dance in Peterborough [New Hampshire] one time. You went in and parked your car and there were pine trees all around, and the Contoocook River was flowing by, there was a waterfall there, and you went into this old barn that had been fixed up into a studio and it had a spring floor. The dance had started and you could hear the music coming out through the windows. McQuillen was playing the accordion and John Tromblay was on piano; Russ Allen and Dick Richardson on fiddle, Junior was playing bass and Ralph was calling . . . and I'm telling you that was just beautiful, the way the sound came out, this high pitched sound coming out, and the thump of the dancers feet. There were a lot of local people that danced then, a lot of farmers and woodchoppers and some of the summer people, and there was a definite style, it was where I really saw that clogging for the first time, the whole floor was going . . . and it was a total effect I just remembered."

Dudley's been moving ever since. The best place to find him sitting in one place for more than a few minutes is in his car. Like a traveling salesman, he averages a thousand miles a week in his VW, going from town to town running country dances. His time in the car is the space he gets all to himself, like the space between two stanzas of a poem, where nothing is said but the next event is imminent. His time in the car is well spent: he memorizes words to songs, plays the harmonica, and maybe thinks about what he's going to do when he gets where he's going; who's going to be at the dance.

When Bob Fiore and I started to work on our film about contra dance, and Bob told Dudley I was going to help out, Dudley had said: "Oh yeah, he doesn't come to my dances anymore"—even though up to then Dudley and I had never talked at length and certainly had had no personal relationship. I was amazed that Dudley had any idea who I was. But Dudley notices exactly who comes to his dances—and in this case, who does not. Later in the year after we had shown him a rough version of the film before final editing, we talked about his relationship with the dancers:

"Somehow there's a whole space between me and the dancers, and I can see the whole, but I can't feel each one . . . so occasionally to get myself closer to them I'll take the band down on the floor with me where I can feel all that energy that's happening down there. . . . To be a dancer, well, I can't do that anymore, because I'm too busy playing for them. . . . I've become separated from them, and I guess I've sort of forgotten sometimes about that wonderful energy. You see I can't go to one of my own dances to really get that feeling . . . but there is a definite spirit, and there are smells and sounds and things that you see, the way they dress and behave, and for me there's something totally exciting to watch them on the dance floor."

The fall of 1976 marked the end of the Bicentennial summer, a season of seven-day work weeks for Dudley. On a late afternoon in Hanover, New Hampshire—one of those Indian summer days New Englanders covet like gold—Dudley, Jack Perron, a caller from Harrisville, New Hampshire, and I stood on the steps of Wilson Hall at Dartmouth College. I remember this day particularly well because Dudley talked about being very tired, a state of mind and body I didn't think he ever experienced. But he said he was tired, after calling dance after dance, and that he had decided to take the month of September off to rest. He said that sometimes he would wake up in the middle of the night wondering what he was doing. He said: "I didn't know when I started to call full time if it wouldn't drive me nuts, but I had to try it and see." Later I thought about what he had said, and for the first time I realized how hard a caller works. I had always thought of Dudley as a multitude of people: the caller, the dancer, the fiddler, the joke teller, the poet, but never associated any of those roles with hard work. Now I saw that all of these occupations were work for Dudley, and, more significantly, they all were connected, tied together in such a way that helped him create a dance. Dudley has written several books of poetry, and I believe he applies his skills as a poet to the business of calling a dance. He is aware that a poem must have a beginning, an ending, and a meaning. So, too, a dance. He explains it like this:

"You can't predict what's going to happen at a dance. You never know if there's going to be a bunch of regular dancers where you can just do the standard stuff, or suddenly a whole busload of kids from a summer ·camp will show up, and they've never danced in their lives, and I have to be prepared for that. But there's usually enough good dances to do that everybody can enjoy. I try to vary the dances as I go along, doing a line dance and then maybe some squares, or a circle dance or something; and I try and remember what I did the night before in case a lot of the dancers who've been there, so they won't get bored . . . but my inclination is to cater to the total effect of the dance . . . I have to be totally aware of who's on the floor, who's in the band, everything. I think the spirit of the country dance is friendliness, good naturedness and tolerance for beginners, and people who've danced for a long time but are all left feet."

But not every dance goes smoothly. Mistakes are made and problems arise, and sometimes the dancers don't like what's going on. Dudley has to respond to them:

"Some dancers are uptight about doing things 'right,' and it's hard to cope with because I feel that I've done a good job and I've brought happiness to a lot of people. I think my dances are fun things to go to, and then someone says I haven't done a dance 'right,' and I have to expend energy fighting with them, and I don't like to do that. It's difficult to tell somebody to get off my back because it's not in the spirit of the dance, and I get upset when I find someone wants to waste time arguing about it. . . . Sometimes I get hassled from the floor and I find myself getting angry which I don't like. I don't mind people talking to me from the floor but when someone starts telling me how to run the dance and I know damn well he can't do it, I have to put some energy into fighting back. . . . It's just that some people are so hung up on this tradition thing and I really don't concern myself with tradition per se. It's an ongoing thing that's happening now and my job is to take care of those kids who've paid their two bucks to get in the dance, not preserve the tradition of some dance like 'Hull's Victory' . . . I think any negativity should be left outside the door. You should come in to dig the music, dig the people that are there and the dancing . . . I don't like it when people complain that I'm not doing good dances and I shouldn't pay any attention to the people who don't know how to dance—the people who're just getting into it and really enjoying it. But sometimes they come up after the dance is over and tell me about the belligerence of some people who shoved them around. I guess the biggest problem is the dancer who refuses to accept growth, like I'm supposed to protect some memory of theirs . . . but I continue to grow and the dance scene continues to grow, new people come into it all the time, but some people blame me because the scene changes."

Dudley often faces difficult situations. One night I rode over with piano and accordion player Bob McQuillen to a dance being held at the American Legion hall in Seabrook, New Hampshire. It was one of Dudley's many Bicentennial dances during that summer of 1976. Colored ceiling lights had been set up, and a few Legionnaires were hanging around at the bar drinking beer. None of them were waiting for the dance to begin: they thought we were a country and western band or something like it. By the time the dance was supposed to start, a grand total of six people were there, and when Dudley began only four of them got up to dance: the other two had just come to watch. Nobody else showed up. Dudley had to get a couple of the band members to dance to make one square.

The dance in Seabrook was the smallest I'd ever seen. The biggest, the one Dudley called in Oxford, Massachusetts, on Halloween 1975, was also one of the most peculiar. The dance was held in the basement of a Catholic church in Oxford, a little town on the edge of Worcester, Massachusetts. To get to Oxford you have to go through Worcester's "wavy gravy" district, and past a string of sleazy roadhouses. The problem with Worcester and its suburbs is that it's almost, but not quite, a city. The teen-agers there, the kids who came to the dance—about 200 of them, all dressed in the strangest costumes I'd ever seen—were symbolic of the mixed-up culture of Worcester and towns on its edge, like Oxford. They wanted to be something different on Halloween night, something that showed they were in touch with the contemporary scene; as if they were going to the hottest disco joint in Los Angeles and not a country dance in Oxford, Mass. They wanted to be David Bowie and Mick Jagger; about half the boys came dressed in drag, not in raggedy "let's dress up like girls" costumes either, but with sophisticated makeup and wigs. They looked like real transvestites. And a good number of the girls came dressed as prostitutes, the super garish variety.

When these two hundred teen-agers lined up for the dance, the girls and the boys were indistinguishable; mixed among them were kids dressed in gorilla, clown, and cowboy costumes, and three kids dressed in nuns' habits they had probably borrowed from a convent. The scene was uncontrollable. The noise was outrageous, nightmarish, and I couldn't imagine what Dudley was going to do with them. At one moment I remembered that he had once said: "To be a caller you've got to be crazy. They're all cut out of different pieces of paper, but they *all* are crazy." Now I understood. The next thing I knew Dudley was down in the middle of all these kids herding them into lines, moving around the floor gently but steadily getting them into formation. He stayed down there until he had them dancing, and they liked it. The noise never lessened, and they hooted and swung around the room. Their makeup was running with sweat, but they kept on dancing and dancing all night long.

I reminded Dudley of the Oxford dance during an intermission, back with the six dancers in Seabrook. Dudley said: "Oh I'd much rather deal with a situation like in Oxford, anytime!" And then he went off and sat down at a table with the Seabrook people who were sitting at the other end of the room wondering what was going to happen next. Dudley got a beer from the bar and sat down with them. I realized he was doing just the same thing he did in Oxford: getting close to the dancers, making them feel as comfortable as possible. He really cared whether or not they were having a good time. Bob McQuillen once described to me the way he sees Dudley:

"I call Dudley quite a craftsman. He's the artist, painting a picture. He has to have the right music to fit the dance, to hit the mood of the dance as he interprets it. He gets all the different inputs and then he melds them together . . . I can't begin to figure out how he does it, but it seems like the whole scene sort of beats back at him and he gets a feeling from it and then he responds to that . . . he's reflecting what he gets from the floor and then he's happy and they're happy."

Dudley has called hundreds, maybe thousands of dances all over New England. He started twenty-eight years ago, and, as he says, he used to have to go knocking on doors to get dances going. Every dance, like every one of his poems, has its own character. Contra dancing is big in New England now, but it hasn't always been that way, and Dudley's calling hasn't always been as lucrative as it is now. He once explained his view of the current surge of popularity and the outlook for the future:

"It goes in cycles. It's very big now but it'll have a dip. The reason it is always potentially popular is because it fills a need. This time it's filling a need of young people, and the reason I think, is that they need to be involved and active in a community activity that the parents are not involved in, and the contra dance really offers that. . . . It bothers me a little that some of the older people aren't dancing, but it just doesn't seem to speak to their condition. Some older people will come to a dance and say 'Gee this is great!' but then you don't see them for another year, you know because they got to go to their card parties or stay home and watch the TV, and that's alright because that's their life-style, that's what they do. They come from a time when country dancing didn't speak to their needs, and it still doesn't and it doesn't have to, but right now it *is* speaking to the young people and so they are the ones who're dancing. A lot of the older people will say: 'Well we don't like to go because the young people are too fast, or dirty or they're too rough or we just don't feel we have any identity with them,' but I think they just feel they have to have an excuse not to dance and that's what it is.

"Mainly it's filling the needs of young people. I think it has to do with the Back-to-the-Earth movement and all that; and that they feel they are rejecting the 'plastic society,' but the other thing is the music. In America we can go through things incredibly fast; and if you live in some place like Harvard Square in Cambridge, you can learn to play any kind of folk music you want, simply because of the availability of the recordings, the tapes and books, and the concerts. You can start out with Joan Baez or some blues singer and in no time go through it all; you can become a self-styled expert on all of them. So after going through all the different folk styles sooner or later they were bound to find our music, and they did, right about the same time they found the earth, and the need for some kind of community. I just happened to be there at the right age, the right time, you know, Johnny-on-the-Spot, to be able to cope with their demands.

"In the old days there was one way to do it, the dances, and you just didn't change it, but now it *has* changed. A lot of old timers don't like it and some of them have stopped coming to my dances, but in the meantime something new and exciting has developed in the contra dance, and it's not in the tradition per se of doing an old sedate contra dance the way we used to do them. They're much more lively now, because the kids are much more lively. . . . See they've been through the rock-and-roll scene, and they're bringing this whole feeling of freedom of body movement into the contra dance. That's what's changed it, really, so a lot of kids are doing rock steps, you know they're wriggling around, whereas in the old days you stood right still like a lighthouse; you didn't dare move. And particularly you notice that with some of the older Boston dancers: they're just straight and prim and proper! When they dance down the center they go all eight steps and turn right around on a dime; they don't shuffle down at all, and it makes a big difference.

"And it's the music. The kids like the music because it isn't threatening. The tunes are fairly easy to learn and play on a harmonica, or a penny whistle, and it's an economically feasible thing for a kid to get into. If a kid wants to join a rock band he might have to spend thousands of dollars on electronic equipment, and then he might not get a chance to play, except in a garage. And it's a highly competitive thing, whereas country dancing is, although it's becoming competitive to some

# A DANCER INTERVIEW: RICHARD MONAHON

Rick Monahon came to Harrisville, New Hampshire, originally on a temporary assignment involving the restoration of several brick mill buildings in the town, which were slowly falling apart. But after the restoration project was completed, he decided to stay in New Hampshire. Rick goes to contra dances occasionally and made these comments about the dances.

"About two years ago I started going more than I do now, because of the music which I had just gotten into, and discovering that the dancing was really easy, but also a creative, expressive thing to do. What's great about them is that they stay pretty much the same: the music is consistently good and there are always good people to dance with. And it still has the qualities of the old town square dance, you know, the Saturday night get together, which I really like. I like to go and see a couple of older people, some young kids, and just feeling that in any other context, like the city or suburbia, the hierarchies of social interaction would be totally separated; so that you would never see a fourteen year old dancing with a forty-five year old unless you happened to be at a wedding or something like that.

"Of course that closeness works in the reverse too; sometimes I'm really hesitant to go to a contra dance because there might be somebody I don't want to see or something, who I know is going to be there, but that's a product of living in a pretty tight community of people, most of whom do the same things, and the major social expression of those things and those people seems to focus around contra dancing.

"I never feel that there's much of a mating game going on at contra dances. It's almost asexual in a way. There's something about the whole dynamic of the swinging with men and women and the interchange being exactly the same that gives it that quality; so that you have a partner, but you're dancing in a set with other people and in fact sometimes developing much richer dynamics with the other people in the set than with your partner. But sometimes there is a moment, occasionally, when you'll meet someone dancing in a set, and suddenly you're swinging them, someone you've never seen before, and there'll be some quality in the way they relate to you in a swing that goes way beyond your standard expectations, and it's just really nice!

"I'm always interested to see who's dancing with who, and you know there's a lot of strong visual stuff at a square dance: girls dress up a little bit, some of 'em do, and some girls just come and look great, and they look even better when they're dancing than just standing or sitting around. And there's something about the dynamics of seeing a person really moving, that just adds a whole dimension to what they are.

"One of the nicest things that's happened at the contra dances up here is that they seem to have taken on some of the qualities of other kinds of dancing, even rock dance, so that you can waltz, polka, and clog and stomp all in one night to essentially the same music. And that's a very special dimension because in a conventional dancing scene, you either have a rock band or a little quartet doing slow dance music, and it's hard to have a group that does all. I think that the change in the contra-dance style has evolved a lot from the input of the younger people, who have their background in foot stomping rock music, which is more expressive than more conventional forms. But there's the constraint that the contra dance puts on that expression by systematizing it, having a certain number of rituals to go through, that really is not a constraint at all, because it allows you to get much closer to the music in a way that you don't if you're just completely freelancing it in a rock dance.''

*Photo by E.W. Cohn*

Rick Monahon

*Photo by Nevell*

Dudley Laufman playing two penny whistles in S. Amherst, Massachusetts.

# DUDLEY LAUFMAN /
# ON TEACHING KIDS TO DANCE

I first saw Dudley Laufman work with kids at the New Hope Center and the Wheelock School in Keene, New Hampshire. In both cases Dudley exhibited a quality rare in any teacher, fairness to the kids; he treated them like people worthy of respect. I talked to Dudley about his work in schools:

"I had been doing a program up in Wolfboro with the fourth, fifth, and sixth grades and then they ran out of money, but the kids wanted it so they went to the PTA and they raised enough money to get me back for a few weeks. They really like it because it introduces them to a tradition most of them aren't even aware exists, and a lot of them have never seen a live musician before.

"I show them the melodeon, take it apart and show them the inside. Then we do dances and singing games, and I try not to talk down to them. I just treat them like anybody else, as I would at any dance. The half hour in the classroom gets the same treatment as three hours in the dance hall. It has to be a meaningful and worthwhile experience. I try to make it so it's not like a classroom, try to forget that. It is educational to some degree, but I'm primarily interested in the social content."

Dudley once wrote a book of dances, including one for kids called "The Rumford." His description of the dance depicts the spirit of his approach in the classroom.

## The Rumford

"This is a dance for little kids. If you have read *A Hole to Dig,* then you know the kind I mean. Make a circle for as many as will, no partners needed. The boys will probably all gang together on one round of the circle, and all the girls will giggle together on the other, and the poor kids on the ends will squeak and balk at taking the boy or girl's hand. Get going anyway and have them all circle left and the other way. Girls to the center and back, boys the same, and then all to the middle and back. Do the circle thing again, and then have the girls dance to the middle, and circle to their left while the guys circle to the right single file around the outside. Everyone go the other way, and have the girls come back out to the circle any place, it doesn't matter, and after all the squealing is over with, do the circle bit again, and then have the boys dance to the center, etcetera. Circle again, and then have the girls center, face out, join hands, and go round to their right while the lads clap hand in this manner: 1–2, 1–2–3, 1–2, 1–2–3. Girls dance the other way, and then out to the big ring and away we go, and then the boys do the face out part while the girls clap etcetera. Circle again and finish dance off as in the beginning.

"Anyone who walks through this dance beforehand is nuts.

"I call it 'The Rumford' because I first used this dance with some tough little kids at the Rumford School in Concord, New Hampshire. They know why."

*Photo by Nevell*

Dudley teaches a song with his concertina.

*Photo by Nevell*

Dudley teaches the kids at the Tilton, N.H. elementary school how to do a Christmas contra dance.

degree, still not anything like the rock scene. So a young kid can form a little country-dance band with a kazoo, and he can make the kazoo out of a comb and some tissue paper, and he can go out and buy a tambourine for a couple of bucks, and there's your band! And you teach the kid a tune like 'The Muffin Man' or 'In and Out the Windows,' and you show another kid how to call a dance and they're in business. And I think that this appeals to many young people, because it's something they can do! They can get it. And that's why the dance appeals to them because they don't have to sit around like you used to have to at folk concerts. They're in it! Of course it has it's restrictions. It works within a framework, but I think the kids are ready for that to some degree: it's just enough of a framework that it gives them a border to stay within that's healthy, and they can accept that."

# ON MAKING MUSIC FOR CONTRA DANCES

As Dudley Laufman says, you don't need much more than a comb and some wax paper to provide adequate music for a contra dance.

In the history of country dancing, almost every imaginable instrument has been used to make dance music, from fiddles to french horns and even oboes. (Reknowned flautist Newton F. Tolman of Nelson, New Hampshire, has even been known to play the dandelion stem as well as to "lilt"—an ancient tradition of singing the tune using phrases like "deedledee dee" and "da dum da dum.") Ralph Page tells a story about Cecil Nash who used to play the trumpet at contra dances back in the forties. Some time after Nash had quit playing at the dances someone (probably Ralph Page) said: "Cecil, do you think you could play 'Devil's Dream' once more?" And Nash, who had played the tune thousands of times, looked up and slowly said "Yup . . . once."

Basically all you need is a melody instrument and a rhythm instrument, both of which must be loud enough to be heard by the dancers but not so loud as to drown out the caller. The fiddle is the most preferred melody instrument, but nowadays flutes, penny whistles, harmonicas, and banjos are commonly used, alone and together, in varying combinations. Occasionally a hammered dulcimer player shows up but are more common in the South. The Piano is the preferred rhythm instrument, but a guitar with a good loud bass will do when there's no piano to be had.

The best all-purpose instrument for contra dances is an accordion, which can provide rhythm and melody together. A good piano player can do this too. According to Dudley Laufman, recorded music should be used only as an absolute last resort. Others feel that a good record will do the job just as well. Personally, I think whatever suits the dancers' taste is fine. Someday I'd like to dance to a trumpet. Maybe Cecil Nash could manage "Devil's Dream" twice.

The tunes most commonly used for dances are jigs in 6/8 time, and reels and hornpipes played in 4/4 or 2/4 time. It is not difficult to learn how to play these tunes adequately for dancing, but it takes many years to learn how to play them well. Any trained violinist can play them with ease, but technical excellence does not mean danceable excellence.

The good dance musician must, above all, be willing to cooperate with the caller or whoever is running the dance. Steady rhythm is required for the dances to work. The best way to learn how to play for dances is to take your instrument to the dance and, if permissible, "sit in" with the orchestra, playing quietly in the background. It is customary to ask permission from the caller and the musicians for this privilege.

Music is important at a contra dance, especially so in New England where callers use live musicians instead of records. Live music adds a lot of spirit to the dances, lacking when records are used instead, but the caller also pays the price. He not only has to work with the temperament of the dancers but the temperament of the orchestra as well:

"There's no substitute for live music. Anything is better than a record. It's important to have a good rapport with your musicians, but everyone has problems with their band, occasionally. Ralph Page had problems, I have problems, Jack Perron probably has problems with his. But that's all part of it. Just to be a musician is an artistic thing, and there's temperaments involved, so there's bound to be problems sometimes.

"Sometimes one of my musicians might be having a problem with another musician, and then I have to devote time and energy to somehow dispelling that for the time being, and I have to act as the go-between. Or sometimes a musician will pick a tune that just doesn't fit the dance, and so I have to pick one right away, and that might cause a problem.

"But my feeling is that I'm totally committed to the dance as a whole, and the music is for the dancers rather than for the musicians. The musician is there to produce for the dancers, and so that the dancers go away feeling as if they've had a worthwhile experience."

When you work at something for twenty-eight years as Dudley has you're bound to make mistakes, maybe even make a few enemies along the way. Mostly Dudley Laufman has made a great number of people happy and alerted them to a tradition they could participate in, rather than stare at like some museum piece. Dudley has been open to change and growth in the contra dance, in an age when things change at astronomical rates. Some people think that he has not exercised enough control on the form of the old dances, not tried hard enough to keep them "traditional."

"If anything I have an anti-tradition feeling because it's been jammed down my throat, not by the dancers, but mainly by the Country Dance and Song people. My feeling is that as far as tradition is concerned let's just do it and not waste time talking about it. You know we celebrate Christmas but we don't waste a lot of time talking about the traditions involved, we just do them. We know we're going to eat turkey, decorate the tree, open our presents, and other things. Well it's just the same with the dancing. We know one way or another we're going to dance on Saturday night . . . and that is tradition."

For twenty-eight years on, just about every Saturday night of the year, Dudley has been someplace calling a dance. The dances in Seabrook and Oxford were unusual, unique dances, but in a way every contra dance is unique. The nature of a dance ultimately depends on the people who are there. A dancer once pointed out that she felt that the nature of a dance changed every time she moved one progression in the dance. I think Dudley recognizes this characteristic of a contra dance: that if dancing is to remain meaningful to people, it has to change to suit their needs; that the tradition is ongoing, passed from one hand to another, just like the figures of the dance that demonstrate the physical exchange between people. There is something inspirational about that process, about the idea that the contra dance is a progression of people passing along the tradition. It was Becky McQuillen who first got me out on the dance floor. Her father was the one who inspired Dudley to learn the accordion. Dudley describes McQuillen on one of his albums as "this happy man, this laughing giant with steel gray hair." And McQuillen remembers Dudley when he was playing for Ralph Page:

"I can remember when Dudley Laufman first showed up at one of Ralph Page's dances. I don't remember exactly where it was, although it might have been Boston, but I do remember watching him coming up to the stage and he'd watch us play, and the music was obviously a big thing for this young man and he loved what he was hearing."

It is this personal involvement that makes the tradition meaningful, the sharing of the music and dance. Dudley once said:

## ELIZABETH COHN /
## SEAMSTRESS AND STORE OWNER

Elizabeth Cohn came to New Hampshire from Boston in 1972. She now lives in Nelson with her daughter, Sarah, and owns and runs a store in Peterborough where she sells children's clothes made by herself and other local craftsmen.

Sarah and Elizabeth Cohn

"The first time I went to a contra dance I was really nervous about dancing because I was really self-conscious about it, and it looked like an incredible hodge podge on the floor. I didn't understand it, and I was kind of taken aback by the people who were really excited and jumping around and all that. Now I can be the same way they were then, because I'm not so self-conscious . . . I just get out there and dance.

"One of the things for me, I think, that makes it good, is the contact with people, the physical touching of people. It's a really nice way to be with people; putting your arms around a woman when you're casting off and stuff like that . . . you know, because you can't do that normally, you can't walk up to someone and put your arm around their waist, or hold their hand.

"But I was thinking about my background, my family background, and growing up in a way where I was moving all the time, moving into a new home, or a new job, just moving up the ladder, and then I looked at some of the families around here in Nelson and one of the most important things

*continued*

from my point of view is staying put, and not breaking up the land that was your grandfather's, passing it along. And that's something I never had in my life, something I want to give to my child, so the contra dance in Nelson is important to me. It's tradition, you know, anything I can look forward to that continues year after year, or month after month. I know that every first Saturday night of the month I can go to the Nelson town hall and dance and that's really important to me: being a part of a community and starting to form those kind of roots, roots that Sarah can have also.

"You know Sarah and I have been reading the *Little House in the Big Woods* series, and they talk a lot about old-time life, and they talk about going to the grandparent's home for a big square dance, and they danced 'Mony Musk' and 'Hull's Victory' and stuff like that, and Sarah can do that right here in her own town . . . and I like her to be a part of that, because it's a heritage thing that she can relate to. When we read the books I say: 'You know "Mony Musk," you've seen mommy dance that, and you can learn how to dance that too.' And when Paul plays the fiddle I say 'That's like Harvey Tolman playing the fiddle, and maybe Harvey's kids will learn how to fiddle, and you could too, if you want' and she can relate to that. And I think it's good for her, and it's something I always wanted but never had.

"I think everybody's trying to get a piece of that old-timeness, because we've lost so much of it."

*Photos by Nevell*

Dudley Laufman teaches a schottische

"When McQuillen went off to Korea, I thought, and a lot of us thought, 'Jesus, he might be killed or something, he might not make it back.' And so I learned to play the accordion because I felt that someone had to continue what he did . . . and then when Ralph Page stopped calling dances in the area, and stopped using that band, that's when I said: 'It can't stop, it's got to continue,' so that's when I learned to run dances in the same vein. And like Ralph, who adapted to the changing situation and moved on to other things, that's what I've done . . . and now Jack Perron's calling the dances in Nelson, after I lasted there almost twenty years, and he's trying to keep that going, and that's good, that's the way it should be. . . . You know Jack is about the only caller I would trust to do a dance that I could know there would be pretty good music and some nice friendly people around, and just a nice situation."

### III

Sometimes when autumn is just arriving in New Hampshire there are days which are absolutely infectious: warm days that stay with you throughout the winter. In September when winter is lurking behind every tree, I sometimes think it is only the infection of these particular days that carries me through the season.

On one of these days Jack Perron, a young caller from Harrisville, New Hampshire, and I, after sitting on the Dartmouth College plaza in Hanover planning a New Hampshire–Vermont festival of folk arts, took a ride back south, home to Harrisville. On the way Jack told me a story about the times before he was a caller:

"It was in February and it was really cold. I can remember it was cold and I can tell you how I remember it was so cold because I was wearing moccasins and my feet got so cold walking along the side of the road that I found myself looking down and I'd find myself walking along in bare feet, and I'd have to wander back fifty feet or so and find one moccasin, and then wander back a little further and find the other one . . . my feet were so cold I couldn't feel anything, like they were asleep or frostbitten or something. It was really cold.

"I'd started in Northfield. I'd been down visiting Paul Spaulding and I got a ride up to Keene with his father and he let me off in front of that Gulf station on Route 10 going out of town. And then I tried to hitchhike a ride to Acworth where there was going to be a dance that night. But no one would pick me up. I thought it was neat at the beginning not getting a ride, because I was walking up the road where it curves around and there's a stream comes down to a waterfall that's half frozen. This

# BOB McQUILLEN /
# ON MAKING UP TUNES

Bob McQuillen lives in Dublin, New Hampshire. He makes a living as a fulltime school teacher but for many years has spent most Friday and Saturday nights playing piano and accordion for every major contra dance caller that's come through New England: Ralph Page, Duke Miller, Dudley Laufman, Jack Perron, and many more. Ralph Page once said of McQuillen that "He's got the best left hand in the business. You can't beat Bob McQuillen on piano."

Having played traditional dance tunes for so many years, Bob says "I am a part of the music, and the music is part of me, now. It's a total immersement: McQuillen and the music and that's how it is." The results of this marriage are scores of tunes, written in the traditional idiom, inspired by friends and experiences. It started in 1972:

"One day I suddenly had an idea for a tune, and I called the tune 'Scotty O'Neill.' Scotty O'Neill was a boy that lived down in Peterborough. He was an excellent skier and athlete, and he was friendly with my daughter Becky. He used to pull in here every so often and stop and visit, have meals and so on. And one day, I think it was in November, '72, he got on his motorcycle with another kid and went out to Keene. And he hit the crossing there on Route 10 at the traffic lights and he had a tragic accident which he did not survive. Sometime after that, somehow or other, I got a tune that went through my head and I tried to write it out. In truth I had to write it out do-re-mi because that was the only way I knew to do it. I can't write out music directly, in the normal way, and I still can't. But that's the story of Scotty O'Neill, and I got the tune, and it's the first one, and I called it after him, but he started it the way I view it.

"Now they come all the time, some of them fast, some slow. One tune I wrote out in a minute and a half. Just like that. But that's unusual. But sometimes it comes at weird hours, and I feel like I'm a receptor or something like that. I'll wake up a 3 o'clock in the morning and have to go to the john and then I can't go back to sleep because all of a sudden I've got this 6/8 (jig) rhythm coming in, not a dream, but a 6/8 tune and it keeps coming in and coming and coming! And then all through the day I changed it over and over in my head, until I finally got a version of it written down. But I had to keep working at it, and it's still not right. But that's the way it is: I can't tell if a tune's any good until we really start playing it, and then I can tell, if it rings, if it hits just right, then it's OK . . . but sometimes they're just no good.

"But I'm no whiz musically speaking. I use this do-re-mi bit because it's what I was taught in grammar school, and because it works for me. I can literally play a tune on my squeezebox from these do re mi words. Or I can play it from the regular notes, but I can only write 'em in the do-re-mi fashion."

Bob has recently published two volumes of tunes—*Bob's Notebooks*—of jigs and reels and other melodies. Almost every tune is dedicated to someone, or to the memory of some experience.

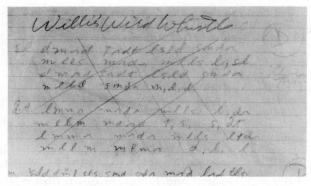

Bob's worksheet for "Willie's Wild Whistle"

A completed "Willie's Wild Whistle"

Bob writing in The Quacker Box

*Photos by Nevell*

was in the morning, about 11 o'clock.... I remember I had my fiddle with me because my old fiddle case didn't have a handle on it and it was hard to hold, it was a real pain in the neck after awhile. But Dudley had a dance and I had to go there. To Acworth.

"But there were no cars and when I got to the top of that hill I started really seriously wanting to get a ride, but no one would pick me up. And I didn't even look particularly grubby or anything. They just wouldn't pick me up. So I just kept walking right up that road, Route 10, and it was really cold."

I realized as we drove south that we were moving over the same ground that Jack was talking about in his story. We bought gas in Newport and then passed through Goshen and Lempster down Route 10. We could see the trees in the swamps, the soaking maples just starting to turn. The sun was hot in the car, and that helped take the chill out of Jack's tale. We passed the turn off to Acworth and he continued his story as we drove through Marlow:

"The most important detail of this walk to me is this: see how it's all flat and desolate along here through Marlow. It's like walking across the tundra or something, but once you get in towards Acworth, it all turns to evergreen and hilly and warm, sort of womblike, and that day as I walked through Gilsum and Marlow, across this depressing flat sandy land, I had in my mind how neat Acworth was going to be. But no one would pick me up.

"By the time I got to South Acworth and I began to walk up that hill to Acworth it started to snow, and it was that kind of crystalline type of snow that you can hear, like rain, a tinkling sound, and that was all I remember hearing. It was like shattering glass.

"Then as I was walking up the hill towards Acworth some guy finally stopped and asked me if I wanted a ride and I said no. I was only a mile more from the place and I figured I might as well finish the walk. And it was dark by now. Back in Marlow I had stopped at the general store and asked how far it was to Acworth and he said that it was about ten miles, and I knew it had been about 16 from Keene to Marlow, so by this time I figured I might as well just finish the walk.

"So I kept on walking up the hill through this incredible blackness, not knowing what the hell I was doing, and wondering when Acworth was going to show up, and then I heard this door slam ... and some dogs barked ... and some kids yelling at the dogs ... and then I could see off through the trees a light from the house, kind of halo like, because there was ice in the air, and I finally got a feeling for the town being there, people living out in the middle of nowhere, like an island in all that blackness.

"When I got there I went right to the town hall and I sat in there. No one was there. It was freezing cold so I turned on the space heater with the fan and sat in front of that for awhile and watched it get darker and darker. I watched the sun and the light disappear through those wavy kind of glass windows you see in old buildings in New England.

"I sat there for an hour or so by the space heater until it got totally dark. And then someone walked in, a girl as it turned out. And she was stumbling around and I didn't know what to do, because I didn't want to jump up and scare her because I knew she couldn't see me . . . and then all of a sudden she says: 'Who's there?' and so I said who I was. So she invited me down to her house, and we sat around a fire and drank coffee and then later we came back to the hall for the dance."

The dances in the Acworth town hall were for those who were really into contra dancing because it is a very difficult place to get to in the winter. The only worse place in New England is Palmer's barn in Unity. But something about the dances in Acworth were special: the dancers felt like they had come together for a special event; they really wanted to be there, enough to make monumental, if not insane, efforts to get there. That in itself made them special dances; obviously this was true for Jack Perron, who had walked twenty-six miles to get there.

"Then after the dance I slept in the town hall. In the town hall. In the back there was Victorian-type sofa with a curved back and one of the legs was broken off. I slept there with a blanket I found and it was warm for awhile and then it got cold.

"So then I was looking around and in the back of this old mirror I found this old newspaper, an 1868 edition of *The New England Farmer* or something, and in it I found these two poems. One of them was a four liner and it went like this:

> I feel like one who treads alone,
> Some banquet hall deserted,
> Whose roses fled, whose garlands dead,
> And all but I departed.

"And that's exactly what my feeling was, walking around alone in that town hall, and everyone had left after the dance. That's when I was really into square dancing and I thought it was the coolest thing in the world. Because it was a bunch of people coming together. Now I don't want to sound corny but it really was a symbolic journey; because just as it was desolate the whole way getting there, and the dance represented life, it sort of summed up the way I was feeling at the time about my life at that time. My life in Boston at Medical school was this blah, meaning-

## DANCER / TINA STALLER

Tina Staller came to the Monadnock region of New Hampshire as a graduate student in early childhood education. Before she moved to Nelson, she had lived in Bennington, Vermont, and often traveled great distances to attend the contra dances in New Hampshire, especially the dances in Acworth.

"It was like a fever. We'd drive two hours to a dance, dance all night, and then drive right back. And then we'd do that weekend after weekend. The first dance I went to was in Acworth, which in itself is something special. Driving up that long hill, and I'd never seen towns in other places that had that wonderful closed in feeling that Acworth has; you know the town buildings, the church, the town hall, and the houses. So coming up there in the winter like it was, and going in to the room where there was a supper going on, and it was kind of cold, but then the music got started and the dancers got up and the room got really hot, and I just remember feeling just incredibly caught up, and feeling like I was in another time, but how timeless all of it really was.

"But I really loved it: the swirliness of it all. You know sometimes you get swinging with someone, and there's that great balance and that great pivot, and you just don't want to stop! Sometimes I'm really transformed at a dance, and I have a hard time coming down from it when the dance is over.

"I think a lot of the quality of the contra dances around here has to do with the fact that they're held in the old halls, with the old wooden floors, and you just have a feeling there that you can't get anywhere else, like in a gym or something.

Photo by Hilary Feldstein

Tina teaches a dance at the Harrisville School.

"Now I like to go to the dances in Nelson the best, and maybe it's because I'm trying to get closer to the original form, you know where just the local community danced with each other. I like to have some people over and then go to the dance. It's important to me to know a lot of people at the dance, to feel part of a true community . . . and you know sometimes there's that feeling at a dance, you know there's a real comfort in the dancing; you know you get passed from one person to another sometimes in dances, and there's never a feeling, a strange feeling of being with strangers, you know what I mean?

"I began dancing when I was very young, and it just became part of my expressive nature, and I was able to express that easily and freely. Then I got into the contra dancing, and there was a discipline, but I appreciated that because it was still dancing; immediately, from impulse to expression, it wasn't chopped by thinking what the sequence is, because your body knows it and executes it, and then if you have that within yourself, then you become part of a whole, part of a whole group of people moving, and you can fit into the whole picture, and that's really what I love about dancing."

George and Judy balance. . .

. . . and swing! in the Nelson town hall.     *Photos by Nevell*

less thing, and I had romanticized the dancing, to the point where I was motivated to walk all that way to one of the dances.

"And I think that a lot of contra dancers have done something probably very similar to that. Because there's a certain point where you first get introduced to it that it just overwhelms you and you romanticize it to the point where you would do almost anything to get to a dance. That was a time where you could almost live at contra dances, just wander around from dance to dance; I remember one guy who literally lived in dance halls. He had a knapsack and he spent all his time at dances or hitchhiking to the next one somewhere. That's all he did for a year.

"So that's why I did it. And I can remember saying to myself how stupid it was to be doing it, but then saying to myself that if I ever stopped doing crazy things like that I might as well forget it, forget living."

I don't know how many dancers have walked twenty-six miles to a dance, but I remember that when the younger generation in New England discovered the dances, there was a fervor, almost a fanaticism on the part of some dancers. They would make contra dancing the central focus of their lives. Time was measured in the days between dances, and space was measured in the distances between the towns where the dances were held: Fitzwilliam, Nelson, Francestown, Acworth, New Boston, Brattleboro, Franconia. There was an unspoken but well understood community of dancers, the ones who went to nearly all the dances, who knew each other only as dancers, not even by name perhaps, but by the style of their swing, or their balance, by the way they looked you in the eye when they danced. These identities were so strong that names often didn't matter. We all came together, almost as a congregation; I suppose some of us were still thinking of the ideal utopian ideas of the sixties, and trying to keep that going.

The dances attracted people from some of the new local communes, as well as people from cities like Boston, even New York; and college kids. There were hundreds of them and each one probably has a story like Jack's, a story that illustrates the power of the contra-dancing tradition. It was a magical power to some people: Dudley was called "The Pied Piper of Canterbury" in articles in New England newspapers. Others didn't appreciate the power that attracted so many young "hippies" to their town halls. The selectmen of Fitzwilliam suddenly set a limit on the number of people they'd allow in their hall, a reasonable enough measure, but then they decided that girls had to wear bras. Different towns reacted differently. Some people predicted that contra dancing would die as quickly as it had sprung up, but the ones who were making those predictions did not understand the subtler but ultimately stronger power of the dance tradition.

There came a point where the dances reached a peak, a point where they really couldn't have gotten any bigger. Like other fads in modern culture, New England contra dancing could have died, but it didn't. Instead it spread out and gained a stronger and broader foundation as callers sprung up in different towns and the dancing became more localized. Dudley had been carrying the bulk of the demand for dances. Duke Miller ran dances in the summer down in Fitzwilliam as he had for many years, and still does. Duke ran a more structured dance than Dudley, but still attracted young people who were not just interested in dancing as a "fad."

Many dancers made a passage from fanaticism to the realization that they just plain liked to contra dance—maybe not every day, or even twice a week, but often enough to fill their need. And they realized that they didn't have to travel a hundred miles to get to a dance. They could wait until there was a dance within a reasonable distance from home, maybe even in their home town, where the people they danced with were generally from the local community. This is what has happened after the "fad." Since the early seventies the dances have become more local in character, although newcomers still freshen the crowd.

One reason the contra dance has blossomed throughout local communities in New England is because dancers have come to learn the tools of the trade from Dudley and Duke Miller and other callers and musicians. When Jack Perron made his walk to Acworth he was a dancer, learning to play the fiddle, who sat in with Dudley's band. Eventually, like many of the new musicians who became so enamored of this traditional music, he joined people such as Bob McQuillen and Peter Colby who formed part of the amorphous Canterbury Orchestra run by Dudley. He became a hired fiddler, playing at dances all over New England. A graduate of Harvard University, he took a leave of absence from medical school and moved back to his home state of New Hampshire:

"When I left medical school the dances were the only thing I had to latch on to, and it was basically an escape from the world I'd been educated in. The dances were a world totally detached from the rest of the world I was involved in, the world of being a doctor. . . . The first thing I decided to do was go live with this fiddler, Allan Block, who played for Dudley's dances, because I wanted to learn how to fiddle. I remember going up to his house in the middle of the night and talking to him about it and he told me the best thing to do was to come to the dances and learn there . . . so that's what I did.

"After awhile I got myself to believe that I could live totally within this make-believe world of contra dancing, and for some time I could, except that eventually it became a real world for me and no longer a fantasy.

"I worked as a fiddler for Dudley, and sometimes for Ralph Page at the New England Folk Festival, which was fine for awhile, but then I got bored with the music I was playing, and developed an interest in other kinds of fiddle music than was being played at dances. I became especially interested in Irish fiddle music which I had heard on some old records of Michael Coleman, an Irish fiddler who lived in New York for awhile, and some other musicians like Paddy Cronin in Boston. . . . I realized that the only way I was going to be able to play these tunes at dances was if I became a caller myself, so that's what I did. . . . I felt that a lot of people really misunderstood fiddle music. You know if you tell them you play fiddle they think of 'Turkey in the Straw' or some other simple tune, and if you tell them you play Irish music they think of 'The Irish Washerwoman,' but in reality I found that fiddle music can be as expressive a form as classical music, and that it takes as much experience, training and exposure to really appreciate traditional fiddle music as it does classical music. A musician can express himself in an incredible variety of ways through these fiddle tunes, and one of the reasons I got into calling my own dances was because I wanted to expose people to as much a variety of music as possible.

## FIDDLER MAKER / JOE DOMINICK

A retired postman, Joe Dominick has been making and selling fiddles since about 1960 at his farm in Winchester, New Hampshire. Joe moved to Winchester from Yonkers, New York, in the twenties, when he was about four years old and spent most of his life growing up in Ashuelot, New Hampshire on a hill called Fiddle Hill. Joe tells how he first got interested in playing and making fiddles:

"Well I had a fiddle when I was a kid and it got burnt up in a fire, and I got to thinkin' about it and I wanted to play one in the worst way, because I thought there's nothing like getting up in front of an orchestra, especially the old fiddler, and I says to myself, 'If that guy can get up there and play that fiddle, boy, I can too.'

"So my father helped me a little, 'cause he was pretty handy with building things, and then I met a bunch of guys and they'd all made their own fiddles, and I started to think 'Well, I don't see anything so extraordinary about them,' and I says, 'by Jesus,' If they can make fiddles, then I can make one, see?

"But there was this guy Sam Tarbell, he was the postmaster here, and I knew he had some fiddles he'd made . . . three or four of them, so I went up there and he showed them to me. I never heard him play 'em but he showed 'em to me, and out in the shed he had some wood, and that's where I got some of my first wood, some of this old maple and the spruce tops from him, see?

*Photos by Nevell*

Joe Plays the "Lisa Marie" while Lisa    Joe holding a new fiddle.
Marie listens.

"The main thing you've got to look out for, part of the fiddle being maple and the other part being spruce, is to get 'em so they're balanced, the top and the back, because the spruce vibrates faster than the maple, it being a softer wood. So I've got to raise the pitch of the maple to catch up with the spruce, and that's how you get your two sides to work together, to synchronize, and that's how you get your power.

"A fiddle's like anything else, though. If you practice every day you get good at it. But every day is different, and somedays, now, why you might pick up the fiddle and, Jesus, it sounds like a thing from heaven . . . and then someday you'll pick it up, and Christ it don't sound like nothin, ya know? There's a sound coming out but you don't like it!

"But a fiddle's as important as a wife, sure, because it's something you love and cherish all your life long. And they're as important as a wife because there are days when that fiddle will pick you up when probably the whole rest of the world just fell on you! But your fiddle comes through and kinda saves you!

"But like I say I don't make a living at it, probably'd starve to death if I tried to, but over all what makes a good fiddle is paying attention to detail and staying right with it. You can't say 'That's close enough,' You've got to get it to do the right thing, and you've got to have patience to no end . . . so like I say when winter comes and the snow's seven feet deep, I'll be whackin' these things out to beat hell! Ya know?"

## ROD MILLER / FIDDLING FOR DANCING

Originally from upstate New York, Rod Miller started out taking violin lessons in grammar school through the eighth grade, until he dropped it. Rod played his first dance "sitting in" up·at a dance in the Acworth, New Hampshire, town hall. Later at Pinewoods Dance Camp in Massachusetts he met Dudley Laufman who subsequently hired Rod to play a dance in Franconia, New Hampshire. Since that first dance in 1971, Rod has become a regular fiddler for Jack Perron at dances all over the Monadnock region, and he recently won first prize at the First Annual Dance Fiddlers Competition held in Concord, Massachusetts. Here are a few thoughts from Rod on what it takes to be a good dance fiddler.

"Mainly you have to feel the music, and play the tunes so the dancers really get something out of it and dance up. a storm. The sign of a really good dance fiddler is one who feels the beat, and gets the dancers on that beat so that they are dancing so well they almost don't need the music. The tune helps the dance, drives it on to a point where the dancers are perfectly in time with the music.

"Sometimes I hear tunes that are particularly good for dancing, like some of the French Canadian tunes, but I don't usually think of a tune as being good for one particular dance, just that it's a generally danceable tune. The simpler the melody and the more beat a tune has, the more successful it is for dancing; tunes that you can really get ahold of. There are lots of good ones in *The Nelson Music Collection* by Newt Tolman and Kay Gilbert: like 'Deerfoot.' That's the kind of a tune that you can put rhythm into. I almost fiddle differently on that tune: I put more bounce in the bow, and an extra little beat on almost every other note, so that there's this chugga chugga beat that the dancers can pick up on.

"But there are lots of tunes, like a lot of the Irish reels that have too complicated a melody and not enough beat. They're not very good for dancing even though they're great tunes to listen to. Also sometimes a tune isn't good for dancing if it's written in a key that's too low, where most of the notes are played on the lower two strings, the G and the D. In that low range the tune gets covered up by all the other sounds in the hall: the piano, the dancers feet and all: so with a tune like that I'll change it to a higher key, so it's played mostly on the higher two strings. Then the tune can be heard by the dancers.

"The mood of a tune is important. Like in 'Rory O'More' the first part is major, but then it switches to the minor key in the second part and a real change takes place in the dancing. I can see it. When the dancers are doing 'country corners' everybody sort of 'gives the eye' more, and I think it's because of the change to the minor key. You know it's kind of sexy when a tune is in a minor key. I know when I used to dance more, whenever a minor tune was played I danced a little differently, changed my style. . . .

"I guess the only unrewarding thing about playing for the dances is if somebody comes up and says they didn't like a tune, which happens once in a while. But, you know, you have to play a new tune in public a few times before they'll accept it, because they like tunes they're familiar with. When you get down to it they'll always pick the old standards as their favorites: 'Mony Musk,' 'Petronella,' stuff like that. They really don't get sick of tunes they hear all the time, but the fiddlers get sick of playing them sometimes, so I'm always trying to learn new tunes and introduce them.

"I don't go to the dances looking for any special reward. I just go and play; but some nights I just want to stay home, but then it is rewarding when you go and play and people come and have a good time; when they don't go home early, but stay and just dance up a storm."

Rodney plays fiddle with brother Randy on piano.

*Photo by Nevell*

"Basically I'm a musician and my main concern is to have the best quality music possible at a dance. You should be able to hear each instrument clearly and distinctly, especially the fiddle, or whatever the melody instrument is. And I think having a piano in a band is essential. Really a piano and one other instrument is all you need.

"The tunes are basically simple to play. Any trained classical musician can play them, especially if they can sight-read music, and it's an awful temptation for a lot of classical musicians who come to a contra dance to get into playing the tunes, especially if they can get paid twenty-five dollars a night for doing so. . . .

"But the competence of the dance musician really depends on his sensitivity to the music and a total understanding of the tunes he's playing.

"Sometimes I've been tempted to give up producing good quality music at dances, because most of the dancers are just very happy with a loud sound. You know, you could have Heifeitz up there playing and they wouldn't appreciate it unless there were three violins backing him up to dance to . . . but I still think it's important and more of the dancers are getting to be more sensitive to the music we play."

The music is undoubtedly the mainstay of the dances. Not only the sound, but the structure dominates the dance. Jack and many of the new callers use the most familiar dances in an evening of dancing, but they also make up new dances based in the traditional form.

"Many of the dances are unique, like 'Mony Musk' or 'Chorus Jig,' and they have certain music that you just don't mess around with too much, but others simply conform to the thirty-two measure pattern, and many different tunes will fit one dance. But picking the right tune is important, and sometimes hard. You have to have the right tempo to fit the dance. We use mostly jigs and reels and depending on the dance, one type of tune might fit better than the other. For example, if you have a real complicated dance and you use a jig, you're going to have some trouble because they go quicker than reels. So if you want to have more time, then you better use a reel. Sometimes I mess up and I have to stop and fix the music. Basically it's simply that the complexity of the tune has to balance the complexity of the dance.

"Making up dances is really not as hard as it might seem. There's a tendency when people make up a dance to make it too complicated. The simpler dances are easier to do and when people don't have to think it tends to be more fun for them . . . but the way I make up a dance is really a very simple procedure. What happens is I hear some great tune that I really like, and the music just suggests certain dance figures to you, especially a balance or a swing. So what I do is listen to the tune over and over again and just imagine what I'd like to be doing to music if I was dancing.

"The reason I make up dances is this: most of the tunes and dances are traditional, but I like to feel like I've put something of myself into the dance. When people come up and say 'That was a nice dance' you can take some satisfaction for their appreciation of the dance as a whole. But that's just sort of a reflection of your personality, and it's difficult for me to take much satisfaction just in my own personality. I have to be more creative, somehow, so I write dances to try and really put some of myself into it."

# JACK PERRON / ON MAKING UP DANCES

Jack Perron has composed many dances in the traditional idiom of country and square dances. I asked him to write down a few words about how he goes about making up a dance and what he uses as guidelines for this process.

"Prompters like myself are occasionally smitten with the urge to compose new dances. While it might seem at first that bad dances are a uniquely modern invention, there is evidence that as early as 1893 prompters were calling poor dances. In an edition of the early dance magazine *Galop* of that year, one writer noted: 'It has been a governing rule in dancing from time immemorial, that a swing should be made as a finishing part of a balance, while of course the swing should be made with a person to whom the balance has been made. . . . For some unaccountable reason, some prompters have made a sad change in this, as invariably the order goes: Balance corners/swing partners . . . thus perpetrating a gross breach of etiquette, as well as awkwardness; almost as direct a cut as it would be to extend the hand to a person to shake hands, then immediately turn away.' The author has neatly identified, I feel, the guiding principles that should govern the construction of best-liked contra dances: first, that each change should flow smoothly and comfortably into the next, with no physically awkward movements; second, that it must be understood that each movement or change is a communication between dancers that has a specific meaning; and third, that these messages must be arranged in a coherent fashion. For example the balance, a formal token of welcome, is naturally followed by a more intimate act, the swing. So I would go further than the above-quoted author and say that principles of courtship, as well as etiquette, should guide the composer of the dances. The balance, the do-si-do, and siding are all flirtatious welcomings, and are naturally followed by the swing. The reverse order doesn't make sense, and shouldn't be attempted.

"In most contra dances, the dancer is primarily involved with his or her partner, and usually progresses through a cyclical relationship which develops through 'welcoming' figures, culminates sometimes with a swing, and then dissipates with 'withdrawal' figures. Partners can withdraw from each other in many ways, for example, by going down the outside, or most seriously by swinging someone else.

" 'Lady of the Lake' is a good example of a dance where the relationship between partners intensifies and then dissipates. They start with a balance, and then they swing. Then they promenade down the center, come back and cast off, with the lady, and the lady with the man, and at this point they begin to withdraw from each other. Then there is a ladies chain, followed by a swing with the next person below, not their partner, the greatest of the 'withdrawals.'

"As mentioned before, partners frequently culminate their relationship with a swing, the swing itself being the most intimate physical figure partners can execute. But very often one swings with another's partner, as explained. It is only the 'promenade down the center' that is done always with one's

*continued*

*Photo by Nevell*

Jack Perron with his Stroh violin.

partner. It is the figure that ultimately expresses the relationships between the two dancers within the context of the whole dance. (The contra dance 'Ladies Triumph' comes close to violating this: in this dance of Scottish origin, a third dancer 'steals' someone else's partner and tries to take them down the center, but is quickly stopped by the proper partner.) The promenade is a powerful figure, allowing one to show off his partner to the other dancers, and as the final and most powerful expression of partnership, then, we naturally expect the promenade to follow the swing, as it so often does.

"I, and some of my friends, have composed a number of dances, some of which the dancers have accepted enthusiastically, and others they have rejected. I once tried to introduce a variation on 'Petronella,' which was heartily disfavored by everyone, and even now I hesitate to claim authorship. The dance has no name and goes like this: it's a duple proper. The first figure calls for the active couple to turn ¼ turn to the right and balance, then repeat that figure, just as in 'Petronella.' But then I have them turn away from the partners and swing the next below. Then they go down the center and back, cast off, and finish up with two ½ turns and Balances as in the first part of the dance. As I look at this dance now I realize that the dance is not only awkward, but violates rules of etiquette and courtship as well. What an insult and waste to turn your back on your partner after TWO balances, and swing someone else! Also I have found that balancing after a cast off is hopelessly awkward. You just can't call a figure that requires movement precisely on the beat, like a balance, after a cast off because dancers are invariably late casting off.

"One of my best dances, 'The Giant's Staircase' (named by Dick Nevell), goes like this: the 2nd, 4th, 6th and other even couples cross over and are active. First the men allemande the left lady, then swing the lady on the right (woman does the opposite on the other side). Then all go forward and back; ½ ladies chain; ½ right and left with couple diagonally to the left; ½ right and left straight across; all forward and back; ½ ladies chain. Then the last time through in the first part all go forward and back; ½ chain. Then the men allemande lady on left, and swing their partners on the right. Now here is a dance where one 'flirts' with everyone but his partner, and yet the promenade (in the form of two right and lefts) is always done with the partner. Here there is no courtship of one's partner, but partnership is clearly demonstrated and dominates the basic pattern of the dance, overshadowing all that 'flirting' going on otherwise. It's just a hunch of mine, which I can't prove, but I suspect this dance to be most popular with mature, predominately married couples. See what you think."

The rules for composing dances have been debated for years, and most composers from Thomas Wilson to Jack Perron have tried to answer the question "What makes a dance good?" No one has succeeded yet as far as I can tell: probably because there are too many variables involved in a dance, many of which have nothing to do with its choreography. The mood of the dancers, the musicians, the caller, the moon, and who knows what else can spoil a dance that looks great on paper.

Whether or not a caller makes up his own dances, he has to orchestrate the overall dance, the whole evening or event. Jack explains some of what he's learned about that:

"At the beginning of a dance, especially on cold winter nights, it's a good idea to start off with a dance where everybody's moving all the time. If it's cold you can't do a dance like 'Mony Musk' where only two out of every six people are dancing. You've got to do something with a lot of swinging, where everybody's active. Of course you have to get a feeling for the dancers when you first get there, so I kind of look around and see who's there, because I don't want to turn off people who don't know how to dance. That's really important. Sometimes there's lots of people I recognize as good dancers and so I'll start out with something a little more complicated. But other times I'll get to a dance hall and I won't recognize a person, so I have to start out with something a little more simple. And if there's lots of kids I try and do something fast, but if there's older people I do something a little slower. Speaking of kids, if they get a little rowdy I've got three or four dances that'll really get them tired and it helps to do those to kind of quiet them down a little.

"Basically I try to dominate the evening as little as possible. I try to say as little as possible, prompt as little as possible. Some callers have been able to kind of engineer the mood of the night, but never for very long. I really have to let the dancers develop their own pace, and I try to judge how people are feeling and respond to their mood rather than try to get them to respond to me. It's very difficult to generalize about because every dance is different. But you have to be a performer in some ways, you know, always in a good mood, and I've found that if I'm in a sour mood it really makes a difference to the dancers. And I have to be very careful about the way I interact with the dancers. It's very easy to make them feel foolish, or out of place at a dance, especially people who haven't done it a lot. It's really easy to look down on them and give them the impression that you think they're really stupid, and then they feel foolish and insecure. I try to be sensitive to that, and I've found that the best way for me to avoid doing that is just to get into it myself and have fun. It happens most often with a small crowd, where there isn't so much noise, and so they naturally feel more inhibited. And if I feel detached from them and give them the feeling that I wouldn't be caught dead down there dancing with them, then they really feel conspicuous and foolish. The best indicator, the way you can tell right off, is if they won't swing. If they won't swing then you know something is really wrong. And one of the best ways to solve the problem is just to get down there and dance with them and eventually, hopefully, they get over it. I remember once doing a dance with some kids at a public school. They were seventh graders and we were out on a baseball field. I couldn't even get them to take a partner. I had to line them up—boys on one side, and girls on the other—and say 'there's your partner' and still they wouldn't dance; until finally I got myself and some other adults right in there with them dancing and they felt a lot better about the whole thing. But you have to watch yourself, and stay away from that feeling of sep-aration between you and the dancers. You have to remember that it's newer to them than it is to you, and be careful not to discourage them.

"Of course it doesn't always work the way I want it to. Since I've started calling I find that there's a greater distance between me and the dancers. People are really reticent to come up and talk to me. I don't get a chance that often to get down on the dance floor, and I don't have much of a chance to talk to people. They come up and want to talk and I have so much on my mind, trying to give everyone something to do, then I just don't have that much time to spend with one person. I think I've made a lot of enemies that way, you know, of people who wanted to talk and I had to cut them off in mid-sentence."

Nelson, New Hampshire, is a town with a strong tradition of contra dancing, largely because many people who've been important in the dance live or have lived in Nelson. Ralph Page grew up near Nelson. The Tolman family—including Newt who has published a wonderful collection of dance music with Kay Gilbert—and Harvey Tolman, a great fiddler, have played an integral part in the maintenance of the con-tra-dance tradition there. So Nelson is a town where the caller really has to be on his toes because people are used to having the best there; they don't settle for second best. When the big revival of interest in contra dancing took place in the sixties and seventies, the Nelson people sud-denly found their hall filled with outsiders from all over, including Cam-bridge, Massachusetts. They were used to having outsiders there in the summer, but in the winter the local people didn't expect their dances to be as crowded as the ones in the summer. A lot of local people didn't like it and stopped coming to the dances. Now the dance fad has dissi-pated to a large degree, but the Nelson dance that Jack Perron runs is still predominantly attended by young people, and by very few Nelson people, especially the older citizens of the town. Jack is sensitive to this issue:

"I'd like to feel there was a greater cross section of people at the dance. There's a whole sort of group of people that won't come to the dances because word gets around that they're only for kids or something. And it's particularly frustrating because it really isn't like a town function as it probably used to be."

Nelson, like the whole Monadnock region of New Hampshire, is changing, and it's difficult to maintain a sense of cohesion in a changing community. One day a year Nelson has an Old Home Day, as do many towns in this part of New Hampshire, and at the dance held on that day

## DANCER / RUSS THOMAS

Russ Thomas moved to Nelson a few years ago and since then has worked as a mason, built his own house a couple of times over due to unfortunate fires, and been a regular at the contra dances around the Monadnock region.

"Every dance is different. Sometimes they get too crowded and you just can't dance, but generally it just feels really good when you're in a set with people who know how to dance, and aren't too pushy. It's a great thing to be moving with the music, almost like everybody is part of some kind of Busby Berkeley movie, you know everybody's moving together, and I feel like there should be a camera overhead catching all of it, this well-ordered movement.

"I think that people definitely go to meet people, but it's not like going to a singles' bar or something like that. I like contra dancing because unlike in rock and roll dancing you get to touch your partner! You know last time I went rock and roll dancing, I couldn't stand just standing there all by myself jiggling around so I grabbed ahold of the woman!"

Russ working on his table saw.

Left Hand Star in Nelson

*Photos by Nevell*

Jack Perron and the band in Nelson.

you see more local people than at the regular monthly dances throughout the year. But on the whole it's not the old timers who come to the
dances on a regular basis. Jack has some ideas about why this is:

"The community of people who come to the dances are, I think, more
homogeneous than dance groups have been in the past. They're more
liberal; and they don't choose to come to the dances because of their
geographical location, but more because of their political outlook. I think
there are basically two types of dancers around here: the ones that have
always done it, and still come because it's right next door, and then there
are the ones who came up here because of the whole 'back to the earth'
movement. And most of the people who do it now are in the latter
group, and they are aware of the significance of it, aware of what they're
doing, and they tend to take great pride in being 'good' dancers. It's really a different atmosphere in the Monadnock region, because a lot of
the people still just come to have a good time. They don't want to do
complicated dances, they just want to swing and talk to people, meet
their friends. They're the ones who've done it all their lives, you know,
their parents did it . . . but that group is diminishing, fewer and fewer of
those people are left. So the community of dancers is really a very trans-
itory community. When you have gas and you can move around you're
not really forced to get along with your neighbors. The group that
comes to my dances don't live together generally, they don't work together. They're scattered all around, and so the major social link between those people is the dance."

The Dance. It is a major social link between people in the Monadnock
region, but it still has to compete with the movies, bowling, a slew of gin
mills, but probably most heavily of course, with television. Ray Hull once
said that the simplest explanation for the decline of interest in dancing
around where he lives in Vermont is television. Modern culture has
quickly changed from a participatory one to a nonparticipatory one, and
the change stretches across all age groups, all economic groups. We are
no longer the doers, but the watchers: fragmented, sitting alone in
rooms bathed in hazy TV screen blue. Some people, including Jack Perron, think that contra dancing has value because it is a group activity:

"When I went to my first contra dance, the values that were most
stressed that got you through a dance were: you really have to cooperate
with the other people and you have to get into the spirit of the whole.
You can't just go off and do your 'own thing' during the dance. When
someone comes to the dance who's not into that, who's just into doing his
own thing, you know 'Play man, for me,' they always get taken down a
few notches because that just doesn't work, it screws up the whole thing.
I tell my dancers that my basic philosophy is this: all I ask is that they

don't mess anybody else up. They can do whatever they want: like if there's a swing and they don't want to swing, they want to do something else, fine, I don't object; so long as it doesn't mess someone else up. The contra dance is a powerful instrument for teaching people to cooperate, to think about other people, and I respect it for that."

Once Jack said: "When I was a kid growing up I never went to a junior high school dance . . . I never got into rock and roll and the twist and all that stuff. I thought that stuff was the stupidest stuff in the world. I was the most antisocial kid you'd ever want to meet in your life, really! I never went out on a date. . . . There was a whole aspect that I never experienced and now I'm just beginning to really groove on it, acting in a social way with a large group of people.

"I like being the vehicle through which people meet each other. I think other callers probably feel the same way. It's like being a kind of matchmaker, and that's really an attraction for being a caller. It wouldn't make much sense to just entertain people for four hours: it's the personal contacts that are made that you feel partially responsible for.

"Sometimes as the caller I feel out of it, not in the center of whatever is happening there at the dance. I feel as if it's everybody against me, and I'll go away feeling really bad. But whenever I'm calling, whenever I'm running a dance, whenever I've taken the initiative to hire a hall and hire some musicians, and invited people to come: and they come . . . then every smile that I see is a reward to me, because I really like to see people having a good time, and it really makes me feel good when people do. I watch the dancers' faces all the time, and if I see them laughing it really makes me feel good! like the comedian who can make people laugh. It's the same sort of fulfillment, letting people enjoy themselves. Wow, that's a good feeling, a good spirit, you know, because I've really reached out! And deep down I hope that something of that spirit continues after the dance is over, you know what I mean?"

## Some Favorite Contra Dances

Contra dances, also known as longways, string, or double column dances, are danced in a number of different ways. In this brief explanation we'll just look at the simplest types of contras so that the reader can easily understand how they work. (Note that during an evening of contra dancing some plain quadrilles are usually called, these dances being simple square dances like those explained in the Western square dance section.) The best place to learn them is on the dance floor, so we'll use that model here, imagining ourselves at a dance somewhere in New England on a cold winter night where everybody's dancing because it's the only way to keep warm. The caller announces the next dance, a contra, and you and your partner take your place at the head of the set. If you're the man you stand to the caller's right, opposite the woman who is standing to the left of the caller. The caller says: "Every other couple is active, count down the set!" This means that you, the first couple, and every other couple (3rd, 5th, 7th, etc.) is "active." Being active means that the calls are directed toward you most of the time. Being inactive (the 2nd, 4th, 6th couples) means that you only dance as a result of an active couple approaching to dance with you.

ACTIVE MAN    ACTIVE WOMAN

KEY

INACTIVE MAN    INACTIVE WOMAN

| DUPLE PROPER CONTRA | DUPLE IMPROPER CONTRA | TRIPLE PROPER CONTRA | TRIPLE IMPROPER CONTRA |
|---|---|---|---|

After everyone's been squared away as far as who's active and inactive, the caller will generally walk through the dance slowly, without music, to make sure everyone understands how it works. Let's suppose the first call he gives is "First lady Balance the second man." This means that the 1st, 3rd, 5th, and 7th ladies balance the 2nd, 4th, 6th and 8th men respectively for the first four measures of the dance. The next call is "Swing partner," which means *only* the active couples swing (1, 3, 5, 7). When the swing is over—which, by the way, lasts another four measures—the 1st man (also 3, 5, 7) balances the appropriate inactive lady, the partner of the man the 1st lady (also 4, 6, 8) balanced with (the call for this is "First man Balances second lady"), then goes back and swings his partner again for four measures.

At this point you have completed half of the dance. Why half? Because contra dances are danced to tunes which usually have two parts of eight measures each, which are repeated. If you've been keeping track of the measures so far, you'll see that they add up to sixteen (the first part of the tune has been played twice):

| First lady Balances 2nd man | 4 |
| Swing partner | 4 |
| First man Balances 2nd lady | 4 |
| Swing partner | +4 |
| | 16 |

This particular dance is called "Durang's Hornpipe," named after John Durang, a famous American dancer of the nineteenth century who wrote the tune called by the same name. Like most contra dance tunes, "Durang's Hornpipe" has two parts, an "A" part and a "B" part, each part being eight measures long. For dancing, the tune is played in the following fashion: the "A" part is played through once for the first eight measures of the dance:

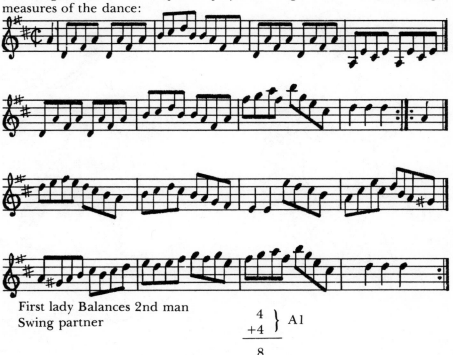

First lady Balances 2nd man
Swing partner

$$\left.\begin{array}{r} 4 \\ +4 \end{array}\right\} A1$$
$$8$$

and then played through again for the second eight measures:

First man Balances 2nd lady
Swing partner

$$\left.\begin{array}{r} 4 \\ +4 \end{array}\right\} A2$$
$$8$$

So at this point you have completed half the dance known as "Durang's Hornpipe." Now let's look at the second half.

The next call is "Down the Center," which means all active couples (1, 3, 5, 7) dance down the corridor formed by the two rows, for four measures; they then turn around and dance "Back to Place" for four measures. When the active couples get back to place, they "Cast Off" with the couple below them (2, 4, 6, 8). To Cast Off, you just put your arm around the inactive person's waist and turn around together so that you change places. So there you are: the two men on one side, places changed, and the two women on the other, also having changed places.

By "casting off" you have progressed one place down the set. You will do this through each cycle of the dance until you reach the bottom. The next call is "Right and Left Over" which lasts for four measures, and then "Right and Left Back" which lasts for four measures (see diagram below for Figure 9, "Right and Left," in "Basic Figures"). And that's it! During the second half of the dance the "B" part of "Durang's Hornpipe" is played twice:

| Down the Center | 4 | } B1 |
|-----------------|---|------|
| Back to Place   | 4 |      |

*(Cast off is tagged on to the end of B1)*

| Right and Left Over | 4 | } B2 |
|---------------------|---|------|
| Right and Left Back | 4 |      |

With this sixteen measures of music you have completed one cycle of the dance. The next cycle begins immediately as the "A" part of the tune starts up. The dance follows the same pattern; only now the active couples have moved down one place and are dancing with a new inactive couple. In this case you, who started as number 1 and first danced with couple 2, are now dancing with couple 4. Meanwhile number 3 who started with 4 has gone on to dance with 6, and so forth. You will now dance with all the initially inactive couples until you get to the bottom of the set, when you will become an inactive couple. Meanwhile all the inactive couples have been moving up the set and when they get to your original place they become number 1 and active. This is why contra dances are called "progressive" dances.

Now we have walked through only the simplest kind of contra dance—but fear not, they all work basically the same way, just with slight variations. Sometimes the active couples are numbered 1, 4, 7 (every third couple); sometimes the tunes are longer because they have more parts. But these variations will throw you only if you're not listening, or if the caller makes a mistake, which happens—they're human, after all.

Your set for "Durang's Hornpipe" can be as long as the hall allows, but it's usually more fun to split up into sets of six or eight couples so no one has to be inactive for very long. If you're a beginning dancer it's best to start out at the bottom of the set in an inactive place so you can watch the other active dancers, who hopefully know what they're doing.

So after all this explanation and a walk-through, you're ready to dance. The caller gives the signal to the musicians to begin, you get ready, and he calls "First lady Balance to the 2nd man." Good Luck.


Lots of people have written about dancing style. Dancing masters of the nineteenth century, Henry Ford, and others in this century have encouraged, if not demanded, a refined and exact style. Personally I've found that to have a good time dancing doesn't require a lot of rules of decorum and fancy footwork. To me, the good dancer is one who is in balance with himself and the other dancers on the floor. This means being aware of the music, the caller, the other dancers, and the space within which you can dance without usurping someone else's space. Good dancing is just being responsible and, with a little practice, graceful.

## Petronella

"Petronella," known to some New Englanders as "Pat'nella," is as standard a dance there is. In *The Country Dance Book,* Page and Tolman say of this dance: "Obviously this is not a dance for the pickle faces," and indeed it isn't. Back in the thirties, according to the authors, then dancing "Pat'nella," ". . . they used this dance as a showpiece for their cloggings and pigeon's wings."

During the current revival of interest in contra dancing, "Petronella" has remained one of the most popular dances and, as in the thirties, the modern dancers have used the dance to show off new steps, many of which are a result of the influence of rock and roll dancing. As the dancers turn to right and balance, they add their own ornaments, characterized by some as "wriggling around." But an even more significant addition to the dance is the inclusion of the inactive couples in the first part of the dance, normally reserved for the actives. This version has been named "Citronella" by Dudley Laufman. As far as the music is concerned, Ralph Page mentions in *The Country Dance Book* that other tunes were substituted for the original one of the same name. The same is true today, but my guess is that most dancers prefer the traditional tune. The dance is in contra formation, with every other couple active and not crossed over. Dudley calls the dance as follows:

A1 { Go Around to the Right and you Balance to Your Partner
Go Around to the Right and Balance Again. } 8 MEASURES

A2 { Go Around to Your right and you Balance to Your Partner
Go Around to the Right and you Balance Once Again. } 8 MEASURES

B1 { Now go Down the Center With your Own
And you Bring that Lady Right Back Home } 8 MEASURES

B2 { And you Cast Off and you Right and Left Over
And you Right and Left Back Home again. } 8 MEASURES

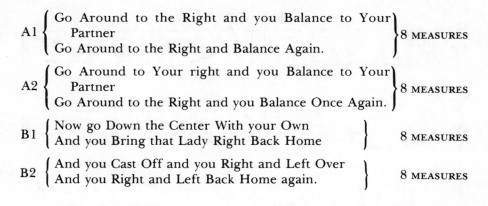

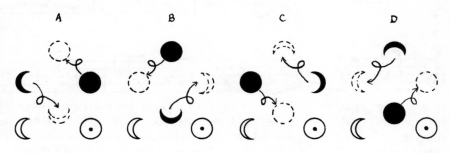

The principle of "Petronella" can be explained by using the analogy of a baseball diamond. On the call "Go Around to the Right," the active man and woman turn to their right and move into the center of the set so that the man ends us facing the caller and the woman, her partner. The man is now in home place for the first balance, while the woman is on second base. For the second balance, the man turns and moves to first, the woman to third; for the third balance the man moves to second base, the woman to home plate; and finally the first active man goes to third base and the woman to first, where they balance, facing down the set, ready to go down the center.

For "Citronella," the inactive couples join the actives in A1 and A2 by also turning and balancing opposite each other; they then follow literally in the footsteps of the actives as they move from position to position around the floor. The inactive man and woman start on third base and first base respectively, and move around the bases in the same order as the active couple. It's a lot of fun if you can figure it out. (Dudley Laufman points out that it is the active couple's choice as to whether or not they desire the company of the inactives.)

Thanks to Jack Perron for the baseball analogy.

## Rory O'More

It is a rare night when Jack Perron fails to call this extremely popular contra dance, "Rory O'More," at least when the dancing crowd is relatively experienced. It is one of the more difficult dances to learn. The difficulty lies in the execution of the figure called "Country Corners," a figure wholly unique to the contra dance, and which appears in only a few of them. With the help of the illustration, I hope this figure and the whole dance make sense. Like "Petronella" this dance has its own tune but can be danced to others, notably a popular tune called "Saddle the Pony." Here's the way Jack calls the dance, one of his favorites:

Every other couple is active and not crossed over.

A1 { First couple Crosses Over to the opposite side and goes down one place on the outside. } 4 MEASURES
They come into the center and cross back to place, the lady in the lead and Cast Off with the couple below, man with the man, lady with the lady. } 4 MEASURES

A2 { The active couples give right hands to their partners and Balance in the center. } 4 MEASURES
Then they step to the right past each other and join left hands and Balance in the center. } 4 MEASURES

B1 { From that spot they turn Country Corners. } 8 MEASURES

B2 { Then they meet in the center where they Balance and Swing. } 8 MEASURES

A1      from Rory O'More      Country Corners

Country Corners is really not as difficult as people make it out to be. Very often the figure is simply explained badly, or people don't listen while it's being explained. It goes like this: the active couple is standing in the middle of the set. The man is looking at the women's line where he sees an inactive woman to his right and an inactive woman to his left. Similarly, the active woman faces the men's line and sees an inactive man to her right and an inactive man to her left. When the call "Turn Country Corners" comes, the active couples join right hands in the allemande position. Then they proceed as follows:

1. The man goes to the inactive woman to his right. The woman goes to the inactive man to her right.
2. They each Allemande left with that inactive person in a U turn and return to the center.
3. Then they join right hands again, Allemande-style.
4. And the man goes to the inactive woman to his left while the woman goes to the inactive man to her left.
5. Again they Allemande those inactives in a U turn and return to the center.

# Canadian Breakdown

"Canadian Breakdown" is a contra dance whose authorship is attributed to Ralph Page in the Sets in Order book, *Contras* by Don Armstrong. It's a little different from "Petronella" and "Rory O'More" because it does not have its own tune and, every other odd couple is crossed over: the active men stand in the women's line and the active women stand in the men's line. Elizabeth Cohn from Nelson, picked this as one of her favorites. As for the music, any good reel with two parts will do. Jack Perron "Sandy McIntyre's Trip to Boston," by John Campbell, for this dance:

Here's how the dance goes:

Every other couple is active and crossed over (active men and women change places).

A1 {
Actives Balance in the center, then Do-Si-Do their partner.
Actives Allemande Left the one below (man with lady, lady with man) and Balance four in line: across the set so that the men are facing down the set, the women facing up at the caller.
} 8 MEASURES

A2 { Active Couples Balance and Swing in the Center. } 8 MEASURES

B1 {
Active couples Go Down the Center.
Active couples Return to Place and Cast Off, man with lady, lady with man.
} 8 MEASURES

B2 { Active couples Right Hand Star with inactive couple below once around. } 8 measures
Active couples Left Hand Star with inactive couple below once around

## Elegance and Simplicity

When I asked Barbara Piscitelli what her favorite contra dance was, she had a tough time deciding. Eventually she ended up picking a dance called "The Bishop," because it has some unusual figures, but mainly because she likes the flirtatious nature of the dance. As she said: "I could get in a lot of trouble if I did that dance too often!" In second place came "Elegance and Simplicity," which I have decided to present here because it's a dance she only did once, with Ralph Page, and I think that fact—that she remembers it so well after one performance—is worth all the flirtatiousness in the world. Besides, it's a great dance.

"Elegance and Simplicity" (which Ralph Page discovered in *The Ladies and Gentleman's Companion Containing the Newest Cotillions and Country Dances* published in 1803 in Dedham, Massachusetts), is not done very often because it uses the most unusual of the contra formations—the 1st, 4th, 7th couples are active and crossed over. It's a tough dance, requiring some practice, but worth it when you get it right. Dance it to a good jig, such as: Bob McQuillen's "The Naughty Noochie."

A1 { First couple does a Right Hand Star with second couple halfway around.
First couple does a Left Hand Star with third couple halfway around. } 8 MEASURES

A2 { First and third couples Right and Left halfway across the set.
First and second couples Right and Left halfway back to their original places. } 8 MEASURES

B1 { First couple Goes Down the Center.
First couple Comes Back Up and Casts Off, man with second lady, lady with second man. } 8 MEASURES

B2 { First couple does a full Ladies Chain with the second couple. } 8 MEASURES

# IV
# SOUTHERN APPALACHIAN
# MOUNTAIN DANCING

I went South with a list of names a mile long, of people who were supposed to know something about "dancin' " (unlike "dancing" in country
dancing, or square dancing which is done all over the United States,
"dancin' " is only done in the southern mountains). The names included
all kinds of people, from college professors to fiddler gas station owners
to friends of friends of friends "who might know someone up there."
"Up there" meant a community in the mountains where I hoped to find
some of the dancin' I'd heard and read about. I had already written to
some of these people, and those who had replied added more names of
people who might know somebody or someplace in the mountains where
a community danced—but no one had a definite place to recommend.
This was hard for me to understand because my impression was that
dancin' went on all over the place, all the time, by everybody in the
southern Appalachians. I soon found out different.

I took off early one April morning from New York, crossing under
the Hudson, and made my way through the surprisingly lovely western
hills of New Jersey until I joined the interstate in Pennsylvania. From
there it was due south on Route 81, roughly twelve hours, to Knoxville,
Tennessee. There isn't a great deal you can do in a car for twelve hours.
I still honk at cars from my home state, although that custom seems to
have lost popularity in recent years. It must be that people are just too
used to driving long distances. Driving South used to be more of an ad-
venture, too. I remember driving the coastal route with my family about
twenty years ago. My father had been warned about the speed traps in
Georgia, the Ku Klux Klan, and grits, and so he passed the warning
along to my sister and me who sat terrified in the back seat as soon as we
crossed the state line into Virginia. Now all these years later as I drove
along the Shenandoah Valley I realized how much things had changed
with me: I was eager to get into the South, in spite of the popular
stereotypes derived from *Deliverance* and "Ode to Billy Joe."

So I drove on through the western Virginia hills, past towns that
looked like New England towns. But there was no snow, just yellow
winter grass leaning and spinning in the wind. The interstate seemed
like a conveyor belt after awhile. It squeezed the land into ridges on
either side. As the sun went down below the oaks lining the western
ridge, I imagined what I would find in the mountains: a Saturday night
dance, fiddlers galore. Then I came around a big curve and saw a house
at the end of a road, red in the light of sunset. The house had black

shutters and a white porch and stood next to a green pond. Above the pond a hill swept up like a sand dune. Stretched over the hill the rows of black apple trees looked as if they were lined up, ready to dance. Soon it was completely dark. Six hours to go.

It was very, very late in Knoxville when I came to the end of my twelve-hour trip. I pulled off the interstate and found a pay phone. I took out my notebook with the list of names and called up Loyce Stracener, a friend of a friend who had offered to put me up for awhile and help me find the people I was looking for. She told me to come right over. The drive took me through the center city of Knoxville and then out the Clinton Highway, a strip of shopping centers and twenty-five cent car washes, to Murray Road, which is opposite the "Big Orange" liquor mart. Everything in Knoxville is "Big Orange" this and that because orange is the color for UT, the University of Tennessee, and around Knoxville, UT is about all that anybody cares about. When I arrived at Loyce's house we exchanged formal hellos and I quickly went to sleep in the guest room.

When I woke up the next morning and looked out the sunny window, I saw a tree with budding, light lime leaves all over it. Below the tree was a barn with horses, including a young colt, around it. A big meadow stretched up a hill behind the barn, where a line of trees was also greening. It was spring. Loyce and I sat out on her porch and drank coffee as the sun rose, getting hotter and hotter as noon came on.

There's still a lot of country around the outskirts of Knoxville, and there are even central parts of the city where people have chickens or hogs in their back yard. I spent my first day wandering through the city noticing different things: the men chewing tobacco, UT coeds dressed in their spring fashions, big blooming magnolia trees. The next day I drove east to the country, toward the Smokies, to the Highlander Center. I had been told that Guy and Candie Carawan worked and lived there, and they "knew everything about music in the mountains." Myles Horton, the retired director of the center, was also there.

I had tried to call up Guy Carawan and his wife before I left Knoxville, but no one answered. I went anyway, just to see the foothills of the Smokies. I could leave a note if the center were empty when I got there. As I drove up the gravel drive past the sky blue mailbox and approached the first wooden building, the land opened before me and I could see what seemed to be the entire Smoky Mountain Range on the horizon. But the buildings on the hill seemed empty. I knocked on the door but nobody answered. The door was open and I almost went in, then decided not to. The hill was quiet; then on the wind that blew across the huge sloping meadow behind me, I heard a voice. I looked up to the top of the hill and I could see someone, then a group of people standing around a modern wooden building. I drove up to the main building at the top of the hill, met Candie Carawan, and discovered that Highlander was sponsoring a songwriters' weekend workshop for mountain songwriters—writers from all over the Smokies and from cities where mountain people had emigrated: Atlanta, Chicago, Cleveland, and so on. About a dozen songwriters had gathered there. Led by Guy Carawan, the writers would compose songs and share them with the others. There were songwriters who wrote topical songs and some who wrote love songs. Some were professional writers and performers, and others were amateur songwriters. The one thing these people had in common—a pretty lady from Nashville and an insurance salesman from back-country Georgia—was that they all wrote songs about the mountains and mountain people.

I had arrived at lunch time, and right after lunch they had planned a square dance. I happened in at just the right time. It was my first taste of southern mountain dancin', and it was free and very casual. The kitchen people came out and danced, and some people just watched. There were three musicians playing fiddle and guitar and banjo; Jon Sundell from Gatlinburg, Tennessee, called the Appalachian Big Circle dances.

A lot of songwriters just watched or sat outside in the sun, which was very hot. When one of the Big Circle dances stopped and the fiddlers kept on playing, a man got out on the floor all by himself and started doing a dance I had never seen before. It was a very fast dance: he was kicking his heels and doing a kind of tap dancing to the fiddle tunes, making lots of noise with his feet. Everybody was hollering at him and the music got faster and he kept going on and on until he almost collapsed, until he just couldn't go on any more. He was breathless. I didn't know exactly what I'd seen, except that it reminded me slightly of step dancers I'd once seen from Ireland; and sometimes at home in New Hampshire, dancers would stamp their feet in time to the music. But this was clearly different because he kept it going, and it was a much wilder, uncontrolled kind of dancing in which he deliberately exhausted himself. I asked the dancer what he had done and he said: "Buckdancin' is what you call it when one person does it, but when you get a whole bunch of people together they do the figures like we were just doing, and that's just called plain old dancin.' " Then I asked him where he learned buckdancin' and he laughed and said, "Oh I don't know; I guess I just kind of picked it up." I asked him if he could teach me how to do it and he just laughed, looked at me in a funny way, and didn't say anything.

Later that night a man I hadn't seen before came over to the table I

# THE APPALACHIAN SQUARE DANCE

The basic figures of the Appalachian square dance, like New England contra-dancing figures, only number about a dozen. In the Appalachian dance, however, there are more figures which involve the whole Big Set, whereas in a contra dance the only figure everyone does together is "all go Forward and Back." The basic figures for Big Circle dances derive from a combination of sources: some traditional ones and some from children's singing games, and others that are untraceable but have been given an American name. Some of them will be explained at the end of this chapter.

*Figures for Big Circles:*

| | |
|---|---|
| Wagon Wheel | Georgia Rang Tang |
| Raise the Window | The Twirl |
| The Basket | Shoo Fly Shoo |
| Balance All | London Bridges |
| Break and Swing | Rights and Lefts |

When the Big Circle splits into several small circles of two couples each, more figures are available for the dancers. Like the Big Circle, these figures derive from a variety of sources. Some of these figures will also be explained at the end of this chapter.

*Figures for Small Circles:*

| | |
|---|---|
| Four Leaf Clover | Lady Around the Lady |
| Right Hand Shake | Adam and Eve |
| Double Bow Knot | Little Side Door |
| Gents Fall Back | Four Hands Across |
| That Old Figure Eight | Open Up Them Pearly Gates |
| Birdie in the Cage | Mountaineer Loop |
| Ocean Wave | Roll the Barrel |
| Swing at the Wall | Shoot the Owl |
| Go Downtown | Wild Goose Chase |
| Black Snake Twist | |

In his book *The Appalachian Square Dance,* author Frank Smith notes that when Cecil Sharp .saw his first square dance in Appalachia, what he saw was a four-couple dance, the same formation as the modern Western square dance and the New England quadrille. This formation is called the Kentucky Running Set, because Sharp saw it at Pine Mountain, Kentucky. Smith points out that there is no difference between the actual dancing style of a regular Big Circle dance and the Kentucky Running Set. Dance Historians have tried to determine for years why Sharp saw this peculiar formation in Kentucky, but none have been able to really solve the mystery. It is worth noting that the four couples are numbered in the same fashion as a Western square, not like the New England quadrille; but my best guess is that what Sharp saw was simply an accident of history that probably resulted from any number of factors: a chance visit by a dancing master from the East on the way to the West; some other traveler knowledgeable about the dancing.

# APPALACHIAN SQUARE-DANCE TUNES

The music for a Big Circle dance or a Kentucky Running Set is provided usually by live musicians: a fiddler, banjo picker, and guitar player, playing traditional tunes. Unlike contra dance music which includes jigs in 6/8 time and reels in 4/4 or 2/4 time, the Appalachian square dance only uses the reels, 4/4 or 2/4, and they are generally played at a very fast clip.

The tunes are traditional, many of them traceable to traditional Scottish, Irish, and English tunes. Because of the speed at which they are played, most of the tunes are quite simple and tend not to be heavily embellished.

The basic structure of these tunes is the same as those used for contra dances: two parts, each part eight measures long, played either A B A B etc. or A A B B etc. depending on the structure of the dance.

"Cindy"

"Cripple Creek"

was sitting at and introduced himself. It was Myles Horton. He said that he'd heard from his wife Candie that I was writing a book about country dance. We talked about dancin' but also more generally about his experiences in the labor movement and the civil rights' movement; especially about the people who danced to keep their spirits up during times of crisis. But, I asked him, looking out at the mountains to the east, "Don't people dance out there anymore?" Did they have public dances where people came from the local community and participated in the casual way we had danced after lunch? I told him that I had hoped to find a remote place in the mountains where this kind of dancing went on as it did in New England. Myles freely admitted that he couldn't answer my question. I found out that nobody could, at least no one among the people there. It seemed to be an almost a mysterious kind of issue. I was beginning to seriously doubt if I would ever find my imagined community of dancers. No one really would come straight and say "Yes I know where people dance in such and such a town" or "No, people just don't do that anymore." Instead there was general talk about mountain life, about the traditional folk-life customs like dancing, which somehow had been very difficult to keep alive through the years. I began to realize that if I was going to understand this struggle I would have to do some of my own research into the history of the southern Appalachian region.

Highlander has a wonderful library, and the next day I sequestered myself in it and read everything I could on the history of the mountains. I found some writings of Emma Miles, a collector of southern Appalachian customs, in which she states, in 1905, that "the old music is supplanted by cheap Sunday school song books, and the old dances are given over to rowdies." Then in 1913 Horace Kephart wrote: "The mountaineers have a native fondness for dancing and music, which, with the shouting spells of their revivals, are the only outlets for these powerful emotions which they otherwise conceal. Whenever the church has not put its ban on 'twistifications' the country dance is the chief amusement of young and old. . . . In homes where dancing is not permitted, and often in others, 'play parties' are held at which social games are practiced with childlike abandon . . . (but) most of the mountain preachers nowadays denounce dances and play parties as sinful diversions, though their real objection seems to be that such gatherings are counter attractions that thin out the religious ones." Then in 1921 John C. Campbell wrote: "Dances in the mountains have been so often connected in the past with drinking, shooting, and evil of all kinds, as to have gained the hearty disapprobation of most of the steady church going population."

I found these observations repeated over and over by writers who had studied the folk life of the mountaineers, so that eventually I was able to draw some conclusions about why Myles Horton and others could not be specific about where I might find some old-time dancin'. First, the church had had a tremendous influence, mainly negative, on the propagation of dancin'. Second and most importantly I concluded that, as in New England, the folk customs of Appalachia could not be described or located in general terms because life in the mountains was innately localized, customs could vary radically between two communities only one hill apart, and unlike New England, they lacked a town structure where people would know what was going on.

In 1955 Frank Smith wrote of dancing in the southern mountains: "Square dance figures, calls and tunes are the common lore of the mountains. Yet, contrary to popular belief, few mountain callers are familiar with a wide range of figures. When one considers what are the dance customs in mountain communities, this is easy to understand. Dances are held infrequently; a lot of people come to them for social reasons, not because they follow dancing like city folks who join a square or folk dance club. And so the mountain caller has often only a limited and well known routine, which is traditional in the community." This seemed to sum up the problem for dancing in the mountains: clearly its survival depended on the survival of each local community. Now local communities have had a very hard time in the southern Appalachians. Small towns have always led a fragile existence throughout the history of the region, which in truth, has never really been a united one. Smith wrote, also in 1955: "The social forces of easy travel and communications; the desire for novelty . . . commercial incentives, such as the sale of dance records and special clothes for dancing; the holding of numerous festivals and dance workshops, at which the variety of traditions used is astonishingly wide: all these factors tend to break down dance traditions."

Comments such as this made me pessimistic about finding a remote "holler" somewhere unaffected by the social forces Frank Smith talked about. I put all the books away and walked up to the top of the Highlander Center hill, where Myles was working in his garden. I said something like: "Myles, now that I've learned a little about the mountains, what do you think I should do?" I thought for sure he'd just say something like: "Go back north," but instead he said, with a characteristic chuckle, "Well, you're sure not going to find any dancing in those books, so if you want to find dancin' in the mountains, then you'll have to go into the mountains, meet the people . . . and who knows, you might just find what you're looking for." Then Myles added: "But before you go anywhere else you ought to go see Wilma Dykeman in Newport . . . she might be able to give you some clues, maybe a direction to go in."

Wilma Dykeman lives in a house overlooking Newport, Tennessee, which is the county seat of Cocke County. Cocke County, I discovered, is well known as the home of many snake-handling fundamentalist churches and is plagued with a fairly high rate of crime. The town used to be merely a trading center for farmers and mountaineers who came from their respective homes for supplies, but when the area became more settled, Newport became the center of legal and business activities for the county. I walked around Newport looking for a pay phone to call Wilma Dykeman and finally found one in a dry goods store. She said I could come up in about an hour so I wandered around the town. There were a lot of farmers dressed in overalls. The center of activity was still the county courthouse, where old men, chewing tobacco, traded conversation and sometimes goods. Across the street a funeral procession passed by, then the normal traffic resumed. It included a host of noisy hot rods and a freight train. I stoppped into the local newspaper office and asked a woman if there was any square dancing in the area. She said "You mean square dancin' clubs? Yeah there's lots of them all over the place." And I said no, I meant old-time Appalachian dancing and she said "Oh, no, you won't find that around Newport, but if you go out in some of these small little places you might find something going on, but I doubt it." So I thanked her, and she said, "You're welcome," and "Y'all come back!" I headed across the street to my car, thinking about what the newspaper woman had said about square-dance clubs. I realized that, of course, there would be square-dance clubs in the area, since Western square dance had become a nationwide activity, but I wondered if the local callers ever used any old traditional southern dances in their routines. I found out later that they didn't, and I also found out that live musicians were never used. It became clear to me that here, where the tradition of music and dance was at one time strong and local in nature, Western square dancing had virtually taken over as the standard "square dance" style. I asked one more person on the street about buckdancin', and he said, "If y'all wanta see some buckdancin' just go out to some of these roadhouses on a Friday or a Saturday night, and you'll see some buckdancin'; when these boys get a few in 'em they can really dance!" Did they dance to fiddle music? "Hell, no, they just dance to the juke or the band, or nothin. . . . No, they just get it on when they've had a few." I asked the guy for the name of a place and he said, "Oh you just go to any these old bars, but y'all watch it, now; some of them boys can get mean!" I thanked him and he said "That's all right, now y'all come back."

A short time before I arrived in Newport, a tornado had whipped through the town, in fact directly through Wilma Dykeman's front yard, taking down one of her favorite trees. We sat on her front porch and talked about what I was doing and what she has done. Wilma Dykeman is a writer who has specialized in historical novels based on the lives of southern mountain people. Myles Horton had suggested that she could give me some clues about places in the mountains where country dancing might have survived the forces of change, as well as a good perspective on the overall effects of those changes, especially on the maintenance of community life. Myles was right. Here is some of what Wilma Dykeman said:

"The dance was simply a part of all the hard work it took to build a community: the log rollings, the cabin raisings; and these were made into social events, even though they were basically utilitarian, because nothing said the people couldn't enjoy themselves along the way. But later, dancing was frowned on by many in the mountains, and thus was created this dichotomy, almost as serious as the families torn by the Civil War, of people who danced and those that didn't. I can remember hearing stories when I was young about people who'd been 'churched' because they'd been to a dance; and it was believed by many, and still is today by many, that one stands a great danger of earthly repudiation and eternal damnation if you attend a dance, much less if you participate in it, for this was and is the 'devil's workshop.'

"Nowadays the continuation of these traditions takes hold where someone makes a conscious effort to preserve it, because your average person around here just isn't interested in it . . . it isn't glamorous to square dance because people don't see it on television.

"So I don't know what you'll find out there, but I will tell you this: one of the things about the dance in Appalachia was that it was all inclusive, old and young could join in. It wasn't confined to just two and two, or an age group, or even class groups. It gave you a real sense of community that you cannot manufacture. You can't just say 'We will now have a sense of community!' as so many people now think you can, just by declaring it in some way."

Then she said, very much as an afterthought, "You know, someone who might be able to help you is Jean Schilling up in Cosby. I think they've been having some dances up there, and she'd know about them as much as anyone. Now why didn't I think of her before?" She laughed and then she said, "Now I think you should go up there to Cosby right now and talk to Jean Schilling." So that's what I did.

## II

The road to Cosby from Newport crosses the interstate, which, if you glance to the east, eventually cuts through the heart of the Smokies. Then the road becomes progressively hillier as you drive away from the river valley into the foothills around Cosby. All along the highway, which continues to Gatlinburg, the roadsigns are clearly designed to appeal to the tourists who invade the area during the summer months. Cosby is roughly halfway between Newport and Gatlinburg, two towns that couldn't be more different. Gatlinburg is a Tiajuana-style town designed to exploit, with a minimum of taste, the local resources or natural phenomena—in this case the Smokies, the mountaineers, and the Indians (who long ago lost control of their native land to commercial interests). The biggest seller in Gatlinburg and other "gateway to the Smokies" places are cheap gifts fashioned in the "hillbilly" or "injun" motif. The only place worse than Gatlinburg in the Smokies is Cherokee, a town in the middle of the reservation, where Indians stand around in front of cheesy souvenir stores dressed in phony costumes with plastic Day-Glo feather headresses, selling little tomahawks to the tourists gawking from their Winnebago motor homes. More than the interstate has cut through the heart of the Smokies.

The only communities in the mountains that have escaped "the cut" are the more remote areas, far enough from the National Park that they have as yet little commercial potential. Some of the outlying communities of Cosby, the neighborhoods tucked into the most obscure regions of the mountains, fit this description. The way of life for many people in these communities has remained relatively untouched from generation to generation since the area was first settled in the nineteenth century. Many still operate small farms producing minor cash crops of tobacco and foods for their own consumption. Two of these settlements near Cosby are called the Bogard and the Wilhite communities. The Bogard Road community is in Cocke County and the Wilhite Road community in Sevier County. Built right on the county line is a large wooden building called the Sunset Gap Community Center, where local people have benefitted from different kinds of social service programs since 1923. Originally built as a grammar school in 1923, the Sunset Gap Center, though part of a widespread Presbyterian organization of settlement institutions in Appalachia, reflects a particular community need. When the original school was about to fold in 1923, local people gave land, lumber, and manpower to build a new school, which since then has been given over to regional education. Now the center focusses on filling other community needs such as preschool education, activities for the elderly, and the encouragement of native crafts and arts—weaving, music, and Appalachian square dancing. The center also offers regular church services and religious education to a small congregation.

It's hard to say whether or not the community that centers around Sunset Gap is a "typical" mountain community; I found out that nothing is typical in the mountains. I ended up at Sunset Gap because of a series of accidents and coincidences, which were a result of meeting people, almost none of whom were on my original list of "resource" people in the southern mountains. There are a lot of places in the mountains today that have become meccas for people looking to "get in touch" with Appalachia; outsiders like me usually end up at Berea College in Kentucky, or the John C. Campbell Folk School in North Carolina, get a taste of "Appalachian" folk culture, and then head home thinking that everybody in the region makes dulcimers and dances all the time, when they're not out trying to stop a strip mine. What I liked about Sunset Gap was that it seemed removed from these trappings. It was serving a fairly local community and nobody had ever heard of it. Nobody was making any money from what was going on there. Yet the center is not isolated, nor is the community totally cut off from the problems of modern Appalachia. I feel it serves as a good example of a place in the southern mountains that has retained some of the old customs, at the same time realizing that forces of change are inevitable and can be put to good use.

There are basically three types of people in the Cosby area: people who have always lived in the mountains, people who came from somewhere else, and people who grew up there, moved away, and then moved back. The fourth type of mountaineer is the one who left and never returned. Following Wilma Dykeman's advice, and directions from a country store clerk, I went to see Jean Schilling, who grew up in Cosby, left, and then came back:

"All through the years I grew up around here most people looked on dancin' as a sinful thing to do. My family was against it. It was believed that anything that wasn't work was a waste of time, that any kind of creativity, whether it was with your hands or your feet or your mind, just wasn't done. I had an aunt who wrote poetry all her life but no one knew about it until she got into her eighties, because that was considered a waste of time. You were supposed to be out in the fields working, not wasting time inside dancin'!

"I never knew anything different until I moved away from the mountains for awhile and realized that all of these things, not just the folk dancin', but the whole way of life of the mountain people, their arts and music, was important to me. And now I've overcome the feeling imposed on me by the church, that it was a shameful thing to do, but because of this very heavy background it comes hard to me.

"Of course not everybody around here was against dancin' like my family was, which is how it's survived at all. There were basically three factions here: those that didn't dance, those that did who believed they were forgiven so long as they went to church on Sunday, and those that danced whenever they felt like it! The total sinners! But it could be hard to estimate what percentage of the community danced because the different factions just didn't communicate much with each other."

Jean and her husband, Lee, help sponsor community square dances at Sunset Gap; once-a-month affairs preceded by a potluck supper. I was curious about the reaction of the local community to these dances. Jean replied:

"People are more tolerant now than they used to be. Some of the staunch supporters of the center that go to Sunday School every week, won't come to the square dance on Saturday night. But they'll be there at Sunday School the next morning sitting right alongside someone who was at the dance and they treat them real friendly."

On a cold Wednesday afternoon I went to see Bob Davis, director and minister at the Sunset Gap Center, and Bill Eirich, the center's institutional aide and one of the callers at the monthly dances. We huddled around an electric heater in Bob's office and talked about Appalachian dancing. First Bill had taken me to the hall upstairs where dances were held. It was empty and cold, but he said that on Saturday they were having a dance and wouldn't I like to come? Then he had showed me the room where they held Sunday School. Where I grew up Sunday School was just for kids, but in the mountains it's a general term used for everybody of all ages who goes to church. Back in the office we talked about the community served by the center. Bob Davis has been director since 1965 and was able to give me a useful description of the area:

"This used to be a very low economic area, basically because it is nothing but two huge ridges with steep slopes that come down to a narrow roadway and kind of a little valley, and this is what we call the Wilhite community. You aren't able to grow very much here, and there isn't enough grassland for cattle. I suppose that in its time it's had as many stills as any other place in the county, mostly because there are good clear streams with nice water, and if a guy could afford the other ingredients, it was kind of a natural thing to get into.

"But over the last ten to fifteen years the area has really changed. Industry has come into Newport to a certain extent, so the men who want to work can. But before they had to leave the area if they wanted to work, and many of them went to places like Dayton, Ohio, or Cleveland or Cincinnati. They'd come back to visit but they had to live someplace else. Now some of them are able to move back because they're able to get a job."

Bob went on to explain that this influx of people who had moved out of the area and had come back, plus the young people from outside the area who were coming in, were causing the area to experience an era of transition. The biggest effect, he explained, seemed to be a change in the widespread acceptance of the fundamentalist, antipleasure doctrine propounded by most of the local churches:

"The majority of the local preachers are still against dancing. No one ever danced here at the center until we came ten years ago. At our public high school in Cosby where our youngsters go to school, they didn't start having proms until twenty years ago, and it wasn't until five years ago that they began to allow the kids to dance! They'd bring in a band and they could sit around and listen to the music but they were not allowed to dance. It was the same way in the old days: the people sat around on their porches and listened to music, you know, banjo pickin' and all, but they couldn't dance to it, no way!

"Now we're sort of the black sheep of the churches around here because we not only allow dancin' to happen, but we encourage people to participate in this. But we don't have a large number of people yet, anxious to dance, because a lot of these local preachers say it's bad, and the people get caught between these guys and me who says it's fine. So unless they're pretty free wheeling and independent, they're probably not going to get involved to a great degree. But the churches in general are beginning to be not so well attended anymore, and consequently some of the feelings that have been held very strongly by some are beginning to break down. And especially those people who've been elsewhere, outside the area, come back and questions are raised, and just because the local preacher says 'no' to dancin' doesn't mean that much and the younger people especially are staying away from the churches.

"But it hasn't changed much, I'll tell you that. You go down the road here to the Church of God, and if you mention dancing to that preacher down there, why he'll tell you where you're going real quick!"

I asked Bob who was coming to the dances—were they local people from the immediate Bogard and Wilhite areas, or did they come from farther out in other parts of the counties?

"The people who usually come to the dances are those people that have moved back to the community, or into the community for the first time. Some of them have had a good experience with square dancing someplace else and want to get into it here, and others are just looking for something to do that they can do with other people. Most of the people come from around this general area, close to Newport. A lot of the old-time local people, because of their association of dancing and drinking, think 'Well if they're having a dance then they must be having drinking,' and every once in a while, after we've publicized that we're having a dance, we always have a few guys who show up pretty inebriated. They look in, and maybe they'll participate, or maybe they'll just sit on the sidelines and watch, but it's only been once or twice we've had anybody give us a hard time. It's a problem we're trying to deal with as tactfully as we can because we feel that dancing is a great thing to be involved in and that you can probably enjoy it much more sober than you can when you've got a few drinks under your belt. We don't condone drinking. But it's still a big problem in this area. I have to say that in spite of that I think we've convinced a few families, some of the old families around here, that you can have square dancing on a level of fun, recreation and good fellowship, and some of these people come back now when we have these dances, sometimes to dance and sometimes to just watch."

Bob had to return to his work, so I spent some time talking with Bill Eirich about the last dance he had called at the center, the previous month. Bill recently graduated from Berea College, where he was involved in the dancing programs there. Now that he was out working in the center he had begun to notice the tremendous differences between the dancing he had done in college and the dancing around Sunset Gap:

"A lot of people have got the idea that everybody in the mountains dances, but it's not true. People in this area don't really know the local square dances of their ancestors. I think for the most part we've been getting a local crowd for the potluck supper and dance, and it was amazing to me that they really had no familiarity with the Appalachian square dances at all. So I just started them out with some simple stuff: the 'Tennessee Mixer,' and some of the easier Big Set figures, and after a while people started to catch on pretty well. I guess the most enthusiastic people in the group were the younger ones, but it was about half and half, and the older folks seemed to enjoy it pretty well. I would say in general that the younger people are discovering something that's new, fun and not that hard to do. A lot of them are shy of it, but the Big Set dance is simple enough and fast paced enough that people seem to get involved pretty easily. When I was at Berea we did a lot of complicated country dances, but around here there's no formality to the dancing; they just want to get out on the floor and do it. I think that's one of the most appealing things about the Appalachian dancing . . . you just don't have to fool around with the fine points because mostly people just want to have a good time."

I realized as I talked to Bill that these dances at the center were in a very undeveloped stage. Unlike contra dances in New England, which are relatively professional, and Western square-dance clubs, which are so carefully organized, almost rehearsed, these dances at the center were almost like ones I'd seen for children. The people had to be baited a little, lured into it, either because they were shy or had been taught that it was bad. And the dances were totally noncommercial. Neither Bill nor the musicians got paid; anyone could come to the dance for free. Bill explained that they had live music provided by "two fellas from Grassy Fork: Haskell Williams who plays guitar, and Ralph Ford, an old-time banjo picker. . . . They like to come and play because they don't get together that often."

Did Bill think that the people who came to the center's dances would continue to come and if so, was there some kind of need in the community that the dances were fulfilling?

"I hope the word will get around," he said, "and I do think they will continue to come . . . because it's one of the best social atmospheres there is. It's a good place to meet people, and I've tried to promote it here as much as I can. It seems that the younger generation is going back to find out something that an older generation knew, and I guess it is because people are starting to realize that these things are dying out, and if we don't learn these things from our grandparents we're going to lose them . . . and I think these young people are becoming really committed to keeping these things alive, so I feel we've got the possibility of getting a good community thing going here."


It was a dark and rainy Tuesday afternoon when I left Sunset Gap. The next dance would be the following Saturday night, so I had a few days to kill before I would have the chance to see what I had heard described. As I drove down through the Bogard Road community toward the highway, I decided to try to get over to Grassy Fork before nightfall. I wanted to meet Ralph Ford, the banjo picker, and his wife Sadie, whom everyone had described as the best buckdancer around. Bill had said that Grassy Fork was "somewhere between here and North Carolina." I had checked out my roadmap and headed in that general direction. It seemed to rain harder as it got darker, until even on the interstate it became almost impossible to see. After crossing the Tennessee–North Carolina border at least twice looking for an exit for Grassy Fork, I finally gave up and went back to Gatlinburg where I was staying. That night I watched the results of one of the early presidential primaries which was won by Jimmy Carter, much to everyone's surprise at the time. All the news commentators talked about the "new image of the South" personified by Carter—how in someways Carter's candidacy meant the rebirth of the South. I couldn't help thinking that what I was discovering at Sunset Gap was another kind of rebirth, one more basic and rooted than what the TV people were talking about. Smaller maybe, but just as significant.

By morning the sky had cleared, the rain had crossed the mountains into North Carolina, and I drove up toward Grassy Fork once again in search of Ralph and Sadie Ford. The highway was occasionally clouded by patches of morning mist. Somewhere just south of Cosby I passed an apple orchard just beginning to bloom, and beyond it cows stood in a pasture stretching halfway up a hill.

I found Ralph Ford easily. He was standing out in his yard fixing something when I drove up. I got out of the car and we stood looking at the mountains surrounding the little valley where his house had been built a hundred years ago.

"They call this Grassy Fork," he said. "There's a creek that comes down over here on this side of the ridge over there, and then there's that big creek over there that comes in and meets the other one and they call that Grassy Fork." I told him I'd had a little trouble finding the place the night before and he said: "Now then you can go right up there and just go right across thataway and over on the other side and then down the creek over there and come in down yander, or you can go right back down here to this store and go over there and hit the interstate at the Carolina power house."

Now that I was properly located, Ralph Ford and I went inside his house where I met his wife Sadie, the famous buckdancer I had heard about from everyone in Sunset Gap. The house was neat as a pin. There was a television in one corner next to a heater, where the fireplace used to be. There were lots of pictures on the wall: of Sadie's parents and of Ralph playing at various concerts and dances around the area.

"This is a big old log house," said Ralph. "My daddy built it way back around the Civil War. I was born here in it on February 29, 1896, and I've lived here ever since. I done a lot of hard work, too. Mostly loggin', way back yander in those hills. I worked hard all my life, but a man's lucky to live this way. My daddy lived to be ninety-seven."

Ralph was anxious to play a few tunes, so he got his banjo out from underneath the bed. The banjo was a fairly modern, expensive Gibson Mastertone.

"When I first started out I had an old homemade banjo that didn't have no frets on it, and it had those old fashioned wooden screws up here to tune it. I watched my sister's boy play, just picked up the banjo and watched him play, and I'd just thump around on it 'till I'd get the tune. I play the old way. There ain't nobody plays like I do I don't reckon, around here. They just come from everywhere and wants to play the way I do, but most of them plays with picks on their fingers, and I don't never play with 'em, I just play it out. I play just the old tunes from way back yander: 'Cripple Creek,' 'Cumberland Gap,' all of them like that; 'Sally Ann,' 'Sally Goodin.' "

Ralph played a few tunes, some of the ones he'd mentioned. Then I played a couple. It was warm in the house. One of their daughters came in to get some laundry and talk to Sadie. Ralph and I kept on talking about music and I asked him if they used to have dances around Grassy Fork.

"Well," he said, "we ain't done none around here in a right smart bit, but we used to now, a long time ago. They used to have square dances in people's houses. Now we used to go places up here in the holler; my brother used to live up yander and we'd go up there, say this comin' Saturday night; and then maybe the next Saturday night we'd go up to some other boy's house and have one. Sometimes they'd have a cornshuckin' and they'd have a square dance after they quit cornshuckin' . . . . They'd put 'em about a gallon of whiskey right in the middle of that cornpile, way down! And when they'd get that corn shucked out why they'd drink that whiskey and have a square dance."

Sadie had come back into the room about halfway through this conversation, and she smiled as Ralph described those old dances.

"And you should have seen this boy play," she said. "He would pick for an hour and a half at a time for a square dance."

"Yeah but then they stopped havin' 'em," said Ralph. "They just plumb quit. Some of 'em went off one way, some another and they just quit playin'. I don't know why . . . I guess maybe some of 'em would act a fool, you know, they'd get 'toxicated and want to raise trouble . . . so we just quit playin', just walked off, quit playin' and dancin'. . . . My brother died, and there was an old man over yander, old Bob, he'd have 'em at his house and then he died out. . . . And the young folks didn't pick it up. . . . They wanted to take after an old car or somethin' and they'd just get in those old cars and wouldn't stay long enough to do anything. They'd just go off this way and thataway. There ain't many young people around here now. They all gone off, moved off, gone workin' someplace else." Ralph looked over at Sadie. "She's got two sisters and three brothers up in New Jersey and one over in North Carolina."

"All my people's gone ain't they?" said Sadie.

"Yup," said Ralph. "So they just quit havin' 'em cause most of 'em moved way out yander."

On my way up the road into Grassy Fork to see the Fords I had noticed that a lot of the mailboxes had the name "Ford" on them, and that one of them in particular belonged to the "Reverend Roe Ford." I asked Ralph and Sadie how the local preachers had felt about the square dances they used to have.

"Oh the preachers don't care," said Ralph. "Back then they didn't care and they don't care now around here. My old uncle lived right down the road here and I asked him one time 'Are there any harm in playin' music and dancin' and stuff like that?' and he said, 'No there ain't no

harm in it 'cept what you make harm in it.' He said you can make harm
out of anything, and he said 'you just get up there and make your music
and there ain't no harm in it.' Old Uncle Ike Ford. He wasn't a preacher,
but he was a good old fella, and that Reverend Roe Ford, he says there
ain't no harm in it."

Ralph said he didn't know what anybody thought outside of Grassy
Fork. That was just the way it was in his community, the way he knew it,
and he hadn't played for a dance in years until one day Jean and Lee
Schilling got him and some of his friends to go over to Sunset Gap for a
dance.

"They got to havin' dances over at Sunset Gap; yeah they have good
ones over there. Jean and Lee got acquainted with Leona over there, the
one that played fiddle, and they was going to have a dance over there
one night, and they wanted Leona to play. So Leona said, 'Well, I'll go
up there and see Ralph.' They call me Ralph, and she asked me if I'd go
over there, and I said, 'Yeah, we'll go over there.'

"Well, we went over there and they had a house full, all of 'em there
for the pie supper and a square dance. You know, so we went in and
then they said 'They'll get some music now we've got that Grassy Fork
bunch! You just watch 'em sweat now!' And when we get playin' the
sweat's just bilin' offn' us . . . because they like them fast ones when they
square dance over there, there ain't no question about that! And some of
them come up and they said that there music beat anything they'd ever
seen, or ever heard tell of . . . they'd just take a fit over it. We'd have
some awful good music over there, and they have a time of it!"

I remembered what Bob Davis and Jean Schilling had said about
Sadie's buckdancing, and I also remembered the fellow up at Highlander
who laughed when I asked him if he could teach me how to dance it. Jean
had said that everybody wanted to dance like Sadie: she'd get up and
dance and all the girls would get up and try and do it the way she did. I
asked her how she learned it:

"Well I just picked it up," she said. "I just learned it myself, you
know."

"Her father was a good dancer!" added Ralph. "I reckon she takes it
after him. And then she's got a brother that's a good dancer, a good
buckdancer, but he lives up in New Jersey now."

"Oh but I can really dance when I feel up to it, 'cause I've been down
with the flu lately." Saide said, kind of sadly. "But over there at Sunset
Gap they just all try and do it the way I do it!"

"I couldn't dance." said Ralph. "I can't dance at all. Never could!" I
asked Sadie how she got to be such a good buckdancer, and how it was
possible to tell a good one from a bad one. She blushed a little, and then
she said:

"I just know the steps I reckon . . . I hear the music and I get the feelin' to dance and I just start in, that's all . . . I don't know what makes me good, though. I guess it's just like anything else; the good Lord just give it to me that's all."

The sun had risen to its peak in the sky when we walked outside, and there was still a frosting of white on the trees on top of the mountains between Grassy Fork and the Carolina border. One of Ralph and Sadie's neighbors down the road was stacking wood. I was going to leave, but before I did I wanted to take some pictures. When I'd finished taking the pictures Ralph said, "Now you take those pictures and show 'em them hillbillies you know! OK buddy?"

A car roared by at a high speed. Ralph watched it disappear down the road, and he said:

"Back in the old days they'd all just gang up, like I told you; forty or fifty of 'em at one house. But it was different back then. Now they seem like they don't appreciate one another like they did back then . . . like they don't know one another or somethin'. Back then they'd stop and talk with ya for half a day, now half the time they won't speak to ye hardly, just pass and go on. Livin' too fast I reckon.

"We used to play a lot of baseball up here," he continued, "and I was pretty good, and they used to try and get me to go, you know, out yander, to the big leagues. But I wouldn't go. They tried but they couldn't get me. I reckon I just thought there wasn't nothin' like these mountains!"

## BUCKDANCING

Buckdancing is the simplest and yet the most enigmatic kind of southern mountain dancing. Essentially, buckdancing is a dance for one but can be for more than one; the dance itself involves nothing more than moving your feet in time to the music. The origins of buckdancing are unclear. The name probably came from the Indians who may have had a ceremonial dance danced by a brave costumed as a buck deer. The roots of the step are really untraceable. I see it as a mixture of different influences: I have seen American Indians, French Canadians, a Boston Irish step dancer, New England cloggers, Appalachian cloggers, Cape Bretoners, vaudevillians, and black entertainers such as James Brown, all do essentially the same dance.

The uniqueness of buckdancin' as it's done in the southern Appalachian area lies really only in the name. It is worth noting that in New England, no one ever gets up and does this dance by him or herself, as people will do during breaks at a dance in the southern mountains. Also no equivalent of buckdancin' exists in the modern Western square dance. *continued*

The choreographer of the buckdance is the instinct of the buckdancer, and the length of the dance is dependent upon the individual's energy. But make no mistake about it, it is not easy to buckdance. It takes practice, inspiration, and stamina.

Martha Lee Hyatt and Monk Summey—cloggers.

*Drawing by Randy Miller*

Sadie Ford, buckdancer, and husband Ralph, banjo picker.

*Photos by Nevell*

Mary Ann Brosnan—Irish step dance teacher from Cambridge, Mass.

## DANCER / DARON DOUGLAS

Daron Douglas grew up in Georgia. After attending the state university in Athens, she played violin in the Richmond, Virginia Symphony for two years, then she moved to Tennessee, taught tenth grade in Gatlinburg and became a full-time weaver. She lives in the back country of Cocke County in a place called Bybee, which used to be called Lick Skillet. In the summer she helped teach weaving to visitors at Sunset Gap where she regularly attends the square dances. One night I talked with Daron concerning her feelings about the dances at the center, and a little about her life in the mountains.

"My grandmother was from Madison County, North Carolina. I always wanted to belong somewhere and I liked the mountains and the fact that my grandmother had been here. So I moved to the mountains and took up weaving.

"I guess I moved to the country because, like others, I have ideals about what I want to do with myself, you know things like trying to 'find yourself,' or find truth and freedom, things like that. Sometimes I think of Ingmar Bergman, the filmmaker . . . you know he has this island, and after spending time on that island a person can find his own rhythm, by trying to get as many outside influences out of the way . . . I think that's why I'm here partly.

"I did some square dancing when I was real young, but it wasn't until I moved up here that I began to really get involved in it. I go to the dances in Knoxville at the University, but the dances at Sunset Gap are different. There's a real community of people here in Cocke County, but it's difficult to put your finger on it because it's so spread out. So the dances here are a special event because it's one time the people can get together. And the dancing is different here, because of the people, I think. Everybody really wants it to work here, so it feels different . . . even though the dancing isn't as varied and advanced, because the important thing is being with those people. And these people are very natural, more natural than in Knoxville, because they're not trying to prove anything.

"There's a certain amount of courting going on at these dances, and I think that it can serve as an important function. Maybe people wouldn't admit it right away, but they probably would later. But here it's a lot less devious than it is in a bar or something, because here it just seems to fit with the dancing. After all it's perfectly natural that my partner is a man, so the framework is already set up. It's something that two people are going to enjoy together, and nobody's trying to get anything. It's possible to dance with someone without the idea that they have to go home together. That tension isn't there.

"The dancing itself is a kind of statement: but it's kind of contained and removed from talking or trying to think of reasons . . . and it's complete . . . it's just a motion, an opportunity to free myself . . . but that's just puttin' words on it!"

The Sunset Gap Community Center

Saturday night at Sunset Gap.

*Photos by Nevell*

# DANCERS / JOHN AND LYN PARKER

John and Lyn Parker have lived in Tennessee around Cocke County for five years. They came here after living in Colorado and Florida. They have a young daughter who goes with them to the dances and the Sunday School at the Sunset Gap Community Center. One day I went to see them. We ate food that they had grown and raised, drank a little moonshine someone had left behind in their house, and then an old man came by with some ramps, which look like little onions but taste twice as powerful as onions and garlic combined. I ate one raw, which is a kind of initiation into the mountaineer community, then the old man said: "Don't go expectin' anyone to get near you for the next couple of days." In the meantime we talked about the dances at the center and the Parkers' feelings about their new community.

*Lyn:* "We've been here in Cosby since 1975. We're basically the same people but I think we've grown up a little since we moved here. We're not trying to impress anyone anymore."

*John:* "I think we just appreciate life a lot more, which probably sounds corny, but I think it's true, and I think we'll live a lot longer too."

*Lyn:* "This is an open place. When we first came here we didn't know how we'd be accepted, you know with John's long hair and all, but we found there's a lot of young people around and they're trying to make something of it around here like we are. . . . And they're trying to preserve the old mountain ways. So it's not as spectacular as the Rockies but it's a little more quiet and we like it for that . . . "

*John:* "In fact it's so 'country' it shocked me. There's this one girl at the dances that breast feeds her baby right out in the open, and I'm a city boy and I'm just not used to seeing this in a public place."

*Lyn:* "We started going to church there because of the dancing. We got to know some of the people there eating and dancing with them, and then of course a part of what makes it there is the people who run it . . . Bob and Kay Davis just accept everybody, all the different kinds of people, and Bill really takes the time to teach everybody. We probably sound like weirdos saying that we love it so much, but we do! We love it because it's a family thing. We don't have to get a babysitter . . . It's the first family thing I've done since I left the farm I lived on in Minnesota when I was fourteen. There we used to have church socials and stuff like that . . . It's a country thing that I've been out of touch with for a long time and I'm glad to have found something like this."

*John:* "It's the contact with people. I remember more about the Boy Scouts than I do about Viet Nam, and I can remember when we were kids we'd get out and play baseball or something and there was no problem of contact . . . but it seems now you can't touch, you can't touch anybody, and I think the square dancing does away with that one phobia. The more I dance it just feels better and better. And I just never danced before."

*Lyn:* "Yeah, we used to go to these rock bars and he'd never dance with me and now he's found out he likes to dance. The square dances are nice because I don't have to worry about some drunk trucker climbing all over me. . . . A lot of people around here just spend their time getting drunk, and I think one of the reasons they get wasted is because they're looking for something to make their life happier. But instead of trying to get out and dance they just get screwed up . . . "

*John:* "Sometimes it's hard though . . . but I haven't lost faith in human nature. That's why we go to Sunset Gap, because I'm trying, I'm trying with everything I got to enjoy life; but sometimes I feel like that's the only friend I got in the world (points at Lyn) . . . but I feel really good livin' here . . . "

*Lyn:* "It seems like Americans are just getting away from fellowship . . . they just don't take the time. They go to movies in couples, or go out to bars alone, or to shoot pool, or they go to the bowling league . . . but this gives us a chance to meet other people, and talk to them."

A circle dance at Sunset Gap

Bill Eirich and Walt Williams

*Photos by Nevell*

I got into my car and started it up, waved good-bye, but before I could turn around Ralph came over to the car and said: "Now to get back there, you just go down this here blacktop road, cross that creek down yander, go up over that hill there and you'll hit the interstate, OK buddy? Now you take it easy! And we'll see you at the dance Saturday night."

I went to North Carolina to the mountains for a few days, then I headed back down from Madison County through the Pisgah National Forest, then through towns like Hot Springs, Sleepy Valley, Del Rio, and when Saturday finally rolled around, I ended up in Grassy Fork. Ralph and Sadie weren't home so I went on to Cosby and got there in the late afternoon. The days had been sunny but still fairly cool, and as the sun went down in the Gap we could tell there might even be a frost that night. I was sitting downstairs in the kitchen of the Community Center with an old friend of Ralph Ford's, Walt Williams, an eighty-five year-old-man from the Wilhite community. We stoked up the coal stove, and he told me what he knew about this area, where he had grown up and lived all his life.

"Now my daddy he always got the prize, for playin' the fiddle, but he never played for dances, not around here, because they didn't have none back in his day. The preachers around here didn't like dancin', but there was a few like my daddy who had a homemade banjo or a fiddle or something, but not many . . . and my folks never danced, it just wasn't in fashion. But now up there in Grassy Fork, where Ralph lives, they had 'em up there. And that Ralph can play that banjo . . . I'll tell ya! He's a good old boy, that Ralph Ford."

As we talked some of the people started arriving for the potluck supper, and everybody came over to say hello to Walt. Then people really started pouring in, with all kinds of food for dinner: baked casseroles and breads, salads and lots of pies and cakes. We all lined up to get our supper, but before anybody ate, someone said grace. Then we sat down to eat. There were mostly younger people there; a lot of families with kids, but some older and middle-aged people too. Everybody seemed to know each other fairly well because, as Bill Eirich observed, many of the people had been to the dance they had given the month before. Some of them were regulars from Sunday School.

After the supper everybody went upstairs for the dance. Nobody was in a hurry to begin; they just gradually migrated up to the hall. The only person who seemed to be a little bit worried was Bill. The Grassy Fork band hadn't shown up yet: Ralph and Haskell and Todd Wright, a young fiddler from near Grassy Fork. But eventually they came, much to Bill's relief, and they started right in playing. Bill called the dances, mostly the simpler ones like the "Tennessee Mixer," the "Virginia Reel" and some of the Big Circle figures. The band played all the time, whether anybody was dancing or not. They kept right at it, because some people would get out and buckdance: first there was Sadie, and then some of the young girls who got out on the floor and tried to dance like her. She loved that, obviously enjoying the dancing even more when other people joined in with her. As I watched Sadie dance I began to understand why everybody looked at me strangely whenever I asked how they learned to buckdance. It was a dance that was clearly so individualized that it seemed to have no fixed pattern or style, no real beginning or end. Her style was much gentler than I expected. Her feet barely left the floor, completely unlike the high kicking style of the buckdancer I had seen at the Highlander Center.

Somebody else got up and started in buckdancing in his own style, different from but similar to Sadie's. Then Jon Sundell, whom I had met at Highlander, got up and danced, and even though they were doing individual dances, the two men were still dancing together in a way that seemed natural.

The whole evening went along in this fashion. Bill would call a few dances, then Jon would call one, but the band virtually never quit. It was a marathon music session. There was no public-address system so the band had to play as hard as they could, and the caller always danced with the dancers, shouting out the calls as loud as he could, which is damned hard in that situation because there's always a lot of whoops and hollers from the dancers. And if the music got too slow, the caller would pass the word as he came around by the band and yell out "Faster! Faster!" and they'd speed it up.

Not everybody danced. Some people were too shy to get out on the floor but enjoyed watching the dancing and listening to the music. And some of the people danced all the time, mostly the younger ones. The kids got into the middle of the dance every once in awhile, so somebody did a play-party game for them, and adults enjoyed the game as much as the children.

About halfway through the dance, Walt Williams, who'd been watching from the sidelines and not dancing, decided to go home. He was tired he said, and besides he had to get up early for Sunday School. I wondered how he viewed the dancing and asked him if I could come visit his house to talk the next day. He said that would be fine, so we said "good-night," and Bob Davis gave him a ride home.

The dance ended when the band quit, after playing straight out for almost three hours. People left the hall as slowly as they had come in, lingering to visit and say good-night. They collected their dishes and pots and pans, empty after the supper. By midnight they were all gone. Only Bill and I were left in the hall, sweeping up the floor. He said he was very pleased with the turnout which had included a lot of local people, many of whom come to the Sunday School; and he also thought more

people had tried the dancing than at the last dance. He felt encouraged
and hoped that the dance next month would be even better.

It had become very cold when we closed up the center and walked over
to the house where Bill lived. A few cars passed as we crossed the road. I
said good-night to Bill and climbed into the little Airstream trailer where
I was spending the night. As I went to sleep I could hear dogs off in the
distance. Some hunters were out after coons.

The next morning was clear and you could tell there'd been a frost, but
as we walked over to Sunday School it was beginning to warm up. Walt
Williams was there already and some of the other people were starting to
arrive, a few of them dressed up in their Sunday best, others in regular
working clothes. The worship service at the center is very simple. It
centers mainly on the singing of old hymns written in "shape-note" harmony and on a simple lesson from the Bible which is taught by a different member of the congregation every week. The people took turns
choosing the hymns, and the whole service had a feeling very much like
the dance the night before: free and casual but meaningful.

After Sunday School Bill and I went down the road to Walt's house.
He'd invited us over to visit for the afternoon, and I was glad to go talk
to him about the dance the night before. When we got there he was outside sitting on a tree stump next to his house, which, like Ralph and
Sadie's, had been built by his ancestors out of logs. He lives by himself
most of the time, keeps a surprisingly large vegetable garden, and grows
a small tobacco crop for cash. He still plows with a horse and uses tools
he's had for fifty years. While we talked he worked on carving a new
handle for his axe.

"They call this the heads of Sugar Count and Yaller Britches" he said.
"You go over here to the other side of that hill and it's called Sugar
Count, but down here this is called the Heads of Yaller Britches, but it's
not on the map. Then some old man came in here, old man Wilhite, and
that's where they got that name. I don't know where they got Yaller
Britches, but that's what they call it. Then my relatives settled this valley.
My daddy owned this land plumb up to the schoolhouse and plumb back
over to Wilhite and then when they died out it was divided up among
us."

We walked around his land a little bit; past his tobacco patch, down by
the stream and then up to where his tomatoes would eventually be. By
now the sun was hot, and we returned to the tree stumps and talked
about the dance the night before.

"When we used to go down to the Wilhite church there was a missionary Baptist preacher there and he was agin' it. And he preached that
the Scripture was agin' it, against dancin' and pleasure. But now there

might be some things the Scripture call pleasure that we wouldn't. It's accordin' to what a man knows and believes, you know. I don't think there's any harm in it but there is if you go and know it ain't right for you and then you feel condemned, and you know you'll be chastised for it. But God didn't put man here to be a dummy, did He? No, He put us here to enjoy ourselves, and He wouldn't have allowed some men to make all this music and dancin' if it wasn't going to be used for some purpose.

"Now I know there's people doin' this dancin' now, here and maybe out yonder, and I think they're just looking for something to satisfy them. You boys are young boys now but ten years from now you're going to see a great difference in the world. It's gettin' critical now, and it's everywhere, not just here, everywhere. People don't care for one another no more, they don't care nothin' but for themselves. It's dog eat dog. But you talk about these people comin' down there and dancin' last night, I think it's better they're up there than out trying to steal something from somebody else's house. No I don't think anybody came there to that dance to any harm. I know I did not and I don't think any of the rest of them did. They just came to be neighborly and there ain't no harm in that, now is there?"

Leaving Sunset Gap I drove out the Bogard Road past the antidance Church of God that Bob Davis had mentioned. I thought about one other thing that Walt Williams had said as I thought about the preachers who even today take a strong stand against a simple folk activity like the square dance. Walt had said: "Now next time you see a preacher that tells you the Bible says you ain't supposed to dance, then you ask him what David did, and see if he didn't dance for the Lord . . . it says right there in the Bible that he danced with all his might and all his power, so that proves that one man did dance for the Lord, and oh how I would have liked to have seen him!" As I thought about Walt and the other old timers like Ralph and Sadie, and also the newcomers like John and Lyn Parker and Daron Douglas, all of whom shared the same useful experience in spite of their differences in age, religious beliefs, and political outlooks, it seemed unbelievable that this kind of community activity wasn't blossoming all over Appalachia. It had, after all, been difficult to find any kind of public square dance with live music, a dance that catered to the local community; and I was glad to have found Sunset Gap, where a person can go into a hall and dance for the simple fun of it, without having to give anything but his own will to dance or to play the music. As I again headed out of Cosby toward the interstate, I thought of one of the things Wilma Dykeman had said to me that seemed to get to the essence of what I had seen at Sunset Gap. She said:

"One of the things that's interesting about Appalachian life, and something the world might well copy, is that we didn't have it all so compartmentalized. It was all part of the totality of life in Appalachia, the dance and the music . . . and don't you feel it would be useful if we could get back to some of this in our life today?"

III

Before I left the North, and as I traveled around the South, people I talked to and wrote to about dancing in the mountains always mentioned "clogging" first. By the time I left Sunset Gap I had a rough idea what clogging was. Lots of New England contra dancers clog as they dance, intermittently stamping their feet in time to the music, especially in dances like 'Mony Musk'; but as I talked to people around the country and in the South especially, everyone made the point that I had to see a clogging demonstration, or better yet a clogging contest. I started to realize that clogging might be as organized an activity as Western square dancing.

I remembered that when I had asked the first buckdancer what I had seen, he had said it was buckdancin' when one person did it, but cloggin' when a group of people did it. Today clogging is a synthesis of two old-time arts: the traditional Appalachian square dance, the Big Circle figures, combined with the footwork of buckdancin'.

My first look at clogging was in Knoxville, at the Dogwood Festival, a fair staged by the city to stimulate interest in the commercial district downtown. The center of the festival took place in the downtown shopping area of Knoxville. There were booths set up for local craftsmen and merchants, and in the middle of the area a stage had been mounted for music and dancing—primarily clogging. A blackboard announced the clogging groups: the first was a team from North Carolina, and they would be followed by other teams, some of them from Tennessee.

The first group of dancers came on the stage in Knoxville dressed alike, in costumes that resembled Western square-dance costumes except that the girls' hemlines were higher. They wore patent leather shoes, white or black, with taps on them. The group was called the Tennessee Mountain Cloggers, and the essential step they used was the same used in the buckdancing I'd seen, except that the dance itself was flashier, with much higher kicking and a wider repertoire of "fancy" steps. Some of the time they danced simple, old-fashioned Appalachian Big Circle figures, but often they would fan out into a straight line, which reminded me of the Rockettes. Then individual dancers would come out from the line and do a short routine from their own special trick step repertoire—high kicks and twirls—but except for these moments when individuals "did their stuff," everyone executed the same step, in a very choreographed, precise way. It seemed clear they had been taught the dance in a fairly uniform fashion.

I saw three different clog teams that day. All of them performed in a similar fashion, which I found out is not surprising because there are literally hundreds of these teams scattered throughout the mountain region. I had a chance to talk to the leader of one of the groups, Ralph Pierce of the Tennessee Mountain Cloggers, whose team I had seen at the Knoxville Festival that day. The group has three different teams within it: a senior team of teen-agers usually in high school; a junior team who are more or less junior-high-school age; and a "pee wee" team of grammar-school age kids. Ralph explained that the attitudes toward dancing had changed considerably since he was a boy growing up around the Knoxville area:

"It used to be that if you acted anything like a 'hillbilly' you were immediately made fun of. The worst thing in the world you could do was listen to country and western music. Now it's changed, I think largely because of the rising popularity of Western square dancing and the bluegrass music. And the kids themselves have a great influence, because they are a little more of the attitude that if you like something, just do it."

Ralph explained that most of the clogging teams included boys and girls the same age as his. His group was fairly new: only six months old at the time. He explained that his team was modeled after other teams around the Smoky Mountain area, but that most of the teams came from North Carolina where clogging, at least in its modern form, had originated.

"Over there," he said, "up there in the mountains in North Carolina, being on the town clogging team is like being on the first string of the local football team around here. But it hasn't come along that far here yet. It's on the rise, no question about it. More teams are popping up all the time."

It seemed clear to me, after talking with Ralph Pierce, that clogging was the most popular dance of the modern mountaineer. It retained some of the traditional character and movements of the Appalachian square dance but had evolved into a clearly modern folk dance, heavily influenced by contemporary fashions, and danced to contemporary music: "bluegrass," the stylized, ornamental version of traditional fiddle music. Like Western square-dance music, clogging music emphasizes the beat rather than a melody; and like Western square dancing, the costume had become an integral part of the dance. As Ralph Pierce explained: "The kids like the short dresses, because the clogging emphasizes leg movements; so the reason for the high hemlines is this, plus simply that it's what they want; it's their modern-day tradition, fashioned from the Western square-dance outfits but with a modern touch to make them look snappier and sexier." But though I now knew what clogging had become, I had little understanding of how it had gotten there. I left Knoxville, got back on the interstate, and headed through the mountains for the heart of clogging country: western North Carolina.

Every summer in Asheville, North Carolina, the city sponsors a Mountain Dance and Folk Festival. It was founded by Bascom Lamar Lunsford, a lawyer by profession and a folklorist on the side. Lumsford collected folk songs from the western North Carolina area as well as dances, and even wrote a small manual on the Appalachian square dance. He started the festival in 1927, but it wasn't until 1938 that the dance part of it put emphasis on competition between teams of cloggers. The first clogging group was called the "Soco Gap Dance Team" founded by Sam Queen. Queen is generally acknowledged as the inventor of modern clogging team activity. Until he died, Sam Queen was a caller of square dances mainly for tourists in Maggie Valley, one of the mountain towns that caters heavily to the tourist trade. Today you see signs all over for Maggie Valley's "Ghost Town," a tinseled tourist attraction. Curiosity took me to Maggie Valley; partially to see where Sam Queen had gotten his start, and partially to see if Maggie Valley had been developed as much as Gatlinburg, Tennessee, the other "gateway to the Smokies." Although not as extensively as Gatlinburg, Maggie Valley has become a strip of motels, amusement parks like "Ghost Town," and fast food enterprises. But the most interesting places to me were two rundown buildings in the center of town. One was a typical, decrepit souvenir and junk gift shop, with a big sign over it that read: "Hillbilly Fun House, Real Hillbilly Music!" Unfortunately the place wasn't open, so I didn't get to hear the "real music." Down the road was another building, set back slightly, also with a big sign. It read: "Maggie Playhouse/Square Dancing" and sported a painting of "hillbillies" who were "square dancing." There were similar commercial establishments all along the stretch of road through the valley, most not as blatant as these two. They reflected the kind of attitude that a great many natives of the mountains had complained about: the derogatory and disrespectful attitude for the mountaineers and their culture. It was bad enough to be parodying their customs and crafts, but at the same time they were using the "hillbilly" image to make money.

Sam Queen's Soco Gap Dance Team won the first clogging contest in 1938 at the Mountain Dance and Folk Festival in Asheville, and won the contest periodically over the years after that. One summer a young man from Canton joined Sam Queen's team. He was only sixteen and his name was Floyd King, known as "Flos" to his friends. Now, thirty or more years later, Flos directs, calls, and dances with the current champion clogging team, the "Southern Appalachian Cloggers" from Canton. Flos and his wife "Poochey," who also dances with the team, live in Canton. Floyd works in the Champion Paper Mill, where most of the men on the team work, and Poochey works as an insurance agent for another company in Canton. Unlike Ralph Pierce's very young Tennessee Mountain Cloggers, this team from Canton ranges in age from about twenty-seven to fifty-seven, the average age being somewhere around forty-five.

When I went to see Flos and Poochey, I had already seen them dance an exhibition in Greenville, Tennessee. It was essentially a Western square dance but had been organized to raise money for a local facility that served the mentally retarded. The cloggers had been invited to help attract more people to the dance. I arrived at the local public gymnasium after driving all over Greenville to a hundred wrong halls. When I finally found the right hall, Flos was standing outside smoking a cigarette with the other men cloggers, and the women were sitting around sipping Cokes. It was dark but I could tell they were the cloggers because they had taps on their shoes and were wearing identical costumes.

I wondered whether the clogging I was going to see here was going to be any different from what I'd seen in Knoxville at the Dogwood Festival. I realized then that these people were not kids; that alone would make a difference. I introduced myself to Flos, and he started introducing me to some of the other team members. I began to anticipate something very different from what I had seen in Knoxville. I was right. When the Western square dancers cleared the floor and the cloggers came out dancing, I immediately felt something very strong; an excitement passed between me and the dancers, a quality I hadn't seen in any country dancing except in Vermont with the Ed Larkin Dancers. There was a maturity in their dancing, an ease. It must have been that they were just having a good time. I thought: this is what Lloyd Shaw's Cheyenne Mountain Dancers must have been like.

When I arrived at the King's house in Canton a couple of days later, Flos and Goon Rymer, another clogger, were working underneath the team's bus, which had a failing generator. Poochey was inside the house, and I talked with her for awhile. She explained that when she was a young girl she did not go to the square dances because her family felt that the environment at the dances was not an appropriate one for her.

"My mother and father didn't have any objection to the dance itself, but the crowds were generally pretty wild, the early ones anyway, and it started to get a bad name, because people would get to drinking and the parents who were very strict and Victorian wouldn't let their kids go.

Then I married Flos and I learned how to dance, but before we were married, he used to go and I couldn't, which caused a little trouble sometimes! Then when this team was formed about six years ago I decided that I really wanted to dance too!"

I told her of my visit to Maggie Valley and some of the feelings I had about the apparent exploitation of the hillbilly image.

"Well," said Poochey, laughing a little, "we do get fun poked at us constantly: about the way we pronounce our words, you know, and we're asked if we go barefoot all the time, and this is what some people really think. But we take it very well; it doesn't bother us at all, because we're proud of these mountains and proud of our people." Flos had come in at this point, with Goon, to take a break from the bus. He had strong ideas about the commercialization of Appalachian music and dancing.

"Now Sam Queen to a certain extent was against capitalizing on the dancing, yet still he did make money out of it, and we believe that it should not be used as a money-making venture at all . . . because it's part of the culture. But we do have some people who like to capitalize on things of this nature and that's what hurts it. There are people who have come in here and capitalized on other aspects of mountain life; you know, the milk stools and dulcimers and the quilts, and the dancing, like over in Maggie Valley at the Playhouse. The mountain people, a lot of them, are proud of their culture and it hurts them when somebody comes in and capitalizes on it. It used to be that if you knew a mountain person that made dulcimers, and he was your friend, he might make a dulcimer for you and not charge you for it. But that's a way of life that's going fast, and there's only a few interested in keeping it alive. The rest of them are just trying to make a buck, and that just hurts it."

"We moved away for a few years to Michigan," said Poochey, "right after we were married, and it was the first time I'd ever been away from the mountains, and oh how I was homesick."

"Then we came back," added Flos, "and we found that there were clogging teams all over the place. Our son was about seven or eight and he got on the YMCA clogging team, where I had originally learned to dance when I was a boy. Then Poochey and I got involved with a group, the Canton Old Timers, around 1960 and danced with them for about three years. Then we quit and didn't dance for awhile until 1970 when we started this team. I just got the idea that some of the people who were running these clogging teams were going about it all wrong. Some of them were trying to make a buck out of it; there was a lot of drinking going on, and it just seemed like nobody really cared about the fact that this dancing was an important part of the mountain heritage. You know you can go up to the mountains and see Maggie Valley and the Blue Ridge Parkway and all of that stuff, but it doesn't tell you anything about how this land was carved out by the mountain people.

"And another thing that's hurting it is the increase of what we call 'precision' clogging. This is where someone takes a bunch of kids and teaches them the basic 1–2–3 step, like a tap dancer, and then they teach them some of the old traditional mountain figures, add a few twirls and high kicks and fancy costumes. Which is all right, except then we go to a festival and they advertise 'authentic' mountain clogging, and what we see are these precision teams; and I know it isn't authentic. I've got people on this team that have been dancing almost fifty years and they know it's not authentic because they didn't see it until about ten or fifteen years ago. It's the rage but it's not authentic."

"I think the reason this has happened is because it's easier to teach," adds Poochey. "You know the music teacher in a school can just get the kids to do the basic step and off they go; but I don't think you can really teach this dancing because it has to come from within; it's a dance of self-expression, and I feel that was the original way it was; so what really is authentic, I think, is in the individual himself."

Flos then continued to explain how the team got started and what the purpose was behind it:

"I wanted to have a team that could travel around and show people the authentic way the mountain people dance. So I started to lay the groundwork and it took about a year to get the dancers I wanted. We were very selective about it: we didn't want anyone that drank and we wanted to have people that had danced all their lives as much as possible. Now most of our cloggers are basically buckdancers, because that's the way they learned to clog, was by buckdancing when they were little.

"The other thing was that these other teams didn't explain that this clogging was a part of the way we grew up, that it was part of the mountain heritage, because most of the people in it at that time were just trying to make a buck out of it. We charge for our demonstrations but the money all goes into a fund for costumes and the bus, and if for some reason the team is disbanded then the money automatically goes to charity.

"The main thing with our team is we're trying to bring it back with a little dignity in it. And if we don't show these young people the real mountain clogging, in twenty years it'll be gone."

"This is part of our trying to preserve it," says Poochey. "We get them right out there with us on the floor. Each dancer takes a member of the audience and we put 'em through the paces, so they know how it feels to do this dancing. But only a person that's from here can feel really deeply about it. Because when it's been a way of life, and you see the people that have been that way of life go out, you hate to see it go out with them: you want to preserve it somehow so that generations later can say 'Well I knew of this.' There will always be changes, but by the same token I want my children, when they have children, to know how it was. I

# CLOGGERS / ANDY AND JANE SMITH

Andy and Jane moved to Clyde, North Carolina, which is next door to Canton, from Alabama, where they had lived for three years. Andy grew up all over because his father was in the military, and Jane grew up in New York State, around Buffalo. When they came to North Carolina, neither one of them had ever seen or heard of clogging, although Andy has been interested in fiddle music for a long time and plays the guitar. Realizing that in order for the team to continue, Floyd and the other Southern Appalachian Cloggers must bring in new people to dance with them. Andy and Jane learned to clog, by a sort of osmotic process.

*Andy:* "When I saw people dancing to that music I just had to try it. I'd seen modern square dancing but it didn't turn me on the way clogging did. When I saw Flos and them clogging at the Waynesville Festival I just couldn't believe it."

*Jane:* "They looked like they were having so much fun and that impressed me as much as anything."

*Andy:* "Yeah, when I saw them do it I just knew I wanted to do it too, whether it was hard or not never really crossed my mind. Then I met Flos at the mill and he said, 'Come on down to practice.' The first night I was really apprehensive, because I'd never gotten out in front of people and gone wild like that, but he just said, 'Get out there,' and I never had a chance to back out.

"It wasn't hard to learn the figures, but the dancin' part is harder . . . that takes time. It's funny because the music just taught me naturally, but Jane sort of learned it more mechanically . . . Poochey and Martha Lee helped her out a lot."

*Jane:* "It's really a matter of balance, like a bicycle."

*Andy:* "Just like a bicycle. One day I just started feeling it and I could do it! And now we're influenced a lot by the other dancers, but gradually we're beginning to develop our own styles."

*Jane:* "We found out when we moved here that the people are very proud of their mountains. And it comes out in the dancing. Seeing the team was the first time I was really affected by something like that. There's a tremendous amount of team spirit. They can get into scraps, but when the music starts and they start dancing . . . "

*Andy:* " . . . it's a different world. We're all half crazy I guess, but the people are close, and loyalty holds the group together because sometimes it's hard to dance if you're tired, but the pride holds them together. I guess somehow the dancing symbolizes the area, the people and their customs . . . and I think it's mostly a feeling of being close to your neighbors."

The Southern Appalachian Cloggers

Flos King—caller

*Photos by Nevell*

## CLOGGER / BUCK FINNEY

Fifty-two-year-old Buck Finney, like Flos King, danced on Sam Queen's Soco Gap Team. He also appeared in a movie, with Tex Ritter in 1964, *The Girl from Tobacco Road.* He remembers the old-time square dances in people's houses when he was a young boy four or five years old. That was over forty years ago, and now Buck dances with the Kings and the other Southern Appalachian Cloggers:

"I learned how to dance from the time I could walk! Then when I grew up we'd drive around and go to dances just about every night of the week . . . at the old Piedmont Hotel on Tuesdays, the Armory on Friday night, and lots of different places. Anywhere you went there was live music. We just did the old buck and wing dances, that's all we ever dance around here, some call it 'flatfoot,' or 'cloggin,' 'buckdancin'' but it's all the same.

"There wasn't so much courtin' going on then . . . just a bunch of boys and girls getting together. This one girl had an old '37 six-cylinder Ford and we'd all pile in that thing and go to Canton Armory and square dance, and we'd have to push that old thing up the hills and coast down the other side, but you know, we just all went together in a crowd and danced together.

"But I really learned to dance myself . . . just by watchin', especially Aunt Idy Mullins. Now that old lady could flatfoot dance! She was just as light on her feet, just like a puff of wind could blow her down, that's how light she looked to me; and I've tried to imitate her but I can't do it . . . but she danced plumb up until she was in a wheelchair and couldn't dance.

"This is the best cloggin' team I've ever been on. The other teams I've been on there was always a lot of drinkin', so half the time you'd go and you couldn't find the dancers, you know, they were good dancers, but some of 'em when you needed 'em they was drunk. This team they don't allow no drinkin'.

"We do more figures on this team too. On the other teams they do a lot of Promenadin', and walkin' the Highway and all. But it's a lot more fun to do it with a lot of figures and it's really a prettier dance that way.

"Now there ain't two people on our team that's got the same step, but it's all got the same beat . . . and that ain't like the precision dancin' that's drilled into you. But I think that precision stuff is flat goin' out and the old mountain dance is comin' back in, because there's just too many people who want to see it.

"I guess I just like to square dance. . . . When you get to meet so many people and all, people that I never would have met otherwise. And when we go and dance we put our hearts in it, and I mean every dancer in the team puts his whole heart in it because he likes to please everybody and he wants them to feel good."

Buck

Martha Lee, Poochey and Peggy          *Photos by Nevell*

have two children and I'm going to let them fill their wings, I'm going to give 'em their rope because that's the way it is these days, and maybe they'll leave the mountains, but I know they'll be back . . . it may be twenty years but eventually they'll come back to the mountains, because it's deep within them and you can't take it out, you can't take the mountains out of them. So I just listen to them when they say they'll never come back, although they might not, but I know it's just youth speaking . . . because I know eventually they'll say 'Oh, that's home.' That's *home!* That's the word! So eventually they'll come back home, no matter how long it is, because they're mountain people, and it's in there. For good!"

Flos and Goon went back outside to work on the bus. Poochey and I stayed in the kitchen and continued to talk about clogging, but more specifically about the actual dance and the music:

"Usually we have a live band that goes with us, like the Stoney Creek Boys. The tunes are infectious. You might get one that's got a good beat, but it doesn't do anything for you personally, but then you'll get one that just tears you all to pieces, and you just get out there and bust a gut! Like when they hit 'Little Liza Jane' or 'Ragtime Annie' you're going to see a bunch of wild people! And if you've got a wooden floor, it gives you a sound that you just can't beat. This is when you can really feel the crowd and that self-expression comes out, and I don't even know what my feet are going to do next! Then there are other days when I get out there and I feel very mellow and I want to dance in a smoother way, and this is why I think it's an inward feeling that it comes from.

"Then the whole team picks it up and even though they're all doing their own individual style of clogging, somehow it all comes out working together. And I think it's because we use the old mountain figures in a way that all our people flow together, so that every movement is flowing; otherwise it just doesn't work. And once we get that rhythm going, everybody together, there's just no way to change it."

I asked her if dancing affected other parts of her life: as a mother, a wife, a working woman.

"The work I do is a mental strain and so when I get out on the dance floor after a while my little brain just sort of clears up. I know sometimes on practice night I think I'll stay home because I'm too tired from work or something, but I don't and after I've danced I'm usually in a pretty good mood. But it's a stimulant, and afterwards I have to unwind. I can still visualize the dancers when I come home; the dances go through my head as I'm trying to go to sleep, and I just keep on dancing in my head. But I dance because I enjoy it, and because it brings me closer to the other dancers and the audience. It's really the closeness that matters the most. When I was growing up around here, it was much different than it is now. My Daddy worked for two solid weeks for my mother and us seven kids. The only place you could buy anything was at the company store, and he would come home after two weeks of work with the groceries and with not a cent left over. But we thought nothing of it. Mother would put out a bowl of pinto beans, and a dish of slaw, and a cake of cornbread and a cobbler big enough for an army. And when that bowl went around the table you didn't let it go by because it wasn't going to come around a second time! We were very close, and we took care of each other. It was a good life and the dancing is just a part of that life that we want to keep. It's a way of remembering it, and keeping it alive in spirit."

Two nights later I attended the regular Wednesday night practice of the Southern Appalachian Cloggers. They practice two nights a month in Canton, where they can't wear their taps because they damage the floor. The other two nights they go over to the Legion Hall in Waynesville, near Buck Finney's, where the taps are allowed.

Practice night was fun. They don't have live music, but I was amazed to see how the cloggers seemed to enjoy dancing with themselves as much as they do in exhibition. Flos was clearly in charge, telling people where and when to dance, but the atmosphere was casual and it was evident that these people come together for the simple reason that they love to dance with each other. Some of the cloggers' kids were there, running in between the dancers as they practiced, but nobody seemed to be upset about it. During the breaks they stood around visiting each other, and when practice was over there was no rush to the door to get away. People lingered outside the hall in the cool, damp air. Then they slowly got into their cars and drove away, and as I watched them go off one by one I thought of Poochey King who hadn't stopped dancing yet, who wouldn't stop dancing until she fell asleep sometime later that night.

I don't know if it was fate or just coincidence, but as I headed out of North Carolina the next morning, planning to turn north on the Interstate 81 and leave for New Hampshire, my car suddenly contracted a problem which forced me to turn around: the exhaust system had fallen apart. I couldn't face driving eighteen hours with the deafening roar of my engine. I struggled back to Knoxville to Loyce's house in hopes of repairing the car and leaving the next morning. I went immediately to an auto parts store and bought a muffler repair kit, went back to Loyce's and spent the rest of the day fixing the car. The next morning I headed out on the highway again and the car seemed perfectly fine, but it didn't last. Twenty miles outside of Knoxville my repair job blew apart. Again I roared back to Knoxville sounding like a tractor-trailer. This time I sought professional help. I found a Midas shop with a welder willing to try sticking two rusty pipes together. He swore I'd never make it out of the city, but it seemed to be fine, and at this writing the weld is still holding. But by the time I had got this taken care of it was nightfall again. I delayed my departure one more time until the next morning.

Upon waking in the morning, I realized it was Saturday and a friend of mine had told me about a festival taking place that day up in Cosby. It was the Festival of the Smokies, an annual one sponsored by the Schillings, up on a hill behind their house. Coincidentally the Southern Appalachian Cloggers were going to be there and I decided without much hesitation, to postpone my leaving even one more day.

I called up my friend, Trisha, and we headed out of Knoxville with the sun hot, and my exhaust system holding up perfectly. But by the time we got to Cosby, the sun had disappeared and a light rain was falling. In spite of the rain I was glad I had decided to stay in Tennessee another day. Just about everybody I'd met in the mountains was there: Bill Eirich and a few of the dancers from Sunset Gap; the Grassy Fork bunch; Ralph and Sadie, Haskell Williams and Todd Wright; the Southern Appalachian Cloggers, and even some of the people I had first met at Highlander during the songwriting workshop; Jon Sundell, Jack Wright and others. I felt that somehow I had chanced into the right place at the right time, surrounded by all these people who had helped me to understand the mountain people and their dancing.

I slept at Sunset Gap that night. Rain fell steadily through the early morning hours, but in the night I heard the dogs barking across the valley. Someone was out after coons again. I woke up before anyone else, just after sunrise, made myself some coffee, wrote a note of thanks to Bill and left quietly. I drove out once again past the Church of God where some parishioners were arriving for the early morning service, then up the blacktop road still wet with morning rain. There was a completeness about my trip to the South, I thought, as I drove along the winding road toward the interstate, a beginning and an end that felt whole. The source of that feeling, I believe, grew out of what had become a deeply rooted faith in the tenacity and the perseverance of the southern mountain people; that in spite of whatever outside forces continued to threaten the survival of their folk arts, their simple and strong respect for themselves would allow those arts to endure. With this thought I remembered the words of a poet I had met in Swannanoa, North Carolina, Billy Edd Wheeler, who wrote:

> And to sing
> One must learn to dance
> Because all of life is a dance.

All of life is a tune
And the feet of men know the tune
Though many have forgotten out
Of sickness and are clumsy into
Their souls. And their feet
Are splintered blocks which break
The harmony and tempo of life.

And as she taught me
She told me: take the child
And let him blossom as he will.
As free of fluffs of dandelion.
Let him hammer in his mind
The music by which he will live.
Let him take the hand of his brother
And dance.
Dance to the fish's tail churning,
The storm, the fire, the tide, the hill.

Dance to work, to love
To beauty and pain.
Let him take the hand of his father
His brother
All his sisters, mothers
Fathers and brothers, all the children of earth
And dance.
      Dance!

Let the circle gird the world
In its rise and fall.
Let the feet of men remembering the tune
To which we are tending
And let them not be ashamed
To move themselves in dance.

Let this be
As it desires to be
A land of dancing men.

from *The Music Teacher*
(*Her Vision of a Land of Dancing Men*)

## Some Favorite Mountain Dances:

## Big Circle Dances

Unlike the contra dance, the Big Circle dances of southern Appalachia
are rarely named and more often than not do not have a predictable or

set pattern. Instead the caller uses a repertoire of figures, some of them from our glossary of Basic Country Dance Figures, and others uniquely popular in that region of the country. So, too, the tunes are chosen on the spot by the caller or the fiddler. Ninety-nine percent of the time reels are used for these dances, played at a tempo significantly faster than in contra dances.

As in the contra dance, the Big Circle has active and inactive couples—called "odds" and "evens" respectively—who perform figures together for a certain amount of musical time, usually thirty-two measures. After each thirty-two measures the active couple then moves on to dance with the next inactive couple and performs a routine of the same length. The Big Circle dances are progressive the same way contra dances are, though the mechanism of the progression involves passing through and never casting off. Also, there must always be an even number of couples in a Big Circle dance.

Now let's pretend we're in a dance hall in the mountains. The caller tells everyone to get a partner and form a big ring, the men with their lady partners on their right. Then he gets the fiddler to play a good old southern tune like "Cripple Creek," and the dance begins.

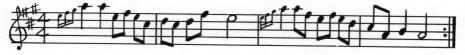

Usually the caller will start the dance with the whole ring dancing a few figures all together: He'll say "All Circle to the Left" for the first time through the "A" part of the tune; then "All Circle Back to the Right" for the second time of the "A" part of the tune. Then he might say, "All Swing Your Partners" for B1; and then "Promenade All" for B2. So the dance would look like this:

A1   All Circle to the Left.
A2   All Circle Back to the Right.
B1   All Swing Your Partners.
B2   All Promenade.

Then the caller will say "Odds (active couples) out and Circle Up Four!" at which point the odd couples move to dance with the couple on their right and circle with the even couple to the left for four measures, and then back to the right for four measures. The group circling routine usually precedes figures performed with groups of four. At this point, then, the Big Circle formation should look like this:

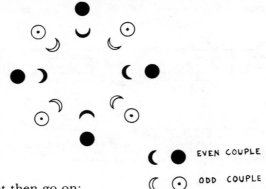

The dance might then go on:
A1    Odds go out and Circle Up Four, then Back to the Right.
A2    Right Hand Star and Left Hand Back.
B1    Swing your opposite lady, Come Back Home and Swing Your Own.
B2    Ladies Chain Over, Ladies Chain Back.

Then the caller again says "Odds move on and pass through to the next!" at which time the odd couples pass by the couple they've been dancing with and go on to dance another routine with the next even couple, starting again with "Circle Up Four" as the first call.

This routine can go on indefinitely, until the caller gets tired of it or the dancers collapse, or until all the Big Circle figures have been used up. The fiddlers are supposed to go on forever!

The southern caller has a long list of figures to call during one of the Big Circle dances. In the following pages a few characteristic figures are described but for a more complete repertoire, I suggest that the reader consult the bibliography for books that teach Big Circle dancing. Better yet, take a trip down South and find some folks who dance, and join in.

## Tennessee Mixer

I'm not sure who gave the dance, "Tennessee Mixer," its name, and neither is Bill Eirich, the caller at Sunset Gap, but around Cocke County in Tennessee this is what it's called. Beginning dancers like John and Lyn Parker like this dance because it gives them a chance to meet all the people in the hall. Bill says you just have to walk through it once to get it, and then once you get bored with it you can start to gradually add some of the Big Set figures (such as the "Georgia Rang Tang," see p. 200, or "London Bridges," see below.) Bill generally uses this as the first

dance at Sunset Gap "just to get everybody acquainted and warmed up."
As for the music, he gets Ralph Ford, Haskell Williams, and the rest to
"play any good old hoedown they like, so long as it's good and quick,
something like 'Cumberland Gap.' "

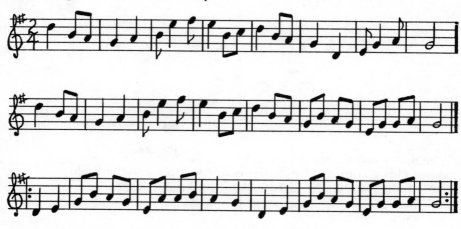

Here's the "Tennessee Mixer," the way Bill calls it.

Everybody gets in a Big Circle with the men standing with their
partners on their right.

A1 { Everybody takes the Promenade position and Promenades right. } 8 MEASURES

A2 { And Promenades back to the left. } 8 MEASURES

B1 { Everyone turns their partner with the right hand (Allemande or handshake-style)
Everyone turns their partner with the left hand. } 8 MEASURES

B2 { Everyone turns their partner with two hands and
Do-Si-Do's their partner passing right shoulders.
Then Do-Si-Do passing left shoulders and the man
dances past his partner and Swings the next lady on
his right. } 8 MEASURES

Don't join this number if you want to dance with the same person all
through the dance—the person you've been waiting to dance with all
night.

*Explanation of London Bridges*

This figure always follows a promenade (such as after A1 above). When
the caller announces "London Bridges" the lead couple (any couple indicated by the caller) turns around and ducks down to walk hand in hand

underneath arches made by all the other couples who have been promenading around in the big circle. The lead couple is followed by the second, the third and each succeeding couple. When the lead couple goes
under the last arch they turn back and make an arch and follow the
couples ahead of them. See the illustration.

## Skip to My Lou

Another kind of dance some of the people at Sunset Gap enjoy is what's
called a singing game or a play-party game. These were often done in
the days when the church prohibited all dancing and fiddling, according
to Jean Schilling, so that girls and boys could have some contact with
each other. Nowadays these dances are still popular with kids and adults
as well.

This particular singing game, "Skip to my Lou," is a common one, not
just by name, but by its form, too, since it employs an "extra" dancer. In
square dances, where this motif is also found, the extra person is called
the "nine pin."

The dance goes like this, with everybody singing:

Everyone stands in a Big Set Circle with partners, except for one extra
man or woman who stands in the middle of the ring.

The singing starts:

> Flies in the sugar bowl, shoo, fly, shoo!
> Flies in the sugar bowl, shoo, fly, shoo!
> Flies in the sugar bowl, shoo, fly, shoo!
> Skip to my Lou, my Darling!

While the singing is going on everyone promenades; as soon as the first verse is over, the "extra" person tries to steal someone's partner and swing her or him; meanwhile everyone else swings, while singing the chorus:

> Skip, skip, skip to my Lou
> Lost my partner now what'll I do?
> Well I'll get another one cuter than you.

And the dance goes on like this as long as everyone can think up new verses to sing, like "Goin' to Texas, two by two . . ." Consult the bibliography for more singing games, for little and big kids.

## Kentucky Running Set

When Cecil Sharp visited the Pine Mountain Settlement School in Kentucky in 1917, he was pleasantly shocked to find some of the people there performing dances which he felt were " . . . the sole survival of a type of Country dance which, in order of development, preceeded the Playford dances (1650) . . . and sometime in the 18th century it was brought by emigrants from the border counties (of England and Scotland) to America where it has since been traditionally preserved."

The Kentucky Running Set formation is not a Big Circle at all, but basically a square or quadrille: four couples numbered 1, 2, 3, 4 counter clockwise, as in the Western style square. The figures used are basically the same as those used in the Big Circle dances, both big and small set, but the small number of couples allows for variations on some of the basic figures, such as Birdie in the Cage, which can be done as follows:

> Birdie in the Cage and three hands 'round you go
> Birdie in the Cage and five hands 'round
> Birdie in the Cage and seven hands 'round
> Bird hops out and the owl hops in
> All hands up and go round again!

It works this way: the first man makes a circle with the second couple while the first lady spins around in the middle in the opposite direction from the circle formed by the three. She stays there spinning as the circle of three increases to five, then seven, as other couples in the set circle. The circle is always moving to the left, and quickly!

Bill Eirich tells me that the Kentucky Running set dances were originally done without any musical accompaniment because the church felt that the fiddle was the instrument of the devil and wouldn't allow it. It's interesting to do the Running Set without music, but you can do it just as well with a good fast southern reel, devil or not.

*Explanation of "Birdie in the Cage" for a small circle.*

When the caller shouts "Birdie in the cage, three hands round!" the number one lady hops in the center of a circle made by her partner and the other couple. They circle left while she spins to the right in place. Then the caller will shout "Bird hop out, crow hop in!" at which time the number one man takes the place of his partner who joins the other couple to make a circle going left. The man, the "crow" spins to his right in place.

## Clogging Routine

A clogging routine is the same as a Big Circle dance during which the dancers are constantly "clogging"—that is, stamping their feet in a rhythmic pattern with or without taps on.

As "Poochey" King tells it, she and the other Southern Appalachian Cloggers are never quite sure what their caller Floyd is going to call when they get out on the floor. This spontaneity is in the tradition of the southern mountain dance, and as Floyd says, "I like to keep 'em on their toes!" But make no mistake about it: a clogging team such as this has to know all the figures they use as well as they know how to eat. One of the most popular of these figures is called the Georgia Rang Tang. It's a figure in which the cloggers work together as a group, but it also allows them to show off their individual clogging styles. It goes like this:

All eight couples dance to the left, hands joined in a **Big Circle**.

All eight couples circle to the right.

Then the lead man drops the hand of the woman on his left.

Then the lead man, still holding his partner's left hand with his right, dances under an arch made by his partner and the man on her right, leading to the right back inside the circle.

Then the lead man passes under an arch made by the second couple, leading his partner behind him, and she in turn leads the second man, and his partner through an arch made by the third couple.

This weaving process continues until the lead man has passed under all the possible arches, and finally the circle is rejoined as the lead man meets the woman who was originally on his left.

No particular tune is best for the Georgia Rang Tang but Poochey King likes one called "Ragtime Annie." She says the tune is "infectious . . . it riles me so that I just get out there and bust a gut!"

# V

# WESTERN
# SQUARE DANCING

Last year I went to a contra dance on Valentine's Day, down in Peter-borough. The highlight of the dance came when someone brought me a pan of brownies specially decorated with a pink heart. The year before that I went to a Valentine's Day dance with Bob Fiore and Teri McLu-han in Bernardston, Massachusetts, a square dance. At the time we had just begun our work on "Country Corners," a film about contra dancing. The dance that night in Bernardston town hall was being held by a local Western square-dance club called the State Line Stompers, in honor of the holiday. I had seen an announcement in a local paper about the dance, and thinking we might show the difference between Western club dancing and the contra dancing we had seen around New Hampshire, we decided to go. It was a cold snowy night.

The town hall was warm and decorated with pink streamers, while crepe-paper hearts hung from the light fixtures. All the dancers were dressed up in special square-dance costumes that matched the colors of the balloons and frilly decorations around the hall: the women with their pink petticoats blossoming beneath their skirts like chrysanthemums; the men in pink and blue cowboy shirts, and fancy boots.

There were two squares, eight couples all together. Some of the dan-cers had come from Connecticut for the special party. The caller used a small record player hooked up to his public-address system. His voice was frog-like and he breathed hard as he stood on the stage and played records and enthusiastically called the dances to the records; but his de-livery was so smooth, so professional and deliberate, that he reminded me of a TV announcer. The dances he called were relatively simple, and he used recordings of familiar songs, changed to suit the square-dancing tempo. "Take Me Home Country Roads" was one of them. The dancing was also smooth, especially when compared to the rather raucous contra dancing I was used to. For a time I couldn't believe the dancers hadn't choreographed all the dances in advance, for our benefit. Teri, Bob, and I sat on the sidelines gaping like monkeys at the dancers who whirled around their squares almost like marionettes.

When the "tip" (a group of dances) was over, one of the women left her square and headed in our direction. At first I thought she was going to invite us to dance. She had on her blouse a badge with her name, the name of the club, and her home town. She said she was the hostess of the host club and was glad we were there. She asked us where we were from and whether or not we were square dancers. She said all of this very fast. We said we were from New Hampshire and that we went to contra dances up there, we weren't members of a club, and that in fact we didn't really know anything about club dancing—which at the time was true. She told us we were welcome to stay and watch while they danced.

During the intermission the caller, who looked to be in his sixties, came off the stage and sat down. He looked very tired. The dancers meanwhile sat in a row of chairs lined up along the wall, drinking pink lemonade. The old caller, it turned out, used to call contra dances but had switched to western-style calling when the club-type dancing started booming. He said it was easier to work with a record player instead of an orchestra, and he was able to make pretty good money working by himself instead of with an orchestra. "But I'm getting old", he said, "and I can't work as much or as hard as I used to. But there's no shortage of new young callers coming up, some good ones, too."

When the next tip began, a new caller took over for the old man. "There!" he said. "That young fella's got good delivery and a good voice. Now a guy like that's got some future." The young caller's delivery and general style reminded me even more of a TV emcee—someone like Bert Parks or Ed McMahon. Every phrase was carefully turned: the calls, the patter, the directions for the dance. The dancers were having a hell of a good time.

We got up to leave after the next tip. The hostess thanked us for coming and we thanked her for the coffee. She smiled and said come back, very graciously. Everybody waved good-bye as we left the room.

That was the first "Western" square dance I had ever gone to, but it wasn't the last. Ten months later I boarded a jet for Denver to begin my research into western dancing as it's done in its birthplace. I would stop first in Colorado, and then in Los Angeles—where I had learned to my own surprise—more people square dance than anywhere else in the world.

On the plane I found myself seated next to a businessman who liked to argue about everything. "Nice day," I said to him, looking across the sunny Boston skyline as we took off. "Too damn cold for me," he said. He looked at my fiddle case and said: "Is that a violin?" I said: "Yeah, but I call it a fiddle, but they're the same thing." He said: "No, they're not, how can they be?" Then he said: "What are you going to do in Denver?" I was afraid to answer, but I told him I was writing a book about square dance and he said, "Square dance? You mean like that stuff they do on 'Hee Haw,' that hick stuff?" I said: "Well, not exactly," and I tried to explain how oversimplified his view was, but I started fumbling for words. I realized that I couldn't explain because I still had too much to learn—all I'd seen was the Valentine's Day dance, which I didn't feel was enough to make a judgment on. So I said: "To tell the truth, I can't really tell you what it's like because I don't know much about it." That really got him. He looked at me as if I was out of my mind and said: "How can you write a book about something you don't know anything about? Jesus!" He wanted to argue about everything.

In spite of that businessman's contrary nature, my conversation with him proved fruitful, for it started me thinking about some crucial issues of modern Western square dancing, particularly my attitudes toward it. I realized that I had no more than a superficial understanding of what I knew to be an enormously popular activity (an estimated 6 million people are involved in club Western square dancing). My only experience with "club" dancing had been the Valentine's Day dance, certainly a fleeting encounter at best. Yet, in spite of these facts, I found that I had some fairly strong feelings about Western square dance, most of them stemming from a refusal to recognize it as a "folk" art. As I prepared for my journey West, I discussed the Western square dance with my contra-dance friends as well as people knowledgeable about "traditional" folk art in America. The predominate attitude among these people was one of disdain for the recorded music, flashy costumes, and required credentials that are the signature of modern Western square dancing. I found that I shared this disdain, and it was not difficult to understand where my prejudiced attitude came from. The connotations of the words "folk" and "traditional" did not include, in my mind, modern trappings from contemporary society, electric music, or "urban" society in any form. And yet I remembered a passage from Curt Sachs, who wrote: "The dance in its essence is simply life on a higher level." I believe Sachs is right and that the modern Western square dance is a reflection of the modern life of many Americans and, in fact, a tradition in the making.

Before I left on my journey west to Los Angeles and Denver, I read whatever I could about Western square dance. It was mostly instructional material—books, pamphlets, collections. In this mass of information there were three items which particularly intrigued me because I never ran across their like in current-day New England or southern country dancing.

One of the items I found was in *Square Dancing*, a book by Clayne and Mary Bee Jensen. It is basically an instructional manual for callers and square dancers, but in the middle of the diagrams, calls, and figures is a list entitled: "Ten Commandments of Square Dancing." The source of these "commandments" was not explained, so I assumed that the Jensens wrote them. Checking further, I found that the Sets in Order American Square Dance Society had published an *Indoctrination Handbook* which listed "Ten Ground Rules of Square Dancing." They were not the "commandments" word for word, but close to it. It was still not clear to me where these "commandments" and "ground rules" came from. In fact it wasn't their source that interested me as much as the fact that they existed at all. Back in the mid-nineteenth century, country dancing became encumbered with long lists of rules of decorum and manners; I wondered as I first encountered these rules if the same thing might not be happening to the modern Western square dance. The "Sets in Order" book prefaces its ground rules with the following statement: "Over a period of years an activity as broad as American Square Dancing is bound to develop a set of rather well defined ground rules. These rules, based on consideration and courtesy, are often taken for granted. Before putting them into print Sets in Order interviewed scores of dancers, callers and teachers to discover those points considered the most important for all square dancers to know. Rules, in this case, are not intended as restrictions placed on enjoyment, but rather as road signs directing the enthusiast along the path that experience will show will bring him the maximum of gratification."

I couldn't put my finger on what it was about these commandments and rules that fascinated me so. My curiosity led me to read on in the *Indoctrination Handbook* where I found "The Square Dancer's Pledge." As with the ground rules, so the pledge was prefaced by an explanation: "Frequently Sets in Order has been asked to develop a code of ethics for square dancers to be used as a measuring stick in the future development of this activity. Because of the folk nature of square dancing and because a code of ethics often sounds like hard and fast rules, we would like to present this little pledge which, by its very nature, puts the responsibility of square dancing's future squarely on the shoulder of every dancer, right where it belongs:

### THE SQUARE DANCER'S PLEDGE

With all my ability I will do my best to help keep square dancing the enjoyable, wholesome, friendly and inspiring activity I know it to be. This I pledge in the sincere desire that it may grow naturally and unexploited in the coming years and be available to all those who seek the opportunity for friendship, fun and harmony through square dancing."

I thought about the commandments, the ground rules, and the pledge as the big jet plane banked into Denver. In the west the Rockies showed off their shining snow. My argumentative neighbor said something about Denver being a "helluva town to visit . . . still a cowboy town . . . lawless and wild!" I thought: how strange that he should say that just as I contemplated a world of Western square dancing which appeared to have a system of laws and ethical values all its own. And then the question I'd been looking for came to me, the one whose answer I would be looking for on my trip West: who or what enforced the laws of square dancing, and how?

## THE TEN COMMANDMENTS
## FOR SQUARE DANCERS

1. Thou shalt—honor thy caller and harken to his voice, for thy success depends greatly on his words.
2. Thou shalt—exchange greetings and be friendly to all in thy group, lest ye be labeled a snob and unworthy of the title SQUARE DANCER.
3. Thou shalt not—ridicule those dancers possessing two left hands but shall endeavor to help them distinguish one from the other.
4. Thou shalt—strive to dance in different squares, thereby giving to all the benefit of thy fine personality and great experience.
5. Thou shalt not—anticipate or dance ahead of thy caller for he is of a fiendish nature and possessed of evil powers to make you appear ill-prepared in the eyes of thy fellow dancers.
6. Thou shalt not—moan and belittle the caller, thy partner, nor the slippery floor when thou hast goofed, for this is likely thine own mistake.
7. Thou shalt—remain silent while thy caller gives advice and instructions.
8. Thou shalt not—partake of strong drink before or during the dance, lest thy mind become befuddled and confused.
9. Thou shalt—clean thyself diligently before the dance thereby creating a pleasant aroma for thy partner.
10. Thou shalt—strive diligently to observe these commandments, and thy reward shall be great; for ye shall have many friends and be called SQUARE DANCER.

Denver is a sprawling city, with towns and new communities popping out of the plains faster than the post office can invent zip codes for them. It is one of the cities of the sunbelt, a city filling up with people from the northeast and northwest looking to escape the dull, cold winters of rain and snow. The sun shines six out of every seven days a week, and the worst weather problem is wind, big winds that send rolling tumbleweeds bouncing off the houses newly built on the plain, where expansive ranches once stood. Denver is the gateway to the West, the place where an Easterner really feels the presence of the cowboy spirit. It was this spirit which Lloyd Shaw sought to revive in the form of cowboy dances.

After his death in 1958, friends and colleagues of Lloyd Shaw, led by his wife Dorothy, started the Lloyd Shaw Foundation, established "To recall, restore and teach the folk rhythms of the American people: in dance, music, song and allied folk arts, as a tribute to the memory of Lloyd Shaw." For years followers of Shaw had come to Colorado to share his efforts to keep square dancing—which he thought of as the American folk dance—alive and unspoiled by commercialism. A small nucleus of people close to Shaw, dedicated to his ideals, saw something happening in the Western square dance they didn't like. According to the organization's brochure these people "continued to workshop material, to research ideas, to teach, and to manifest concern over a growing tendency of square dancers to rely more and more on paid callers, and on limited and complicated patterns, and on 'club' organization; and to make less and less use of the very wide repertory in the American folk dance, and of its free and joyous quality." They felt that a "well taught lesson was already being forgotten."

The Foundation is led by Mrs. Shaw, who lives in Colorado Springs. She is assisted by John and Linda Bradford of Denver. When I got settled in Denver I called up the Bradfords. They actually lived outside Denver, in a suburb called Lakewood, almost an hour's drive from where I was staying. When I arrived we sat down to talk about Western square dancing and, specifically, the questions I had been thinking about on the plane as I flew west from Boston.

John explained how the Foundation had been functioning since Lloyd Shaw died: "Dr. Shaw started the summer workshops in Colorado Springs originally to teach people how to call the Western square dances. The people who came in the beginning for the most part didn't know anything. They had very intensive all-day workshops, and then they would constructively evaluate each other's performances at the end of each day. My mother was a teacher and she had started to learn how to call square dances in Tulsa, and then she came to one of the summer workshops. I came with her one summer and that's how I got into it in the first place. Later they became more advanced workshops, with more nationally recognized callers. 'Pappy' Shaw was always in the forefront of what was going on. The workshops became a place where experienced callers got together to exchange ideas, dances and new calls. Out of those summer classes grew the Lloyd Shaw Fellowship, a nucleus of dance leaders and callers of the foundation who decided to come back to Colorado Springs even after Pappy died, and their purpose is to promote the American folk dance which we're trying to keep alive."

I asked John if he felt the Western square dance had changed significantly in the last ten years. His answer was quick and strong. "The Foundation recoiled in horror at what was happening in the square-dance scene. There was obviously a great schism between the two: us and everyone else." He explained that the cause of the schism seemed to be a direct result of the tremendous growth in the activity which had caused transformations unexpected by even those people in positions of leadership: "Many of the callers who have come into the activity in the last five or ten years have no idea that this activity has any roots. They think it just sprang up from nowhere. Most of them never even heard of Lloyd Shaw. The result is that most callers today have a very cerebral approach to the activity, and that in turn has caused modern square dancing to become much too cerebral and much less fun. I think that anyone who square dances is really yearning for a kind of community which doesn't tend to exist even in your own neighborhood, much less the city. People are isolated and the square dance should be a place where you can go and join hands with people in a circle and do things together. It's a friendly sort of activity and has a feeling of doing something cooperative with other people, contacting other people. Square dancing is not a mental activity, but the modern style has become, for the most part, very cerebral, and not so beautiful . . . and I think this is due to a large part because of a lack of leadership on the part of many callers and instructors. And most of them are so new that they don't know any better; they never saw it done any other way."

I was beginning to understand more about why there were pledges and commandments for square dancers. Square dancing depended largely on the organization of "clubs" which served to create a kind of community where the community no longer existed. Clubs were necessary to the perpetuation of group spirit, which otherwise remains only in small communities of America. When the small communities disappeared a select number of people saw the need to reestablish their spirit somehow: the square-dance club became their community. The square-dance club became an organizational model within which the dancing sometimes became secondarily important to the perpetuation of the new community: hence the rules and growth of organization needed to establish and justify the existence of the community.

The early square-dance clubs, the ones created in the early fifties, were loosely organized: the dances were simple for the most part and the emphasis was on having a good time, to create a feeling of community spirit. Then, as people from the Foundation pointed out, square dancing changed dramatically. The calling had been a shared responsibility, so that everyone could dance; but then as calling became specialized, it turned into a profession for which the caller got paid. This financial question created a new dimension for the "club" community: an economy which had to be managed. The biggest problem was getting enough money to pay the caller and his hired musicians. This meant taking one of two courses: either enlarging the club or increasing the fees each individual had to share in order to raise enough funds. The attrition versus addition rate had to be kept relatively constant or else the balance of the economy would be thrown out of kilter. Callers quickly realized that they could get more jobs with clubs by decreasing their fees;

the easiest way to do that was to lower the overhead, that is, get rid of the hired musicians and invest in a public-address system. This eliminated two problems for the callers: first the problem of dealing with a live orchestra, often temperamental, always costly, and second the problem of being overshadowed by the musicians, especially the fiddlers. Needless to say, the elimination of these problems meant the elimination of what some considered a vital element of square dancing: live music.

The function of the square-dance club had changed. By the late fifties, it had progressed from a casual get-together to a major community organization complete with an economy in need of management. Clubs were now in the position of having to hire callers, whose evening work became gradually less and less cheap and soon equalled what it had once cost to hire a whole band; they also had to recruit new members as people dropped out or moved away. And since the square-dance club's government had to be democratic, elections were held, committees formed, an entire legislative system developed, with an executive branch and a voting constituency. And, of course, eventually there had to be rules: "thou shalt do this and not do this." Square dancing became a business, at least for those who chose to follow the club model. In fact there really wasn't much choice. Self-styled callers started appearing everywhere, inexperienced but adorned with a good public-address system, a collection of records, some flashy western garb, and Texas twangs in their voices. They asked for a lot of money and got it.

Meanwhile the old-time fiddlers disappeared. John Bradford's mother, Mary Jo, who still calls, remembers well the difference between the days when there were live bands and now when even if you could find square-dance musicians, they'd be too expensive to hire for a small dance. The Foundation brochure poetically but accurately summarizes the results of these dramatic changes in square dancing in the last few decades:

> "We live in a furiously growing and frantically active country. . . . Almost, we have gasoline motors for hearts, and wheels for legs. We have become hardened to killing, both of man and beast; to destruction, both in war and peace. . . . Always, we are looking for what is tangible, commercially usable, profitable and immediate. We level the mountain and dam the river to serve our 'needs.' The arts of which we speak (music and dance) are not invulnerable. They too can be exploited . . . levelled down to earth and replaced by something less lovely and meaningful. Inspired leadership will bring them back, only to be levelled again. The American folk dance has been going through a mechanistic period during the past few years, but leadership is bringing it back to grace, slowly, almost slyly."

John Bradford says of the Foundation: "In the past few years we've been able to get together with the square-dance leadership in hopes of infiltrating with a possible good influence. We feel that our influence is lasting and unceasing, and people who know something know that we've got something worth keeping." And of the square-dance leadership: "Bob Osgood, Stan Burdick and Charlie Baldwin organized 'CallerLab.' They're trying to bring a little sanity into the modern square dance, but it's hard to tell if they're succeeding. It definitely has a big effect on the national modern square-dance scene because their three magazines [*Square Dancing, American Square Dance,* and *New England Square Dance Caller*] have a lot of influence. They invite callers to come and discuss new figures, ideas and problems in the square-dance scene, and of course they're trying to influence people. Basically CallerLab is a recognition that if things continue the way they're going in modern square dancing nothing will be left, it'll just burn itself out."

John adds that some people feel that CallerLab is wielding too much influence. "Most of the powerful people in modern square dancing are members of CallerLab. They're trying to standardize the square dancing and some other callers and dancers don't approve of this, because many feel the dancing should retain its regional character."

But, I ask, isn't standardization the inevitable result when any activity becomes as organized as modern square dancing has, and as huge? Linda offered this idea: "Denver, and for that matter the whole country, consists in a large part of people who are very mobile, who don't have any roots, so they don't expect anything to have roots. They never think to ask if anything has history, and maybe that's why people are trying to standardize the dancing. You know, people travel all across the country now, and the first thing they do is check the local newspaper to see if there's a square dance going on somewhere; and if there is they want it to be familiar to them, so they can fit in." What, I ask, is the most damaging result of this kind of yearning for standardized dancing? Linda says: "There's much less variety in the dances they do, and there's a lot of turnover in the clubs. But one of the worst things is that the music tends to be nondescript. It has a regular beat, alright, but musical embellishment gets in the caller's way. In most of the modern recordings the sound of the phrases is diminished and the beat is very dominant. Consequently the flow of the dance is not really related to the structure of the music. So what happens is that the typical modern square dancer just trys to get through the dance as fast as possible to get on to the next figure."

A couple of nights after this discussion I went to dance with the Bradfords and their friends at a small elementary-school gym in Lakewood. I had been thinking about what they had said and wondered what their dance would be like—especially what sort of people would be dancing. We drove over with three of the Bradford's children and John's mother Mary Lou.

I had expected to more or less stay out of the way, since I didn't have much experience with the Western square dancing, but when the first dance was announced by Gib Gilbert Linda grabbed me and dragged me out on the floor into a square. I remembered the night in Francestown, New Hampshire, when Becky McQuillen did the same thing to me. I was gratified but nervous that I might mess up the dance.

The first thing that happened, even before we started the dance, amazed me: everybody in the square introduced themselves to me and shook my hand. That made me feel much more at ease. I soon learned that they went through this custom whenever they started a new square, for anyone with whom they hadn't already been dancing; to the others a wave was sufficient greetings. The greeting was sincerely given, and I was impressed. This was immediately different from New England customs: at our contra dances people were much less forward in their greetings. And after each dance, it was customary to thank everyone in the square for the dance, not just your partner as we do in New England. Later I consulted the "Ten Commandments" and found that number two read: "Thou shalt exchange greetings and be friendly to all in thy group, lest ye be labeled a snob, and unworthy of the title SQUARE DANCER."

Later, as I read over the other commandments, I realized that at the dance the Bradfords and their friends had conformed quite closely to these ten "laws." But there was nothing at all exclusive about their dance. There were people of all different ages and all different abilities as dancers. The dancers were fairly concerned about doing things "right," and some of the beginners became slightly upset with themselves when they made a mistake. But I was making mistakes all the time, trying to learn a whole slew of new calls as fast as I could, and my fellow dancers were very tolerant of my lack of knowledge. One of the older dancers remarked later in evening: "The thing that's so great about these dances is you feel really comfortable. Not like some clubs we've been in where everybody's so concerned about getting everything just right. And you don't find the cliques here like you do in some of the clubs, you know, people who just want to dance with the 'good' dancers." I remembered the fourth commandment: "Thou shalt strive to dance in different squares, therefore giving to all the benefit of thy fine personality and great experience"; and the third: "Thou shalt not ridicule those dancers possessing two left hands but shall endeavor to help them distinguish one from the other." The group I was dancing with were clearly trying to stick to the purpose of real square dancing and avoid the tensions that had apparently spoiled clubs they had been involved with.

When Gib finished calling a few dances, John Bradford took over for a spell; then Linda called a few contras. I noticed that some of the dancers

# THE BASIC PROGRAM OF
# AMERICAN SQUARE DANCING

The Sets in Order American Square Dance Society developed a standard square-dance course, called the "Basic Program of American Square Dancing," during the late sixties. The course, revised in 1977, teaches ninety-eight basic movements, or figures, of modern square dancing. In the preface to the 1969 edition of the course handbook, Bob Osgood remarked that "the circumstances of today's square dancing point to the need for a special program of American square dancing that reflects and can benefit all that have gone before . . . a plateau that will attract additional people to square dancing who have not as yet sampled this activity or who may have dropped out of the hobby."

With completion of the basic program—the course, sponsored by a caller or club, lasts about twenty-six weeks—the new square dancer may join a club. He receives his Bachelor of Square Dancing diploma, credentials to dance with a home club, or to visit a club someplace else in the world.

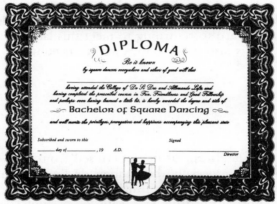

The Square Dancer's Diploma

A square dancing road sign.

*Photos courtesy of Sets In Order American Square Dance Society.*

welcomed the change in dancing style, in spite of a certain amount of confusion about the way to do some of the figures "Eastern" style, such as the New England star. When it came time to swing during one of the contra dances, I spun around with Mary Jo Bradford at a good clip and she exclaimed: "Now, that's a good old New England swing if I ever saw one!" It was then I felt I belonged, that I was home, that I was really dancing again.

The next day my DC–10 lifted ever so slowly, banking over the Rocky Mountain Arsenal on its climb to the Rockies. I was flying to Los Angeles in search of the modern Western square-dance scene. I recalled to myself the start of the big boom in the forties, when Pappy Shaw and Bob Osgood called for 15,000 dancers on Wilshire Boulevard. Square dancing was still growing faster in Los Angeles than anywhere else in the world.

Before I had left Denver I called Dorothy Shaw in Colorado Springs and made a date to visit with her when I returned to Colorado. She sent her regards to Bob Osgood. We had a nice conversation, and already I was looking forward to returning to meet this lady I had heard so much about. But I was also looking forward to meeting the California square dancers.

## II

The changes in landscape as the jet cruised from Denver to Los Angeles were remarkable, especially the sudden decline of the Rockies into the vast southwestern desert areas. But just as suddenly the eastern valleys of southern California filled my eyes with green, and I was finally in sight of a summery vacation. As the plane began its descent into the Los Angeles area, I could look ahead to see what I thought was the ocean at first, but was soon revealed to be a bank of the infamous smog that hovers over the city. As we began the final descent, the smog became thicker and yellower, and by the time the we touched down I could barely see the runway. The air was heavy and hot and wet. I rented a car and headed for the downtown area, making as much sense as I could out of the the freeway system map given me by the car rental people. Eventually I made it to Echo Park where I would be staying with John and Aleka Hankin. Their house stood on top of a very high hill and looked out over most of the city.

I immediately got in touch with Bob Osgood at *Square Dancing* magazine and made an appointment to talk with him the next day.

When I arrived at the magazine headquarters on N. Robertson Boulevard in West Hollywood, I parked my car and walked around for a few minutes, just to get the feel of the neighborhood. There was a big sign that said I could rent a Rolls Royce for sixty dollars a day. That alone convinced me that I was really in fabled Disney country, as far from the New England countryside as I could possibly be. I thought about the comments of my contra-dancing friends, all of whom refused to believe that the next dance I'd be going to would be here in the middle of the biggest, and in their opinion, most inappropriate city in the world for a country dance.

I climbed the stairs up to the magazine headquarters, went through a door, and found myself in a dance hall, which evidently also served as a museum and the "Square Dancing Hall of Fame." There were portraits of famous western callers all along the walls, most of whom I didn't recognize on sight, but down on one end was a face I immediately recognized: Ralph Page. I was surprised to see Ralph Page up there, but then I realized the connection between these two ends of the country, a link that had to do with the personalities of leaders like Page, Lloyd Shaw, and Bob Osgood. At that moment Bob Osgood came out to greet me and took me into his office. He invited Ken Kernen to join the discussion. Both Ken and Bob are callers, and both work for the magazine and the Sets in Order American Square Dance Society. Bob explained how the magazine and Society got started, after "Pappy" Lloyd Shaw brought the Cheyenne Mountain Dancers to L.A. in the forties. Then we talked about the modern square-dance world—its virtues and its problems. I mentioned that the aspect that most interested me about square dancing was the nationwide nature of it, in particular the function of such organizations as "Legacy," a national square dance council or forum with representatives from all groups of people involved in modern square dancing.

Legacy brings together people from fifteen such groups of people—from the International Callers' Association (CallerLab), the Lloyd Shaw Foundation, the Sets in Order American Square Dance Society, area dancers' associations, as well as representatives from the 150–200 local area square-dance publications, the thirty-three square-dance recording companies, the forty round dance teachers' associations, the 150 square-dance callers' associations, and from the manufacturers of square-dance costumes and equipment. The purpose of the group, according to Bob, is to make sure "that all of us aren't going twenty different directions at once; to communicate. We meet once every other year to discuss the issues that are currently important in the world of square dancing. Around 1948 the big boom in square dancing took place, and since then the activity has grown at an unbelievable rate. Faced with this situation we decided to form Legacy, because our whole outlook on the activity is that it should reflect everybody. So Legacy doesn't try to control or impress only one view. We try to show both sides to all the issues."

Why had square dancing become so complicated that it required the kind of diplomatic organization that Legacy was, I asked Bob. He spoke wistfully about what had happened to the old-style square dancing: "When we first started the callers and dancers just found a hall someplace and said 'Gee whiz, let's have square dancing!' and a bunch of people got together. They never talked about having classes or anything. Then the whole thing got big: the caller had to be paid, arrangements had to be made for a hall, and a whole feeling of a need to organize suddenly arose. So they organized clubs, then the clubs organized associations, and pretty soon it really snowballed and before you knew it you'd get two guys meeting on the street and they had to elect officers!"

Ken Kernen explained that southern California and Ohio especially had become "overorganized," so much so that some clubs seemed to choke to death on organization, and so provided less of a folk activity than they originally had. Many clubs were so organized that they spent more time talking than dancing. Ken attributed this development to the enormous number of clubs that exist in the southern California area. He showed me a booklet, close to two hundred pages long, that listed all the square-dance activities in the greater Los Angeles area—for *one* month.

"You know," said Ken, "the club-style of dancing got started as sort of a continuation of the old barn-raising idea. People got together to help somebody else, and then they'd have a square dance afterwards. Well, obviously we don't have barn raisings anymore, but it's still the same idea. I guess it's kind of an idealistic situation. They're looking for something, and they must find it or else they wouldn't keep coming back. We've seen a lot of people come through the classes who previously did not succeed at other things they'd tried. Maybe they tried the ballroom and they couldn't look like Fred Astaire, but they found out if they could walk then they could square dance. In other social circles they may have been put down because of some disability or something, but in square dancing they find out they're just as good as anybody else. So then they found what they were looking for and they joined a club, which most of the time is a happy experience. But you *can* go to some really horrible clubs and be literally shut out, frozen out. There are areas where there are cliques. You get to the door and already they've got their little pads in their hand and they tell you what square you're in, and if you haven't been dancing very long . . . well, you're just not welcome."

"The thing is," said Bob, "that when you have a big city like Los

Angeles you've got to have every kind of club to fit everybody's needs. It's not like being in the country where you've only got enough dancers in your club for six squares which automatically means the dancing level has to fit the average dancer. In Los Angeles you can go square dancing seven nights a week if you want, and become what some people call a challenge-level dancer, which means being familiar with an enormous amount of material [see insert p. 218], or you can just stick to the simple stuff. Now a lot of people will say that if you're only dancing a limited amount of figures then you're a poor dancer, but we think that people should never be judged just because all they're looking for is some easy recreation. Problems arise when some dancers want one kind of dancing, and other members of the same club want something different, and that's why they have to have officers, and meetings and everything. Unfortunately, there's a few people who've been told that the real goal of square dancing is to get to the point where you never make a mistake, and they start to think that the air is very rare at that level."

One of the biggest problems facing clubs is the need to bring new people in to replace those who quit. Most of the clubs sponsor classes regularly which result in the graduation of a large number of beginning dancers who want to join clubs. Usually they want to join the sponsoring club, and this may present problems if the older members resist bringing "low-level" dancers into their squares. "It's a normal, though sad reaction on the part of some poeple," Bob said, "but most people still have the feeling that square dancing is fun, that it's normal to make mistakes, and when it's over you have really appreciated everyone in the square."

Ken explained that the drop-out problem is really serious: "The dancing has become too complicated. Most people come because they want to escape from the everyday pressures of life in the city and they don't want to deal with the same kind of pressure on the dance floor. A lot of people burn out like they do with any kind of fad thing. But then there's the person who somehow makes the transition from being gung-ho and finds something in square dancing other than the game of beating the caller. He begins to like the fellowship and the feeling that he belongs to something."

The game of "beating the caller" arose from the need of some people to compete on the dance floor. Challenge-level dancers execute incredibly complicated dances to the instructions of callers who rattle off the calls at high speed, in the manner of auctioneers, and with little regard for the relationship between the music and the dance. Once dancers have "mastered" the challenge of this "hot-hash" calling, the callers find themselves in the position of having to meet the demands of the dancers, and this can result in problems. Most callers, according to Ken, start out with a genuine love for the activity. All they care about is getting enough

# THE SQUARE DANCING ENCYCLOPEDIA

Every year Bill Burleson of Minerva, Ohio, compiles addenda to his *Square Dancing Encyclopedia* which he originally published in 1970. Bill's encyclopedia, as of spring 1976, included 2,173 different figures (and how to do them) used by Western square-dance callers all over the world. The number is growing all the time as callers make up new variations on basic movements to satisfy the needs of dancers looking for change in their dancing. A lot of people think that all of this creativity is unnecessary, that there are only so many basic movements that a person can dance, but others obviously feel the urge to express themselves by making up new figures.

The choreography of the modern square dance is becoming more and more complicated, and for some callers overwhelmingly so, as they try to keep up with all the new "hot-hash" figures that come along. One of the most interesting aspects in this process of creating new figures and dances is that the creators are using the language of the people who dance to describe their movements; the vernacular of modern square dancing, which incorporates slang and other words not found in the most recent dictionaries, reflects the state of the modern square dancer's environment: technology, the compartmentalization and fast pace of life, also the effect of television, as exemplified by the "Flip Wilson Allemande." Here are some examples of new figures whose language is modern, to say the least:

Acey Deucy
Action Line
All Eight Collate
All Eight Flare the Gears
All Eight Recycle
Alter the Gears
Alter the Yo Yo
Alternate the Beermug
Area Code 1/8

Back Field in Motion
Back Track
Bail Out
Barge Through
Blow a Fuse
Blow Your Top
Blitz
Bomb Thru
Burn Blister and Peel
By Pass

Captivate
Chain and Flip the Gears
Chain Reaction
Climb the Wall
Clover Leaf
Cut the Deck

Cut the Diamond
Cycle Ferris Wheel

Deactivate
Deluxe
Destroy the Line
Detour
Do Your thing
Dynamite

Eclipse
Escalate
Explode

Face the Music
Fall in
Far out
Filibuster
Flush the Tank
Fruit Loop
Full Back

Go Streaking
Gung Ho

Half and Half
Half Breed

Harper Valley PTA
Here Come the Judge
Hit the Deck
Hubs Back Out Rims Go In

Inner Code
In Swing
Isolate

Jay Walk
Jazz the Wave

Left Turnstyle
Load the Elevator

Mesh the Gears
Mess Em Up
Mixed Up and Anything
Motivate

Orbit Circulate
Oscillate

Pass In
Pass Out
Passport
Peel and Streak

Percolate
Pop the Top
Pucker Up

Q.L.T.
Quarter Back

Razzle Dazzle
Reactivate
Re Group
Relay the Yo Yo
Repair the Line
Reverse the Clutch
Ric O Shay
Ringa Ding Ding
Ring a Ding Dong
Rip Off
Rotary Chain

Scintillate
Scramble
Shape Up
Shazam
Shoot the Miami Moon

Short Circuit
Smash the Bug
Snap Crackle and Pop
Sneak Around
Sock It to Me
Spin Out
Strip the Gears
Switcheroo
Swivel
Syncopate

Taggers Dilemma
Taggers Dream
Tandem
Taxation
T Bone Circulate
Throw In the Clutch
T.N.T.
Tootsie Roll
Triple Zoom
Turnpike
Twin Orbit Your Neighbor

U Turn Back

Veer and Spin
Veer to the Right and Left

Walk A Thon
Walk the Plank
WEO
Wham
Wheel and Cheat
Wheel and Deal
Wheel and Merge
Whirlpool
Whose on First

X Formation

You All
Yo Yo Spin

Zam
Zap Out
Zig and Zag
Zip Code
Zoom

money for their records and gas. Few callers can really make a living at it, and the ones who try often run into problems, usually when they move out of their local area. They hit the road and find out that it's a tough business. The dancers are likely to be judgmental and not as tolerant as friendly people in the home club.

"It's an ego situation a lot of the time," adds Bob, who has seen dozens of callers come and go over the years. "One minute a guy who's had a menial job gets a reaction from the crowd and he's a star, and it's hard for this guy to let go. It grows inside him."

"We see a lot of good showmen come and go," says Ken, who is an active caller himself, "because after the glamour and applause dies down they start to drop out. They don't have the depth and background to carry them through. Sometimes they get cocky, or they start getting caustic on the mike, which is a cardinal sin, and then they take a dip. Basically it boils down to really loving the activity and not being in it for the money or the adulation of the dancers."

"The real hero to us," says Bob, "is the guy who keeps the home clubs going. He starts classes, teaches the dances, and that the value of dancing is that it's good fun and a chance to be together with nice people. That kind of caller gets just as much of a thrill out of it."

The square-dance leadership has tried to help square dancers by giving guidelines to callers. CallerLab was formed to coordinate callers' activities and to safeguard the original purpose of square dancing. But, says Bob, "We get criticized for trying to standardize things too much, though all we're really trying to do is help people avoid problems like promenading four different ways." A simple statement in the Sets in Order *Caller/Teacher Manual for the Basic Program of American Square Dancing* summarizes what makes a good caller: "The potential caller/teacher should become the best possible square dancer before he attempts to teach others."

"To some people," says Bob, "the quality of the caller's showmanship might be the important thing, but I think the guy has got to be a basically good person. He's got to be more than a technician, too. He has to have some depth to him, and he has to have a willingness to be part of the people. A good example of that kind of caller is Ray Orme."

Ray Orme is the "home" caller for a square-dance club called "Rip 'n Snort," a Los Angeles area club established in the days when square dancing was just getting started. The first caller for "Rip," as the club is called by its members, was Bob Osgood. Later Ray took over most of the calling duties, although the club occasionally invites other area callers in as guests.

Ray lives in a northern suburb of L.A., Northridge, where he runs an automobile parts business with other members of his family. The day after meeting Bob and Ken, I went to see Ray in Northridge. On the way out of the city, driving past movie studios, strip joints, and Beverly Hills, I couldn't help thinking that Los Angeles was a peculiar place to be researching country dancing. My old prejudices still lingered, though they were fading. The strength of conviction of the Bradfords, of Bob Osgood and Ken Kernen had a lot to do with it, but more important to me was the kindness on the part of the Western square dancers I had danced with. The commercialism and elitism that plagued square dancing were reflections of our American culture, but the square-dance leadership was fighting back to preserve the rights of the average fellow, the easygoing, recreational dancer. As I entered the freeway heading north, I eased into the mainstream of the traffic, which, I thought, is a little bit like the "mainstream" of Western square dancing—the majority of people take it easy, ride along smoothly, keeping up with everybody else. A hot rod came zooming up the passing lane, weaving in and out of the lines of cars. There goes a challenge dancer, I thought: competing, trying to beat everybody else to the same place. A couple of miles ahead a car had broken down, steam was pouring out from under the hood. I thought: that's me, the novice. But eventually somebody comes along with help, and before I know it I'm back on the track, part of the flow, dancing.

I arrived at Ray Orme's auto parts store just after lunch. It was a dry, hot California day. The dust was piling up on the cars in the parking lot. I talked to Ray in his office.

"I started calling in 1947. One of the local Women's Club presidents saw some pictures in the paper of some square dancers down in Encino and she got the idea that we should enjoy the same thing up here. So she pulled the rug up in her front room and invited some couples over to dance.

"Eventually she decided to have bigger dances down at the Women's Club so she hired a caller from Altadena, but since he couldn't get there until nine o'clock I got some notes from him on how to instruct. These were the days before we had any classes, and so I was instructing people fresh off the street from eight to nine o'clock with some of the simple figures: Grand Right and Left, Allemande Left and so forth. By nine they were ready to dance.

"As time went on the dancers started to want more so I taught them some of the more advanced figures like Allemande Thar and Wagon-wheel, and some of them would stay late and work on some of those figures."

Before he knew it Ray had purchased a small sound system and was calling square dances on a fairly regular basis. He attended Ralph Maxheimer's Calling School in the early fifties, where he shared criticism with other callers from the Los Angeles area.

"There was very little new material coming out in those days. Not much at all in the way of new figures. I think Jonesy [Square Dance Hall of Fame Caller Fenton Jones] came out with 'Red Hot' at that time but there wasn't much else. Later new figures were dreamt up to use movements that had never been used before, like the 'Turn Through' which is, I think, the most usable and the nicest figure that has ever come out."

In the later years the callers' repertoires became more and more complex, as hundreds of new figures were invented. Like doctors keeping up with new medical research, callers had to keep up with the latest figures popular among the dancers. Over two thousand figures now exist in modern Western square dancing (see insert on page 218), a far cry from the dozen or so that are used in traditional contra dances and Appalachian Circle dances. Most of the new figures, however, are made up by combining the old ones into new patterns. A good example of this, Ray pointed out, was the family of figures based on the "Cloverleaf."

Ray's relationship with "Rip 'n Snort" was foremost in my mind. As I talked to this very soft-spoken, gentle man I realized that no one could be further from the sort of egocentric, showman-caller that Bob Osgood and Ken Kernen had mentioned.

"The Rip 'n Snort people are great because they're mainly interested

## CALLERS' DANCES

Once the club square dancer has completed his course of instruction, through the Basics or the Extended Basics Program, he's ready to dance. The dances are composed by callers all over the country, and then passed along from one caller to another. Some favorite modern square dances are called the same way over and over (such as "Just Because," see p. 246), like the old contras, but others are made up on the spot by the caller. Bob Osgood's magazine *Square Dancing* serves as a clearing house for current favorite dances by popular callers. Here is a sample of one such untitled dance by Glenn Turpin, a caller from Lepanto, Arkansas.

Sets in Order

# WORKSHOP
FOR LEADERS IN THE FIELD OF SQUARE AND ROUND DANCING

*August, 1976*

IN THE SMALL TOWN of Lepanto, in the Northeastern part of Arkansas, we find one of the most dedicated square dance callers around in the person of Glenn Turpin. Known as the "Arkansas Traveler," Glenn has sent us some samples of the type of patter he uses. Remember, in this feature it does not follow that the calls presented are original with the featured caller, but ones he finds enjoyable.

Sides curlique
Hinge
Lockit
Turn thru
Left turn thru
Back to center and turn thru
Peel off
Star thru
Right and left thru
Pass to the center
Zoom
Square thru three quarters
Allemande left

Two and four spin the top
Boys run
Wheel and deal
Pass thru
Swing thru
Scoot back
Fan the top
Right and left thru
Roll a half sashay
Star thru
Trade by
Slide thru
Spin the top
Scoot back
Fan the top
Right and left thru
Slide thru
Pass thru
Trade by
Curlique
Scoot back
Allemande left

Heads roll a half sashay
Curlique
Boys run
Pass thru
Swing thru
Curlique
Hinge
Lockit
Swing thru
Curlique
Hinge
Lockit
All eight circulate
Swing thru
Girls trade
Boys run
Bend the line
Curlique
Coordinate
Wheel and deal
Swing thru
Turn thru
Allemande left

Heads right and left thru
Ladies lead dixie style
Ocean wave
Boys cross run
Girls trade
Recycle
Pass thru
Right and left thru
Ladies lead dixie style
Ocean wave
Boys cross fold
Slide thru
Curlique (make a wave)
Recycle
Swing thru
Boys run
Right and left thru
Curlique
Coordinate
Bend the line
Star thru
Swing thru
Boys run
Half tag left
Allemande left

# MODERN SQUARE-DANCE MUSIC

With the disappearance of live music at modern Western square dances, a recording industry has grown to fill the needs of the callers, who in turn must meet the demands of their club dancers always looking for new material. Like the pop "Top 40" teen-age America thrives on, the world of square dancing has its stars, some long-time ones like Bruce Johnson and Jim Mayo, and others who shall remain nameless, flash-in-the-pan callers, callers who just don't have the depth of experience men like Johnson and Mayo have.

Every month *Square Dancing* magazine surveys the country to see what the current hits in square dancing are. Chances are most of these records will have fallen quickly out of disfavor by the time this book goes to press.

## CURRENT BEST SELLERS

Fifty dealers and distributors of Square and Round Dance records in key cities throughout the United States and Canada were canvassed to find out just what records were selling in their individual area. The following lists were made up from that survey taken just before deadline.

### SINGING CALLS

| | |
|---|---|
| Paloma Blanca | Hi-Hat 457 |
| Sometime Goodtime Sometime Badtime | Ranch House 204 |
| Grand Old Flag | Hi-Hat 458 |
| Everybody's Somebody's Fool | Red Boot 202 |
| Merry Go Round Of Love | Wagon Wheel 131 |

### ROUND DANCES

| | |
|---|---|
| Humoresque in Two-Time | Hi-Hat 947 |
| Dreamland | Grenn 14224 |
| Snoopy | Hi-Hat 945 |
| Our Blue Heaven | Grenn 14229 |
| Waltz With Me | Grenn 14219 |

Bestsellers from August, 1976

## HOW TO USE THE RECORD REPORT

To get the best possible analysis all singing calls are checked and rated by two sources. First, a rating is made by a square of dancers that actually dances to each record. The records are then sent to another reviewer who rates them on recording quality, instrumentation, clarity of commands, and body mechanics. The final "star" rating is based on a consensus of the reports from both. In all cases and unless otherwise noted, it may be assumed that singing calls are recorded in a medium range. In the case of hoedowns the key will be included.

Each report gives an analysis of the record and the dance. The shaded area in the chart indicates the voice range used by most recording companies. By comparing the voice range letters in each analysis with those on the chart, you should be able to determine the record's suitability to your voice. Occasionally a report will be starred (✱) in which case you will find the call reproduced in the Workshop section of the same issue.

Some of the square dance records reported will have rating symbols at the end of the "Comment" section. These represent the opinion of the reviewing committee. Symbols used indicate as follows: ☆Average, ☆☆Above Average, ☆☆☆Exceptional, ☆☆☆☆Outstanding.

How they rate the records.

Every month "Square Dancing" magazine reviews new records. This rating is from February, 1976.

*continued*

in having fun, rather than learning and practicing all the newest figures. They're an outstanding club in that their relationship goes beyond their excellent dancing. They get together all the time for different events, like a Scottish dancing concert or some other kind of outing.

"You know, I call for other groups, too, and there's a lot of difference in them. Sometimes I call for the high-level dancers. It's very interesting because a lot of them really don't understand how the figures work. They just memorize the pattern and it works fine for them as long as one figure follows another. But if you switch it on them they get in trouble because they don't understand the basic concept of how the figure works."

Ray explained that it was difficult for him to define what it takes to be a good caller because his relationship is different with every group he works for. Some callers, he said, can be great teachers and terrible callers, and vice versa. Others seem to be involved in it simply for ego gratification, but for Ray his reward comes from a deeper source:

"When you get down to it, it's the love that counts the most to me, the love between the dancers and me, especially the Rip 'n Snort people. That's really the only word to express it, and what they give me is the most rewarding aspect of calling, and I think that's what makes me a good caller for them."

As I drove back out onto the freeway, I took stock of what I had learned about Western square dancing in general, and Rip 'n Snort in particular. A great curiosity about Rip 'n Snort was building up inside me—here was a Western square-dance club that was somehow avoiding the problems many contemporary clubs were having.

It is, of course, impossible to determine what proportion of Western square-dance clubs model themselves after the easygoing Rip 'n Snort-style group and how many have bowed to the pressures of commercialism and competition. One thing has certainly changed for all forms of club dancing: the simple "cowboy dances" enjoyed by early pioneers in the American West have been altered drastically; live music has been replaced by records; the actual dances have been so changed that "basic figures" number ninety-eight instead of a couple dozen. Because of this, lessons are required of anyone wishing to join a club, and joining a club is the only way to get to dance on a regular basis in most communities in America. "Open" floor dances are rare. While the lessons are not expensive, they cost enough so that some people can't afford the extra fifty dollars. Modern square dancing is geared toward couples, although more and more singles clubs are starting up in metropolitan areas of the country.

As a major form of entertainment for millions of Americans, Western square dancing has also developed scores of organizations, activities, festivals, and even an Annual Square Dance Convention attended, in 1976, by some 36,000 dancers. It has created a unique subculture complete with magazines, books, records, costumes, and a star system of callers who are in demand from coast to coast. Clubs who want to hire one of these "stars" will often pool resources to sponsor one big "bash" dance. Clearly the world of club dancing is big enough to accomodate many forms of clubs, from the highly competitive amateur kind to those where middle-aged couples dance for the fun of it, to singles clubs which sponsor relaxed, informal "mixers." There could be no doubt about it: Western square dancing in 1977 was in a period of great expansion among all age groups.

When I got back to the city, I drove over to Bob Osgood's house where I was having dinner before the Rip 'n Snort dance that night. Over coffee I asked Bob how he viewed the modern square-dance scene. He said this: "If you just look at what's happened in the dancing itself you can see how the life-style we have here is expressed in the dances, especially in the figures. We have replaced the old style 'cowboy' square dances with a new dance that reflects the mood and the vernacular of modern, urban society. While the standardization of the dances is criticized by some, we feel it is a good influence. A person can go any- where in the United States, and some countries all around the world, and find people who know how to dance just like he does. That's a com- fortable feeling for a lot of people." Bob's words made sense to me. As with any social function, some Western square dancers have clearly gone too far with organization, and standardization has caused a minority of Western square dancers to become competitive and exclusive. Yet the great majority of them enjoy the activity because it fulfills a need not easily satisfied in modern, urban society, a need to be part of something; a community of dancers.

"Rip 'n Snort" is anything but a routine club. As Bob and I drove over to the dance through Beverly Hills, he explained a little bit about how the club works. Instead of having long-term officers, the leadership in the club changes regularly, and even so the "president" really doesn't hold much power. The president is a figurehead who acts as a communication link between different committees made up from the club membership. The committees are based on where people come from. When the club first started, all the members lived fairly close by, but over the years people have moved all over the greater Los Angeles area, so the com- mittee system helps unify the members. Each dance is the responsibility of a different committee, and those people are responsible for all the details: the decorations, refreshments, making the arrangements with the guest caller if there is to be one. Every dance is supposed to have a theme such as "Hawaii," and the decorations and refreshments are pre- pared with that theme in mind. Bob explained that the dance they were having that night was not a regular dance, but instead it would be an evening of modern contra dancing, which was beginning to become more and more popular among Western square dancers. Most of the people there would be members of Rip 'n Snort, but the dance was open to anybody interested in learning more about contra dances.

When we arrived at the dance hall, the same building that houses the magazine headquarters, several of the "Rip" people were already there. Immediately I knew how right Ray Orme had been. In talking to and dancing with the members of Rip 'n Snort and their friends I discovered a group of highly aware, likeable people who were sensitive to the con- troversies in modern Western square dancing. They appeared to have found a solution to the influences of modern society. Before the dancing actually started I had a chance to speak with some of the Rip people about their club. Most of the members are middle aged or older, white collar, many of them professional people. Ray Orme explained that the membership of the club had remained fairly constant over the years because the people were mainly interested in having a good time. Unlike many clubs Rip has a very minor turnover problem, so they have not been forced to sponsor course after course just to keep enough members in to meet the expenses of running dances.

One of the most interesting members of Rip was there that night for the contra dancing. A civil engineer, Ray Jensen first learned to square dance by attending classes run by Bob Osgood back in 1952. In addition to being an active member of Rip 'n Snort, he dances regularly with two other square-dance clubs: "Whoa Nelly" and "Whirlaways." Not a fan of ballroom dancing, he likes contra dancing, square dancing, and round dancing, in that order. "Mostly it provides a regularly scheduled way to get out of the house and away from the television. You know, it gives me a chance to associate with some pleasant people in an active, participatory way." "And besides," Ray said, "it's relatively inexpensive. Also it helps me forget all my trivial day-to-day problems. You know, the caller chooses the music, the calls and the round dances. Our regular caller Ray Orme does a very good job for us." It seemed clear to me from listening to Ray that he was happy to share the responsibility for organizing the dances, but over all he liked best not having to worry about having a good time.

Soon the dance began and immediately someone dragged me out on the floor. My protest of ignorance was useless, so I just smiled and quietly warned my partner that she might have to do some extra pushing to get me through the dance. I felt reasonably comfortable because the formation of this first dance was a contra, but I was in for a big surprise. As the dance was taught I realized that the figures were a mixture of basic traditional ones I was familiar with, plus some modern ones I had never heard of. But eventually I became fairly comfortable with them, thanks to the help of the other dancers whose patience amazed me. Once again I observed that courtesy is an essential part of square dancing. Bob Osgood was calling this particular dance. His style was easygoing and musical, and the dancing reflected his qualities as a caller.

After a couple of tips, there was a break in the action. I began to look again at the portraits of the Hall of Fame callers lined up along the walls of the dance hall. It seemed that these Western square dancers had a strong respect for the history of their modern movement. While trying to catch my breath I had a chance to talk to some of the dancers. Brad and Jane Donovan remarked that the history added to their enjoyment of the dancing. "We realize that that we're part of a long chain of dancers and dancing styles." I asked another couple, Tom and Tootie Banks

## WESTERN SQUARE DANCERS
## FROM *"RIP 'N SNORT"*

Ken and Sharon Kernan are originally from the Denver area but now live in a northern Los Angeles suburb. Both Ken and Sharon work for *Square Dancing* magazine and are members of "Rip 'n Snort." Ken discussed some of the interesting qualities of this club, one of the oldest in America.

"It used to be that the image of the square dancer was of the guy who grabbed a fifth of something and headed for the barn, you know, to see how many eyes he could bloody up. But the people in 'Rip 'n Snort' have taken the square dance out of the barn. They can be a noisy bunch, but they're just having fun. They genuinely enjoy each other, the fellowship involved, and they're not at all worried about becoming a high-level club."

Later some other members of "Rip" told me how they had first become involved in square dancing.

Tom and Tootie Banks. He is a purchasing agent, she a housewife: "Some friends of ours were going to an adult-education class and talked us into going, too. Now it's been our way of life for twenty-seven years. Most of our social life centers around square dancing and most of our other social events take place with our square dancing friends."

Brad and Jane Donovan. A retired aircraft engineer and an attorney respectively, the Donovans were skeptical at first about square dancing. "We had never seen square dancing and thought it must be pretty corny, but decided to go because some neighbors were attending classes and having a

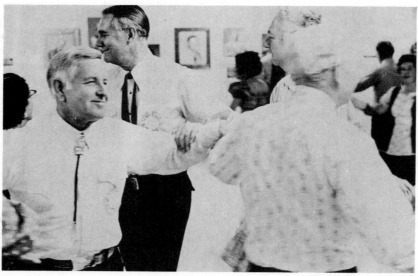

Left Hand Star

*Photos by Tom Vinetz*

Ray Orme calling for Rip.

marvelous time. We didn't intend to dance after the first class finished, but as it turned out we were the only ones who did keep on!"

Ruth Rising is a housewife from north of Los Angeles and has been square dancing for twenty-nine years. In that time she has belonged to many clubs including "Rip 'n Snort," where she actively dances: "I got into it back in 1948 before there were any classes around Los Angeles. My daughter was a Girl Scout and one of the fathers taught square dancing. They got him to agree to teach the troop so the girls could earn a merit badge. They needed male partners so fathers and brothers were encouraged to come and my husband helped. I watched, but we both liked it and soon we started attending dances every week.

Now after all these years of dancing at least twice a week all my friends are dancers. I'd never see them if I quit, especially since my husband died. Besides I can't imagine life without square dancing."

*continued*

Couple promenade.

Rip 'n Snort

*Photos by Tom Vinetz*

what they thought. Tom, who is a purchasing agent, and Tootie, a housewife, have been dancing for twenty-six years. Like the Donovans, the Banks also feel the importance of history in square dancing. "We believe that the more good history there is behind it, then the better base it has to stand on. Then it'll preserve itself as long as people care to record it." After the next tip there was a longer intermission during which I showed the film I helped make called "Country Corners," a documentary about contra dance in New England. All these western dancers who had come out this night to concentrate on learning the contras had a special interest in the film, but I must confess that I was a little nervous about how they would react to it. In fact, they liked it a great deal. They did laugh a little as they watched the young New England dancers barefoot on a cold winter night, but their amusement was not malicious, simply the reaction any Californian would have to the New England winter. I think the film caused some of them to think about different but important issues of Western square dancing. After seeing all the live musicians, the fiddlers and banjo players in New England, some of the Rip 'n Snort people expressed differing opinions as to the value of live, as opposed to recorded music. Ray Jensen, for example, said that he felt "really good live music was preferable to records, but in my opinion it's just not worth the cost. What's more important is the quality of the music, you know, square-dance music has always got to have that strong beat." Several other Rip 'n Snort dancers remarked that the biggest problem was that live music was too expensive. The Donovans said: "We prefer the recorded music. Live music can be great but in the long run we like records better because there's more variety."

After the intermission I was out on the floor again. The next dance was a square, just to break up the night a little. Bob Osgood called this dance, "Just Because," a singing call based on the popular song of the same name. I found that the singing-call dances were the easiest ones for me to do, I suppose because they followed the phrases of the music more exactly, as do the old New England contras.

During the next break I talked to some of the Rip people about their club and why they preferred it to others they had been in. Most of them agreed that they weren't intersted in being challenged by the caller on the dance floor, or by other dancers for that matter. Several of them had been to challenge-level clubs where they had seen people suffer embarrassment and humiliation whenever they made mistakes. "We go to our jobs for that," said the Donovans. "We just want to relax and enjoy the dance." On the other hand, one Rip dancer remarked that she liked a challenge once in a while. But most of them felt that the current trend in modern square dancing toward the challenge level was going to cause the disappearance of dancing to music. I must admit that as I have traveled around to different clubs, especially ones less sensitive than Rip 'n Snort, music seems to be getting less and less important to the dancers and callers. I went to one western club dance in North Carolina recently, where throughout the evening of dancing I never heard one tune. All the records offered was a very strong beat with a melody line so faint that once the caller started the tune was completely lost. Strange as it may seem, this particular dance reminded me of the modern disco dancing I have seen in Boston and New York, where the beat of the music is all that counts.

Another interesting member of Rip 'n Snort is Frank Hamilton, a well-known teacher of round dances and an outspoken observer of the changes that have taken place in Western dancing over the years. Frank is seventy-two years old.

"I learned to square dance from Carl Myles, who was a brother-in-law of Lloyd Shaw's. I got interested because my wife, Carolyn, said that I didn't have to get all dressed up, we'd be home early, and there wasn't any drinking going on. But the thing that really hooked me was that the first night I learned to love to swing! The worst thing that's happened to the modern dancing is the loss of the swing as a major basic. It's still the best part of square dancing."

Frank spent eight years getting his PhD and many years as a round-dance teacher. These experiences taught him a great deal about discriminating between good and bad material. I asked Frank what he thought of the new style of square dancing with all of its complications and especially the huge number of figures available to the modern caller: "Personally I'm not much interested in the new stuff, only the best, proven material. But I do see a need for two or maybe three different kinds of clubs so all these dancers can have a place to get all the material they crave, because after all there's all kinds of different people in any activity.

"The way I see it is this: with a few exceptions I doubt that a beginner of normal intelligence, energy and time can enjoy club dancing until he's been in it for two or three years . . . and even then he's got to dance at least once a week to keep up with all the new stuff. Mostly I think there's just too much new material coming along for the activity to survive and thrive with a large number of participants. The average pace now is beamed at the experienced, trained dancers who have the time and money to dance three or even six nights a week. I don't think this is any way to build a future for square dancing."

After the dance was over a few people stayed for a few minutes to talk. One of the Rip 'n Snort dancers came up to me and said: "You know one of the things that amazed me about that film you showed was how many young people there were dancing those old-time dances. One of the things that bothers me the most about the dancing out here is that almost no teen-agers seem to be interested in getting involved."

I said good-night to Bob, Ken and all the other Rip people. Outside the Hollywood air was warm and moist. I could smell the flowers as I walked along the sidewalk to my car. My evening of dancing and talking with the Rip 'n Snort people had been very enjoyable.

Before I left Los Angeles, I went to see Joe Fadler and his wife Barbara whom I had met at the contra night. Joe is a photographer and has taken pictures of square-dance activities for *Square Dancing* for over twenty years. Now that they live in Downey, a suburb quite a distance southeast of Los Angeles, they do not attend as many Rip 'n Snort dances but have been active in the club for many years. As Joe says of Rip: "Once you're in, you're always in, because unlike most modern clubs, in Rip the basis of the activity is the eight open hands of the square."

As we talked Joe took me out to show me the orchids he raises in his back yard. There were all kinds of varieties, pure breeds and hybrids. Orchids are incomparably graceful, and their basic design full of movement, but most interesting to me were the subtle differences of shape and color. Joe and I talked about the orchids and about costuming which is so important in modern square dancing.

"One of the large selling points that Lloyd Shaw brought to the modern square dance was giving men the chance to doll up without being looked down upon. The Shaw-backed leaders tried to take the square dance out of the barn because I think the educated, sophisticated urban community simply did not want to be caught acting like a country bumpkin. They took the costuming of the farmer and the cowboy to give it some flavor, but they tried to add some decency and put it in a context where the urban dweller could dance and not feel degraded. To a large degree the costuming helps to keep the activity alive."

I remarked that the costumes reminded me a little of Joe's orchid breeding. The new flowers are all the same and produce flowers just like them. Then with crossbreeding the flowers obtain maturity and individual character. "Yes," said Joe, "in modern square dancing the clubs who have costumes that are all alike, that virtually amount to uniforms, are the ones who haven't been around for a very long time. I think they need the boost to their collective ego. They usually wear them when they visit another club, for security because they lack the confidence of older dancers. The success of a club like Rip 'n Snort is that they have avoided that by recognizing that each dancer needs to retain an individual identity. Yet they still have a total club feeling you just won't find in many other groups around Los Angeles. You know, when you have all the same costumes for everyone in a club you're obviously getting away from individuality. At Rip they let the dance do the molding rather than some artificial mold like a costume."

The last thing Joe Fadler said to me before I left Los Angeles was this: "You can go out and find all different levels of modern square dancing, and it is true that this dancing, country dancing if that's what you want to call it, is for the masses. But I think that you really become a dancer only when you build within yourself the realization that you need it, that you need to dance."

Like Joe's orchids, the most interesting dancer is one who comes from a deeply buried seed and a long line of interesting parents with strong natural character. That is the depth that makes a dancer a dancer.

The air was slightly clearer as I entered the freeway for my trip to the airport. I dropped off my car and headed for another plane. As the jet lifted, I could see the ocean and Catalina in the distance, but soon the plane banked around to head east leaving the Pacific lost behind the wall of smog. I headed back to Denver and my meeting with Dorothy Shaw.

## SQUARE-DANCE FASHION

One of the most striking aspects of the modern western square dance is the costuming, which is especially unusual for the men who normally do not get to dress in bright colored, cowboy-style outfits. But like the dancing, the costumes—or dress code—has become largely standardized, certainly reflecting a uniformity of taste, and sometimes in style. Madeline Allen wrote editorials in a magazine called *Square Dance, Where?* which primarily lists where dances are occurring in northern California. In an October 1956 essay entitled "Are You a Square Dancer?" she wrote: "I have been asked several times to comment on wearing special clothes for Square Dancing, and to explain why we think it's important. Of course there are some obvious reasons . . . Square Dance styles are fundamentally beautiful styles. They are gay and colorful and becoming . . . but there is another side to it as well. We feel that as long as a person chooses clothing with the mental reservation that they can also be worn for other things than Square Dancing, he or she is not really with it. As long as you keep one foot in the bottom of the pool you are not really swimming . . . you always seem just about to back out. Women who do not care enough about square dancing to make or buy at least one real Square Dance dress haven't really yielded yet . . . they are not sold on the whole idea. Once you have made a real investment in Square Dancing . . . not only lessons, but dresses and shoes and shirts and boots . . . the chances of your dropping out are much lower. So we say . . . let yourself go! Let yourself have a good time, and be a real 'Square Dancer.'

The modern Western look for men.

*Photos courtesy of Sets In Order American Square Dance Society.*

Petticoats for the ladies.

## III

The wide, strong warp upon which is forever woven,
And forever rewoven the intricate tapestry that is my country
Remains forever the same.

The high clean un-compromising plateau of Colorado,
Wind bitten, sun-gilt, harshly pencilled with snow,
Drops off, east of Limon, into the plain.
The plain sweeps, as it has always swept,
Through Kansas and Nebraska, faintly hostile,
Faintly indifferent—treeless, fertile and splendid,
And then runs imperceptibly into the prairie.
The Mississippi slides silently under the bridge at Rock Island
in un-starred blackness.
The train lights wink into it momentarily as we pass over.

from "*Cross Country*" by Dorothy Shaw

I first read those lines while sitting in Bob Osgood's living room in Beverly Hills. The next time I read them was on a plane flying from Denver to Boston. They were written a long time ago, during the Second World War when, as Dorothy Shaw says:

The middle of my country never looked more peaceful.
The highways lie
Like clean gray tapes, ironed flat and thin with cold,
Untroubled by a million cushioned wheels.
Even the business of simple creatures
Is stayed—and hushed—no harnessed teams step evenly in the stubble;
No cattle graze in the clover that may yet be fragrant.
The little towns are quieter than Sunday
For neither men nor soldiers throng the corners.
March and war are upon it; and war and wind
Have blown it to the bone.

How do you talk about a person you have known only for one afternoon, but for an afternoon that in meaning equaled many days, maybe years? How do I describe this woman? Factually: she was born Dorothy Stott, from Denver. She married Lloyd Shaw; they moved to Colorado Springs and worked together in the Cheyenne Mountain School, teaching their children to dance. Then as their participation in the development of the Western square dance became increasingly important, Dorothy Stott Shaw stood beside her husband and has carried on his work afterwards. She loves chocolate ice cream, especially the kind that she gets from a local dairy in Colorado Springs. She knows all about the NORAD installation, a military fortress built inside a mountain near her house. She is extraordinarily articulate. Her sentences are spoken with strength, uninterrupted by "ums" and "ahs," as graceful as the dance itself. But let me speak figuratively: she *is* dance, she *is* music.

When she wrote "Cross Country," America was just beginning to get reinterested in the country dances. After World War II, Lloyd and Dorothy took their Cheyenne Mountain Dancers to all parts of the country, and before they knew it they watched Americans from all over take up what they considered the native American folk dance—Americans not only in the country, but in the city as well. They saw the old cowboy dances change with each year as they were subjected to the influence of modern urban taste and temperament. Something happened that changed the basic nature of what had been a "country" dance.

"After all," she said, "where is the country? We have such a mélange of things stirred up in our stew, that it's almost impossible to say where it starts. I always think of New England area as being the heart of the country dance. Many of the dance forms that have moved out from New England have gotten spoiled, but the essential country dance is still there.

"We have been doing in other parts of the country what I call computerized dance. It is something utterly new in country dancing and I think it is a reflection of our society; everything that's happening in modern square dancing is a reflection of the terrible mechanization of the American people. We can do almost anything: we can rebuild machines that take us to the moon, but when the man sets foot on the moon that outweighs the importance of the machine. It's simply a comment on our civilization which is so mechanized.

"And the dancers have become mechanized, and their body movements are no longer real because everything they do comes from the cerebrum. There are a lot of people who are influential in the square-dance movement who promote a program of Basic Movements of square dancing. Well, the basic movements in dancing are the same basic movements we've had since mankind stood up on his two legs, and we don't need to go through all this maneuvering. But we Americans have to have everything set out very graphically, written down on paper, and this is where the computer comes in, and it permeates every facet of our dance. And it's gotten to the point where it seems we can't go on without equipment. But what more equipment do we need than the legs and arms and hands and the head of a healthy human being?

"And how do we learn to dance then? Well I'll tell you a story about a little girl. This little girl Erika went to school one day and during the recess period one of her friends taught her to skip. And then Erika came home absolutely enchanted and told her mother that she had learned to skip. But you know you can't really teach anyone to skip. It's one of the most difficult physical activities there is and you cannot explain it to someone with words. But you can teach everybody to skip if you will put the hand of the potential skipper in the hand of the skipper and send them off. It's as simple as that!

"So Erika had learned to skip, and she was skipping around, and singing, and she said: 'I think I'll skip to "Briar Rosebud," ' and her mother thought, 'Uh oh, a skip is in waltz time and "Briar Rosebud" is in 2/4 time, I wonder what she'll do.' Well, all Erika did was let the skipping, the body movement regulate her, and she simply skipped to 'Briar Rosebud' in waltz time. So you see the head just naturally thought up things for her legs and arms to do. And that's how we learn to dance."

There was a breeze that day, a warm day for January in Colorado Springs, and the breeze tossed dry leaves all around the driveway in front of Dorothy Shaw's house. Mrs. Shaw and I walked over to another building on the driveway, where they hold workshops for dance teachers and dancers in the summer months and where she and her friends dance in the winter. Inside, the floor had been damaged by water from some recent accident, but the walls of the interior had not been damaged and on them hung many old pictures—of the Cheyenne Mountain Dancers, other dance groups, and naturally a picture of Lloyd Shaw, dressed in a buckskin coat with a great sky behind him. We stopped for a minute by his picture.

"You know," she said, "you're really much more civilized in New England than we are out here in the middle of the country, because this 'hot-hash' calling has really taken hold here. The callers are just not knowledgeable enough about music. But Lloyd was a superb caller, and it's an art to be caller; not just anybody can do it."

Then we moved over to another picture, this one of the Cheyenne Mountain Dancers, who were performing a particularly exciting figure.

"They were doing the old American square dance, pure and simple, executed as called, and with a great deal of laughter and fervor and joy, and they were doing it with tremendous style." Then she thought for a moment and said: "What's happened out here in middle America is that they've just gotten sloppy. They go on dancing and having a good time, but they've lost their moral sense about it, by which I mean they don't realize that this dance is a treasure of the American people. And what's happened is like not taking any more baths: it just keeps getting grubbier and grubbier, and that is what has pulled down the quality of the American folk dance tremendously. Now pioneer America, they got sloppy too, mostly because of lack of personnel, but also they had to deal with the opposition of the churches in this area. I can remember as a little girl in the Methodist church, being told that dancing was a terrible sin, and I can remember how absolutely out of bounds my father felt it was. But he finally gave in when I turned sixteen and I began to go to high-school dances. And what did we do? We did the polka and the schottische; pretty dull, but at least we were in movement, holding hands and touching each other, and having a great time laughing and dancing. But I don't think my father ever really felt very comfortable about it."

Then we went out of the building and stood in the driveway. She told me that her neighborhood was the oldest section of Colorado Springs and that before the city began to grow at such an astronomical rate, there was more of a sense of belonging to a community. But that had changed and now many people in the area were from all over the country. It was too cold to stand outside as the breeze picked up and the sun lowered over the mountains, so we went inside and had some coffee. The telephone rang, she had a short conversation, and then came back to the room where I was sitting.

She said, "A friend of mine called up one day and asked me if I wanted to go see the gypsy dancers that were performing down in Pueblo. And I said I was very tired and had a terrible cold, and she said 'Dorothy, I think you have to go,' and I said, 'Betty, maybe I do; why don't you pick me up.' So we went to see these gypsy dancers and you never saw anything like it! They had gathered different dancers from gypsy bands all over Europe, and they couldn't communicate with words, but only through the dance, which was just as meaningful. They danced every imaginable kind of dance: a wedding, a murder, they even danced a funeral, but I noticed that the figures they danced were the same figures that we do, and that they were doing these figures in the same order that we do them in many instances. And I thought to myself, there's a reason for that order; we have to go around in order, because we have to be rooted to something, and if you pull up those roots then you're done for. We are, I think, in vast parts of this country rootless people. People who live in one place for a long time, like farmers and ranchers, people who live on the land, are much better off, because there's always those roots that go down. But we don't think of our amusements and our entertainments that way. They're just that, instead of oblations. But if we get in a lonely enough, meaningful enough place, sometimes we start to think 'I need some roots. I've got to put some roots down or I'll just blow away.' And this is what we lack in our dance now. Dance is the people who are doing it, that's what matters, and it doesn't matter what you do, so long as what happens to the people is good."

I finished my coffee. It was getting very dark out and I had to get back to Denver; besides Mrs. Shaw was going to a concert that night and needed some time to get ready. But one question was left to ask, perhaps the most obvious, and I realized this would probably be my last chance to ask her because I was leaving on a plane for Boston the next day. We stood out on the doorstep in the cool night air. She said she often comes out to look at the stars on nights like this. Then I asked my question. Did she think there was hope for the modern square dance; could it regain the grace it once had? Typically, she thought a long time before answering, and just as typically the answer came in the form of a story:

"A man I know, a man who is very involved in square dancing in Colorado Springs, called me up recently. And he said, 'Mrs. Shaw, we need help.' And I said, 'Who needs help?' and he said 'We do, all of us in the Colorado Springs Callers' Association, and the people that dance with us, we need help and I think you ought to help us.' And I said, 'Why me?' And he said, 'Well we make our donation every year to the Foundation and we're about ready to collect something!' And I said, 'Well, then what is it we have that you really want?' And he said, 'We really want what you've got . . . we want to learn to dance again.' And when he said that I could have shot off fireworks!"

It's absolutely impossible for me to relax while a jet is taking off. I just sit there, fingers crossed, my seat belt tight as a girdle, while everybody else reads magazines, watches the city disappear below, or goes to sleep. But when the plane begins to level off, and the landscape below gets too far away to seem dangerous, I settle down and try to figure out what to do with myself for the next few treacherous hours. In this case, leaving Denver, the choices were few. My mind was on square dancing, and especially how I was going to make sense out of all the information I had collected in the West. Out of all the confusion in my head came a host of platitudes: a realization that modern square dancing is merely a reflection of a part of our culture, and that this reflection had as many facets as the culture itself, as many dimensions as there are dancers; but also a realization that, as through the entire history of dance, the evolution of the art would ultimately depend on the wholesale dedication of a few people, people like those I had recently met in California and Colorado. I picked up the book of her poems Mrs. Shaw had given me. I hadn't seen the inscription she had written in it on the first page. It read: "For Dick Nevell, Fellow traveler, Thank you! Dorothy Stott Shaw" Then I turned to "Cross Country" one more time:

> Conflict can be invisible as the wind blowing
> But the scars of conflict are readable and clear
> as the tell-tale prints of the wind.

I knew the conflict she had originally written about was a world war, but I couldn't help thinking that she might make the same observation about the modern Western square-dance world, whose problems were perhaps invisible to many people who are so involved in square dancing that they couldn't step outside, look in and see the scars of their actions. But I knew that Mrs. Shaw would maintain her hope that enough people would see the signs, "readable and clear," and return the dancing to its original form: "Action! Action of the body, and the soul inside the body, just gets up and shouts with joy!"

## Some Favorite Square Dances

The Western square dance is a dance for eight people, divided into four couples. Its most obvious parents are the New England quadrille and the Kentucky Running Set, but what makes the Western square dance characteristically "western" is (1), the speed with which the dances are performed (much faster than the New England quadrilles and more like the Running Sets), and (2), the huge variety of available figures the caller may use. Another aspect of the Western dance is the increased role of the caller. In New England contra dances the calls are "prompted," while in modern Western square dances the calls are often sung in place of the lyrics of a popular song such as "If You Knew Susie"; or given at great speed, in the style of an auctioneer. This auctioneer-type calling is often referred to as "hot-hash" calling, and is most often found in "challenge" square dancing, the most difficult style reserved for only the most accomplished dancers.

Like any popular form of entertainment, Western square dancing, more than any other form of country dancing in the United States, reflects contemporary culture: the calls are made up in the vernacular of the time; the tunes that are danced to rise and fall in popularity just as rock and roll stars or TV shows. The Western square dance is by far the most modern country dance; and yet there are some significant people in the world of Western square dancing who seek to retain some of the older "traditional" calls and tunes. To understand the modern Western square dance it is essential to recognize that this essentially ancient form of dance contains both traditional and contemporary choreographic elements.

To illustrate how a Western square dance works, I have chosen a very simple, traditional square dance, the "Arkansas Traveler." All the movements it incorporates can be found in the "Basic Figures" section of this book.

First we must make a square of eight couples, like this:

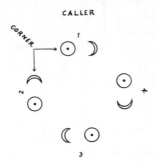

The men are represented by the squares, the women by the circles. The darkened circles are the HEAD couples, the whites the SIDE couples. The "corners" are the ladies to the left of the men, or the men to the right of the ladies. The couples are numbered 1–2–3–4 counter clockwise, starting with the couple closest to the caller, who stand with their backs to him. The 3rd couple faces the caller. The 2nd and 4th couples face each other.

As with contra dances, the "Arkansas Traveler" is danced to the tune of the same name. Also, like contra dance tune such as "Petronella," the "Arkansas Traveler" has two parts: an "A" part and a "B" part. These two parts are each repeated twice, as follows: A1–A2–B1–B2, to complete one cycle (thirty-two measures) of the dance, which goes like this:

A1 { First and 3rd couples go Forward and Back.

A2 { First and 3rd couples go Forward Again and the men Turn the Opposite Woman with the right arm, and Turn Their Partners by the left arm when they get home.

B1 { Everyone Turns Their Corners with the right arm, and Turns Their Corners with the left arm when they get home.

B2 { Everyone Meets Their Corners and Promenades Their Corners once around the ring to the man's original place.

At this point, after one full cycle of the dance, the dancers have all obtained new partners, their corners, the ladies who originally stood to their left. In other words the 1st man is now with the 4th woman; 2nd man is with 1st lady, 3rd man is with 2nd woman, and 4th man is with 3rd.

Like the contra dances, in simple square dances there is a progression. The caller will call three more cycles of the dance, and after each cycle the women will change partners, moving counter clockwise around the square, until finally they rejoin their partner after the fourth cycle.

This is a simple Western square dance, very similar to an old quadrille from New England. To make it "Western" in flavor the caller might add a singing call like:

> Now all turn partners with a left arm 'round,
> And Promenade that corner girl around the town!

As the Western dances became more complicated, with the addition of literally thousands of figures, the basic progressive structure exemplified in "The Arkansas Traveler" became less secure. Many of the dances do not progress in this fashion, and in the "challenge" dances the calls do not always coincide with the traditional melodic pattern of the music, especially those dances written to popular contemporary songs like "Bill Bailey," a dance by caller Ed Gilmore.

## Star Promenade Routine

In Lloyd Shaw's *Cowboy Dances* he describes a figure called the Four Leaf Clover in which the four couples of the square promenade around in the following fashion: The four men form a four-pointed cross, with their left shoulders in the center of the ring. Each man has his partner in promenade position on his right, and the four couples promenade around in that formation. Later this figure was modernized and became known as the Star Promenade or the Texas Star. This "new" figure is really the same as the Four Leaf Clover except that the four men use the "star" hand hold instead of simply leaning their left shoulders into the center, and promenade with one hand. A typical example of how a traditional figure has been changed to suit the modern square dancer's taste, the Star Promenade is also an example of a figure which is part of a "family" of movements. In this case the "family" is founded on the basic Star formation. Finally, it is a good example of a modern figure which

has become part of the American Square Dance Society's Fifty Basic Movements of American Square Dancing.

Here is a simple routine which incorporates the Star Promenade:

> Four Ladies Go Forward and Back
> And the four men Right Hand Star in the center
> And Left Hand Back
> Take your partner's arm around Star Promenade
> And go once around the ring to home
> Four couples go Forward and Back

What happens here is that the four men simply "pick up" their partners by putting their arms around the ladies' waists as they come around in a Left Hand Star ("Take your partner's arm around"), and then continue in the Star Promenade position. This figure is varied at times by having the men passing by their partners as they come around in the Star. When this happens the dance must go through three additional cycles for everyone to rejoin their original partners (as in "Arkansas Traveler"). And sometimes the ladies form the Star by the right hand and "pick up" the men on their way around.

## Rip 'n Snort

Sometimes a modern Western square-dance figure becomes so popular that a whole dance is named after it. This is the case with Rip 'n Snort, an interesting figure because, while it clearly bears the mark of western-style square dance, its actual choreography is almost identical to a very old country dance figure called Strip the Willow.

The figure goes like this: When instructed, the 1st couple dances across the square toward the opposite couple (3rd) who make an arch. Before they pass under the arch, the 1st man clasps his corner lady's hand with his right hand, and similarly the 1st lady clasps her corner man's left hand. The 1st couple then pass under the arch leading the other dancers behind them: the man leading the 2nd couple and the lady leading the 4th couple. As soon as they pass under the arch, the 1st couple separates, the man goes right still leading the 2nd couple to the right, heading back to his original place, the lady leading the 4th couple to the right, heading back to her original place. At the end of the figure the 3rd couple, who have been making the arch, does a simple turn in place and rejoins the circle of eight which is now totally reformed.

A square dance routine using Rip 'n Snort usually takes it name as well, because this figure is clearly the distinguishing figure, the one that makes it more fun than a plain square. Here's the dance "Rip 'n Snort," a favorite of the club of the same name, as written in the Sets in Order "Basic Program of American Square Dancing."

All eight Circle to the Left
The first old couple Rip 'n Snort
Go down the center and cut 'em off short
The lady goes gee and the gent goes haw
Now Circle to the Left with ole' grandmaw

All join hands and Circle Left
Couple number one Rip 'n Snort
Join hands and Circle Left
Allemande Left and Weave the Ring
Promenade home

All join hands and Circle Left
Couple number two Rip 'n Snort
Join hands and Circle Left
Allemande Left and Weave the Ring
Promenade home

All join hands and Circle Left
Couple number three Rip 'n Snort
Join hands and Circle Left
Allemande Left Right and Left Grand
Promenade home

All join hands and Circle Left
Couple number four Rip 'n Snort
Join hands and Circle Left
Allemande Left Right and Left Grand
Promenade home

Bow to your partner,
To your corner,
And the girl across the hall.

"Weaving the Ring" simply means to do a Grand Right and Left without touching hands.

## "Just Because"

I remember this dance from my visit to Los Angeles because it was one that all the Rip 'n Snort people joined in singing as the calls were sung. Bob Osgood called and sang the dance, which is based on the modern song of the same name. When all the dancers came in singing strongly on the "Because just because" part, I was reminded of a spirited night in a dance in Nelson, New Hampshire, when for some mysterious reason Rod Miller, the fiddler, forgot how to play "Mony Musk" halfway through the dance—it didn't take long for a good percentage of the dancers to take up singing the tune and carry it along until the absent-minded fiddler regained his senses and got down to business again! The Rip 'n Snorters didn't have to prompt anyone that night in Los Angeles; they were singing with true dancing spirit and with obvious love for one of their favorite dances.

### "JUST BECAUSE"

It's honors to your partners
And to your corners all
Now Swing that opposite lady
She's the one across the hall

The come back home and Swing your own
You Swing with all your might
And thank your lucky stars
She's the one you brought tonight

Allemande Left with the old left hand
Right to your partner Right and Left Grand
It's a Grand Old Right and Left Around the Ring
Then you Promenade your partner boys
Shout and sing with joy
Because just because!

It's all around your corner
She's the gal from Arkansas
See saw 'round your partner
She's the prettiest in the hall

Four gents center with a Right Hand Star
Star by the old right hand
Go all the way round to your corner
With a two time Allemande

You turn 'em once, turn 'em twice
Then back right off and bow real nice
It's a Grand Old Right and Left Around the Ring
Then you Promenade this pretty thing

Throw your head right back and sing
Because just because!

as on Windsor Records #4144

A "see saw," incidentally, is similar to a Do Si Do. The man passes left shoulders with his partner and moves in a circle around her until he gets back to his starting position. The lady takes three steps forward as the man passes around her, then takes three steps back to place.

# VI
# CATALOGUE

The following catalogue and bibliography are directed to both dancers and nondancers. For people who are already country or square dancers of one kind or another, the books, events, records, and organizations listed here may help you broaden your dancing experience. For nondancers who have read this far and are asking "Where do I go to find some dancing?" this catalogue of resources can serve to direct you toward it. I haven't tried to list every caller, musician, or dance hall I know. Rather, I've tried to give the names of people, places, or organizations that can help get in touch with the person in your community who knows about dancing, music or both. If for some reason you are someplace where there appears to be no dance available—no callers, musicians, clubs, societies—I suggest you look again. Talk to older folks who lived before TV, you'll be surprised what they know. And don't forget to look inside yourself, there's a dancer somewhere in everyone.

## Bibliography

The following bibliography is divided into general sections on country and square dances and sections covering the specific forms of country dancing.

The first section lists major historical works on country dancing; it does not include unpublished dissertations, of which there are a few, usually to be found in the major libraries and archives listed in another section of this catalogue. But do not hesitate to check into the local colleges and universities in your community. I have found that a lot of localized studies have been done, not only by college students, but also by high-school students whose schools offer "Foxfire"-type research projects.

The second and following sections of the bibliography list instructional manuals or collections of dances, some traditional and others original. I have indicated in some cases if a book is particularly appropriate for beginning dancers and teachers of children, or if the book is exceptional for some other reason. Most of these books are available through the distribution sources listed later in the catalogue, or if they are out of print, in libraries.

# General History

Andrews, Edward D. *The Gift to Be Simple: Songs, Dances and Rituals of the American Shakers.* 1970. New York: Dover.

Arbeau, Thoinot. *Orchesographie.* 1588. Reprint.

Ariès, Phillipe. *Centuries of Childhood: A Social History of Family Life.* 1962. Translated by Robert Baldick. New York: Alfred A. Knopf.

Bonnet, J. *Histoire Generale de la Danse.* 1723. Paris.

Botkin, B.A. *A Treasury of Southern Folklore.* 1949. New York: Crown.

Campbell, J.C. *The Southern Highlander and His Homeland.* 1921. New York: Russell Sage Foundation.

Cartwright, Peter. *The Autobiography of Peter Cartwright.* 1856. New York and Cincinnati.

Chujoy, Anatole, and Manchester, P.W., eds. *The Dance Encyclopedia.* 1967. New York: Simon & Schuster.

Connell, Sarah N. *Journal 1805–1824.* 1910. Portland, Maine: Le Fara Towar Co.

Crawford, M.C. *Social Life in Old New England.* 1914. Boston: Little, Brown, and Co.

Damon, S. Foster. *The History of Square Dancing.* 1957. Barre, Massachusetts. Reprint from proceedings of the American Antiquarian Society. Worcester, Massachusetts. (The definitive work on square dancing.)

Dick and Fitzgerald. *Dick's Quadrille Book.* 1878. New York. (There are dozens of these "handbooks" from the nineteenth century.)

Doran, Paul E. *The Backgrounds of the Mountain People.* from *Mountain Life and Work.* January, 1936.

Eccles, Solomon. *A Musick Lector.* 1667. London. (Very rare. Discourse on the evils of dance.)

Emerson, George S. *A Social History of Scottish Dance.* 1972. Toronto: McGill University Press.

Emery, Lynne F. *Black Dance in the United States from 1619–1970.* 1972. Palo Alto: National Press Books. (Though hard to get, this book is worth searching for.)

Essex, J. *For the Further Improvement of Dancing.* 1710. Facsimile edition. 1970. Edited by Raoul Feuillet. London: Gregg.

Greene, Jack P. *Landon Carter: An Inquiry into the Personal Values and Social Imperatives of the 18th Century Virginia Gentry.* 1965. Virginia: Dominion.

Miles, Emma. *Spirit of the Mountains.* 1905. New York: J. Pott & Co.

Pichienri, Louis. *Music in New Hampshire 1623–1800.* 1960. New York: Columbia University Press.

Sachs, Curt. *World History of the Dance.* 1937, 1963. New York: W. W. Norton & Co.

Scholes, Percy, ed. *Grove's Dictionary of Music.* 1950. New York: St. Martin's Press.

Scholes, Percy. *The Puritans and Music in England and New England.* 1934. London: Oxford University Press.

Sewall, Samuel. *The Diary of Samuel Sewall.* 1967. New York: G. P. Putnam's Sons.

Sharp, Cecil, and Oppe, A. P. *The Dance: An Historical Survey of Dancing in Europe.* 1924. London.

Sharp, Cecil. *The Country Dance Book.* Six volumes. London: Novello & Co. (These books have been reprinted by the English Folk Dance and Song Society, E.F.D.S.S., in London.)

Sharp, Cecil. *The Morris Book.* 1907–1913. London: Novello & Co. (Also reprinted by E.F.D.S.S.)

Shaw, Dorothy Stott. *The Story of Square Dancing.* 1967. Los Angeles: Sets in Order "Handbook Series."

Shaw, Lloyd. *Cowboy Dances.* 1939. Caldwell, Indiana: Caxton Printers. (The "bible" of basic Western square dances.)

Shaw, Lloyd. *The Round Dance Book.* 1948. Caldwell, Indiana: Caxton Printers.

Smith, Arthur. "Hillbilly Folk Music". *Etude,* March 1933, p. 154.

Smith, Frank H. *The Appalachian Square Dance.* 1955. Berea, Kentucky: Berea College. (The photos in this book, by Doris Ullman, are wonderful. The book itself is the definitive one on southern mountain dance. Includes some southern fiddle tunes.)

Stearns, Marshall and Jean. *Jazz Dance: The Story of American Vernacular Dance.* 1968. New York: Macmillan Inc.

Tolman, Beth, and Page, Ralph. *The Country Dance Book.* 1937. Reprint. 1976. Brattleboro, Vermont: Stephen Greene Press. (The definitive book on how to contra dance, with some history, and great dance illustrations by F. W. P. Tolman.)

Tolman, Newton F. *Quick Tunes and Good Times.* 1972. Dublin, New Hampshire: William L. Bauhan. (An anecdotal history of contra-dance music in and around Nelson, New Hampshire, by that town's great flautist, including some artful explanation of the nature of jigs, reels, strathspeys, planxtys, etc., with some tunes.)

Whale, Henry. *Hommage a Taglioni: A Fashionable Quadrille Preceptor and Ballroom Companion.* 1836. Philadelphia. (Rare.)

Wigginton, Eliot, ed. *Foxfire.* I, II, and III. 1972. Garden City, New York: Doubleday & Co.

Wilson, Thomas. *The Complete System of English Country Dancing.* 1821. London: Sherwood, Neely & Jones. (Very rare and confusing illustrations of how country dances "work.")

Wright, Louis B. *The First Gentlemen of Virginia.* 1964. Charlottesville: University Press of Virginia.

Ziner, Feenie. *The Pilgrims and Plymouth Colony.* 1961. New York: Harper and Row.

## Books of Dances / General

The following bibliography lists instructional books that are not as specifically focused as the books listed in the contra, square and southern dancing sections. These books include dances from different sources; some indigenous dances from different parts of America and some international dances. I have also listed some older books which were written before country dancing in America became as specialized as it is today. For example, a book like Neva Boyd's *Old Square*

*Dances of America* includes more than just "square" dances. Here, as in other places, the term "square dancing" refers to country dancing of different types.

Ajello, Elvira. "The Solo Irish Jig." 1932. London: C. W. Beaumont. 30 pages. Illustrated.

Boyd, Neva L. *Old Square Dances of America.* 1925. Chicago: Recreation Training School. 96 pages.

Boyd, Neva L. *Country Dances.* 1919. Chicago. (English and American country dances.)

Cazden, Norman. "Dances from Woodland." 1945. New York: American Music Center. 27 pages. Illustrated. (Square dances by a caller from the Catskills of New York.)

Chaplin, Nellie. "Court Dances." 1911. London: J. Curwen & Sons Ltd. 34 pages. (Fancy dances of the court.)

Coles, A. "Old English Country Dance Steps." 1909. London: J. Curwen & Sons Ltd. 31 pages. Illustrated. (Seventeenth century English country dancing.)

Duggin, Anne; Schlottman, J.; and Rutledge, A. *Folk Dances of the United States and Mexico.* 1948. New York: A. S. Barnes & Co.

Durlacher, Ed. *81 Dances: Square, Circle and Contra.* 1961. New York: BerinAdair.

English Folk Dance and Song Society. *Community Dance Manuals.* 7 volumes. 1968. London: E.F.D.S.S.

Everett, Bert. *Traditional Canadian Dances.* 1967. Toronto: Canadian Folk Dance Society.

Fahs, Lois. *Swing Your Partner: Old Time Dances of New Brunswick and Nova Scotia.* 1939. New York: Lois Fahs. 106 pages. Illustrated. (With music.)

Farwell, Jane. *Folk Dances for Fun.* Delaware, Ohio: Cooperative Recreation Service, Inc.

Ford, Henry and Mrs. Ford *Good Morning.* 1926. Dearborn, Michigan: Dearborn Publishing Co. (This book is modeled after the old ballroom prompters of the nineteenth century. More manners and lectures on polite behavior than dances, but a good assortment of contras, quadrilles and round dances: even a minuet.)

Fox, Grace I. *Folk Dancing.* 1957. New York: Ronald Press. 89 pages. Illustrated.

Gilbert, Cecile. *International Folk Dance at a Glance.* 1974. Minneapolis.

Gowing, Gene. "Gene Gowing's Collection of American Quadrilles, Contras and Rounds." (No date.) American English Folkways. 18 pages.

Gowing, Gene. *The Square Dancer's Guide.* 1959. New York: Crown Publishers. 159 pages. Illustrated.

Gowing, Gene. *Square Dancing for Everyone.* 1957. New York: Grosset & Dunlap. 80 pages. Illustrated.

Hall, J. T. *Dance! Complete Guide to Social, Folk and Square Dancing.* 1963. Belmont, California: Wadsworth Pub. Co. 242 pages. Illustrated.

Harris, Jane A. *Dance Awhile!* 1964. Minneapolis: Burgess Publishing Co. (This book has a good bibliography and discography, and lots of good instructional material, mostly on squares.)

Herman, Michael, ed. *Folk Dance Syllabus #1.* 1953. New York: Folk Dance House Pub. 82 pages. Illustrated.

Heaton, Alma. *Recreational Dancing.* 1965. Provo, Utah: Brigham Young University Press. 307 pages. Illustrated. (Has good bibliography and discography.)

Hofer, M. R. *Polite and Social Dances: Historic Dances.* 1917. Chicago: Clayton F. Summy Co. 72 pages. Illustrated.

Hoffer, Marjorie, and Potter, William. *Maggot Pie: A Book of New Country Dances.* 1932. London: Cambridge. 55 pages.

Humphreys, B. "Dances for Party." 1957. London: E.F.D.S.S. 28 pages.

Kennedy, D. and H. "Country Dance Book: 30 Dances from the 17th edition of 'The English Dancing Master.' " 1929. London: Novello & Co. 42 pages. Reprinted by E.F.D.S.S.

Kennedy, D. and H. "Square Dances of America." 1935. London: Novello & Co. 32 pages. Reprinted by E.F.D.S.S.

McConachie, Jack. "The Grampian Collection of Scottish Country Dancing." 1963. London: Imperial Society of Teachers of Dancing. 23 pages.

McConachie, Jack. "Scottish Dancing in the 18th Century." 1963. London: Imperial Society of Teachers of Dancing. 55 pages. (Dances from a manuscript of 1740.)

McConachie, Jack. *The Speyside Collection of Scottish Country Dance Music.* Arranged by Edith Macpherson. 1960. London: Imperial Society of Teachers of Dancing.

Maclachlan, Elizabeth. "The Border Dance Book: Scottish Country Dancing." 1935. Edinburgh: McDougalls Educ. Co. 51 pages. Illustrated.

Mayo, Margot. *The American Square Dance.* 1964. New York: Oak Publications. 1964. 116 pages. Illustrated. (Originally published in 1943. Good bibliography.)

Milligan, Jean C. *99 More Scottish Dances.* 1963. Glasgow: Collins Co., 128 pages. Illustrated.

Milligan, Jean C. *Won't You Join the Dance?* 1951. London: Paterson's Publishing. Illustrated.

Newman Sanders, C. *Scottish Dancing.* 1952. London: Pitman Co. 87 pages. Illustrated.

Playford, John. *The English Dancing Master.* 1650. Reprint of first edition edited by Leslie Bridgewater and Hugh Mellor. 1933. London. (Tunes have been put into modern notation.)

Playford, John. *The English Dancing Master.* 1651. Facsimile reprint of first edition, with introduction by Margaret Dean Smith. 1957. New York: Association of Music Publishers. 90 pages. Illustrated.

Porter, W. S. "The Apted Book of Country Dancing." 1966. London: E.F.D.S.S. 37 pages. (Late eighteenth-century dances.)

Ryan, Grace L. *Dances of Our Pioneers.* 1926. New York: A. S. Barnes. 70 pages. Illustrated.

Sharp, Cecil. *The Country Dance Book.* 6 volumes. 1924. London: Novello & Co. Reprinted by E.F.D.S.S.

Sharp, Cecil. *The Morris Book.* 1907–1913. London: Novello & Co. Reprinted by E.F.D.S.S.

Tolman, Beth, and Ralph. *The Country Dance Book*. Reprint. 1976. Brattleboro, Vermont: Stephen Greene Press. (Good assortment of contras and quadrilles, and some "freak" dances as well.)

Tobbitt, Janet. E.  "16 Dances." 1947. Pleasantville, New York. 48 pages.

Venable, Lucy. "10 Folk Dances in Labanotation." 1959. New York: M. Witmark. 32 pages. Illustrated. (These folk dances by Michael Herman are analyzed with Rudolph Laban's system of recording choreography.)

Williams, Ralph Vaughan, and Karpeles, Maud. "12 Traditional Country Dances." 1956. London: E.F.D.S.S. 32 pages. Illustrated.

Wiseman, Herbert. "24 Favorite Scottish Country Dances." 1939. Edinburgh: Scottish Country Dance Society. 24 pages. Illustrated.

## Contra Dancing

This book section lists contra-dance instruction manuals, those that list traditional dances as well as the modern contras enjoyed by Western square dancers. Some of these books are specifically designed for callers or teachers, and I have indicated this, but even the novice dancer should be able to make sense out of any of them.

Armstrong, Don. *Contras*. 1973. Los Angeles: Sets in Order American Square Dance Society. (An excellent Caller/Teacher manual, with a good selection of traditional and "modern" contras. No music.)

Briggs, Dudley T. *Thirty Contras from New England*. 1953. Burlington, Vermont.

Brundage, Al, and Merchant, R. "Contras Are Fun." 1952. Stepney, Connecticut.

Burchenal, Elizabeth. "American Country Dancing: 28 Contras from New England." 1945. New York: G. Schirmer. 62 pages.

English Folk Dance and Song Society. *Community Dance Manuals*. Volumes 1–7. 1968. London: E.F.D.S.S. (Primarily contra dances, many of which are danced in New England today.)

Gaudreau, Herbie. *Modern Contra Dancing*. 1971. Sandusky, Ohio: American Square Dance Magazine. (Part of the "Callers' Aid" Series.)

Gowing, Gene. "Collection of American Quadrilles, Contras and Rounds." American English Folkways. 18 pages.

Gowing, Gene. *The Square Dancer's Guide*. 1957. New York: Crown. (By a caller who ran many dances in the Monadnock region of New Hampshire.)

Gowing, Gene. *Square Dancing for Everyone*. 1957. New York: Grossett & Dunlap.

Holden, Rickey. *The Contra Dance Book*. 1955. Newark, New Jersey: American Squares. 126 pages. Illustrated. (100 contras. This book is used commonly today.)

Keller, K.V., and Sweet, Ralph. *A Choice Selection of American Country Dances of the Revolutionary Era 1775–1795*. 1975. New York: Country Dance and Song Society. (Contains dances and tunes. A fine book.)

Larkin, Ed. "Contra Instructions." 1948. Montpelier, Vermont: State Dept. of Recreation.

Laufman, Dudley. *Okay, Let's Try a Contra, Men on the Right, Ladies on the Left, Up and Down the Hall or Blow Away the Morning Dew and Other Country Dances.* 1973. New York: Country Dance and Song Society. (A book with the longest title I know of; it contains some fine original dances and tunes.)

Linscott, E. H. *Folk Songs of Old New England.* 1962. Hamden, Connecticut: Archer Books. (This book contains 35 contra dances, with fiddle tunes as well as songs.)

Moody, Ed. "Swing Below." (Available through Ralph Page, Keene, New Hampshire.)

Morrison, James E. *24 Early American Country Dances, Cotillions and Reels.* New York: Country Dance and Song Society. (Contains music and a useful glossary.)

Page, Ralph. *Heritage Dances of Early America.* 1976. Colorado Springs: Lloyd Shaw Foundation.

Page, Ralph. *The Ralph Page Book of Contras.* 1969. London: English Folk Dance and Song Society. (Great tunes and dances; original and traditional.)

Sweet, Ralph. *Let's Create Old Tyme Square Dancing.* 1966. Hazardville, Connecticut. 97 pages. Illustrated. (Contains a bibliography and discography.)

Tolman, Beth, and Page, Ralph. *The Country Dance Book.* 1937. Reprint. 1976. Brattleboro, Vermont: Stephen Greene Press. (*The* book on New England contras, with great illustrations by F. W. P. Tolman.)

Tolman, Beth. "The Country Dance Party." 1937. Weston, Vermont: Countryman Press. (A nice pamphlet on running a contra-dance party. Rare, since it has not been reprinted.)

## Western Square Dancing

This section covers instructional materials for the Western square dance. Some of the books in this section are specialized books for callers and teachers, and if so, this distinction is noted. If there is no special note, the book is easily accessible for any dancer.

Allen, Madeline. *Square Dancemanship.* 2 volumes. Late 1950's. Alameda, California. (Honest editorials from a directory of dancing in northern California.)

Bell, Don. *Calling.* 1961. 144 pages. Illustrated. (For callers only.)

Burdick, Stan. *Progressive Workshop.* Sandusky, Ohio: American Square Dance. (This is basically for callers of advanced square dance.)

Burleson, Bill. *The Diagrammed Guide to Better Square Dancing.* 1971. Minerva, Ohio. (An instructional book for anyone with some square dance experience.)

Burleson, Bill. *The Square Dancing Encyclopedia.* 1970. Minerva, Ohio. (Bill Burleson compiles all the known square-dance figures, over 2,000 in his encyclopedia, and puts out appendixes twice a year.)

Casey, Betty. *The Complete Book of Square Dancing (and Round Dancing).* With 380 Step-by-step Illustrations. 1976. Garden City, N.Y.: Doubleday & Company, Inc. A very complete, well illustrated instructional book on modern

Western Square Dance. This book highlights 85 mainstream basic movements, a list which will need to be supplemented when Sets in Order increases its basic movement list to 98 in June, 1977.

Chase, A. H. *The Singing Caller.* 1944. New York: Association Press. 78 pages. Illustrated. (For aspiring singing callers.)

Clossin, Jimmy, and Hertzog, Carl. *West Texas Square Dances.* 1949. El Paso, Texas.

Durlacher, Ed. *Honor Your Partner.* 1949. New York: Berin Adair Co. (A fine book for all by a famous easterner.)

Federal Works Agency. "Swing Your Partner." New York: Board of Education. 15 pages. Illustrated.

Fraidenburg, Ed. *The Caller's Notebook.* 1970. Midland, Michigan. (250 original figures for callers.)

Gotcher, Les. *Caller and Teacher Manual.* 1965. La Puente, California. 109 pages.

Greggerson, H. F. *Herb's Blue Bonnet Calls.* 1946. El Paso, Texas. 68 pages. Illustrated. (A great little book by one of the best Texan callers.)

Harris, Jane A. *Dance Awhile!* 1964. Minneapolis: Burgess Pub. Co. (A comprehensive manual for everyone. Great for teachers.)

Hunt, Paul. *Eight Yards of Calico.* 1952. New York: Harper & Row. (Good book for a general audience.)

Jensen, Clayne R., and Mary Bee *Square Dancing.* 1972. Provo, Utah: Brigham Young University Press. (Good general book, clearly written and illustrated.)

Johnstone, Grace H. "Girl Scout Square Dancing." 1944. (Typewritten paper in N. Y. Public Library.)

Jones, J. W. *Square Dance.* 1970. Glendale, California: Frontier Publishers. (For dancers, beginning and otherwise.)

King, Jay. *How to Teach Square Dancing.* 1967. Lexington, Massachusetts. 178 pages. (For anyone who wants to try teaching.)

Kirkell, Miriam H. *Partners All, Places All!* 1949. New York: E. P. Dutton. (Forty-four square dances for anyone who wants to try them.)

La Farge, Rod. *Swingo: 20 North Jersey Singing Calls.* 1946. Haledon, New Jersey. 22 pages. (For honey-throated singing callers only.)

Linnell, Rod. "Square Dances from a Yankee Caller's Clipboard." 1974. From *New England Square Dance Caller,* Norwell, Massachusetts. (Mostly squares of the modern variety popular in New England.)

McNair, R. J. *Square Dance!* 1951. Garden City, New York: Garden City Books. (A widely distributed book for general dancing audience. Look in second-hand bookstores.)

Maddocks, Durward. *Swing Your Partners.* 1950. New York: Stephen Daye Press. (Good general book.)

Mayo, Margot. *The American Square Dance.* 1964. New York: Oak Publications.

Michl, Ed. *Build Your Hash.* 1963. Coshoston, Ohio. (For auctioneer-style callers interested in hot-hash calling.)

Orlich, Will. *Gimmicks.* Sandusky, Ohio: American Square Dance. (Part of the Callers' Aid Series.)

Orlich, Will. *How to Be a Smooth Dancer*. 1971. Sandusky, Ohio: American Square Dance. (For dancers.)

Orlich, Will. *Square Dance Choreography*. 1970. Bradenton, Florida. (American Square Dance Caller Aid Series.)

Owens, Lee. *Advanced Square Dance Figures of the West and Southwest*. 1950. Palo Alto, California: Pacific Books. (For callers.)

Peters, Bill. *The Other Side of the Mike*. 1970. San Jose, California. (For callers.)

Phillips, Patricia. *Contemporary Square Dance*. 1968. Dubuque, Iowa: W. C. Brown Co. (Good for physical education teachers.)

Piute, Pete. "The Square Dance Party Book." 1950. New York: Village Recreation Service.

Putney, Cornelia. *Square Dance, U.S.A.* 1955. Dubuque, Iowa: W. C. Brown Co. (Some background material and instructional material for kids.)

Sets in Order American Square Dance Society. *Basic Program of American Square Dancing*. 1969. Los Angeles: Sets in Order. (Edited by Bob Osgood, this is the most widely used manual for callers and teachers.)

Sets in Order A.S.D.S. *Extended Basics Program of American Square Dancing*. 1971. Los Angeles: Sets in Order. (The next step after the "Basic" manual.)

Sets in Order A.S.D.S. *Basic Program of American Square Dance.*. June, 1977. Los Angeles: Sets in Order. This series of manuals for callers and dancers has been updated and revised to include 98 basic figures of American Square Dancing.

Sets in Order A.S.D.S. *Double Square Dance Yearbook 1972*. 1972. Los Angeles: Sets in Order. (Collection of dances from issues of the magazine. Also published in 1968 and other years. Thousands of dances.)

Sets in Order A.S.D.S. *Handbook Series*. 1960's and 1970's. Los Angeles: Sets in Order. (A series of handbook pamphlets on: Basic Movements; Extended Basics; Club Organization; Indoctrination; One Night Stands; Party Fun; Publicity; Story of Square Dancing; Youth in Square Dancing)

Shaw, Lloyd. *Cowboy Dances*. 1939. Caldwell, Indiana: Caxton Printers. (The book that started the square dance boom.)

Square Dance Callers' Association of Southern California. *Training Manual*. 1960. South Gate, California. (For callers.)

Sumrall, Bob. *Do Si Do*. 1948. Abilene, Texas. (From the town where they do the mysterious Abilene Lift.)

Surack, Jim. *High Level Square Dance*. 1972. Fort Wayne, Indiana: Jimco. (Two books actually, one for beginning square dancers.)

Wentworth, Walt. *How to Square Dance by Uncle Walt*. 1970. Uncle Walt Publishing. 114 pages. Illustrated.

WPA, City of Chicago. "How to Square Dance." 1940. City of Chicago. 12 pages. (Many cities offered pamphlets like this during the war.)

## Southern Appalachian Square Dancing

Few books have been written about this form of American country dance. Here are the ones I've been able to find, all of which are appropriate for accomplished and aspiring callers and dancers.

Hendrix, P. B. "Smoky Mountain Square Dance." 1941. Ann Arbor. 38 pages. Illustrated.

Leifer, Fred. *The L'il Abner Official Square Dance Handbook.* 1953. New York: A. S. Barnes. 127 pages. Illustrated.

Lunsford, Bascom L., and Stephens, George M. "It's Fun to Square Dance." 1942. Asheville, North Carolina: Stephens Press. (A nicely designed and illustrated pamphlet.)

Napier, Patrick E. *Kentucky Mountain Square Dancing.* Berea, Kentucky: Berea College. (The most readily available book on the subject.)

Popwell, Sheila. *Clogging.* Sandusky, Ohio: American Square Dance. (A Western square-dance version of the art of clogging.)

Smith, Frank H. *The Appalachian Square Dance.* 1955. Berea, Kentucky: Berea College. (The best book on the subject, with tunes and marvelous photos by Doris Ullman. Available only in libraries.)

## Round Dancing

As with the Appalachian square dance, little has been written about round dancing. Since round dancing includes many dances which been absorbed into what we generally know as ballroom dance, I have listed only a few titles here. Also, keep in mind that many of the books primarily on square and contra dancing include a few round dances tagged on the end.

Hamilton, Frank. *American Round Dancing.* 1973. Los Angeles: Sets in Order A.S.D.S. (Clearly written manual by a member of "Rip n' Snort.")

Harris, Jane A. *Dance Awhile!* 1964. Minneapolis: Burgess Pub. Co. (Good selection of standard round dances.)

Shaw, Lloyd. *The Round Dance Book.* 1948. Caldwell, Indiana: Caxton Printers.

## Children's Singing Games and Dances

These books are dance and song books designed primarily to be used with children, but that fact should not restrict their use. Many adults enjoy these singing games, especially in the southern Appalachians. The books listed here are not the only ones in this bibliography suitable for use by or with children: after many of the books listed in the other sections I have indicated which ones are good for schools or any group of children.

Chase, Richard. *Singing Games and Play Party Games.* 1967. New York: Dover. (Originally titled *Hullabaloo* and published in 1949 by Houghton Mifflin, New York.)

Cox, John H. "Singing Games." *Southern Folklore Quarterly,* Volume 6 Number 4, December 1942.

Gomme, Alice Bertha. *Traditional Games of England, Scotland and Ireland.* 1894. 2 volumes. Reprint. 1964. New York: Dover. (The classic collection by "Lady Gomme.")

Kraus, Richard G.  *Elementary School Square Dance*. 1966. Englewood Cliffs, New
    Jersey: Prentice-Hall. (Gym class dancing.)
Kubitsky, Olga.  *Teacher's Dance Handbook for K–6th Grade*. 1959. Newark, New
    Jersey: Bluebird Pub. Co. (A fairly comprehensive book.)
Jones, Bessie.  *Step It Down*. 1974. New York: Country Dance and Song Society.
Laufman, Dudley.  *Okay, Let's Try a Contra . . .* 1973. New York: Country Dance
    and Song Society. (Contains one marvelous dance for kids, "The Rum-
    ford," by a master teacher.)
McIntosh, David S.  *Folk Songs and Singing Games of the Illinois Ozarks*. 1976. Car-
    bondale, Illinois: Southern Illinois Univ. Press.
Newell, William Wells.  *Games and Songs of American Children*. 1963. New York:
    Dover. (Originally published by Harper & Bros. in 1903.)
Rohrbough, Lynn.  "Playparty Handy." 1940. Delaware, Ohio: Cooperative Re-
    creation Service.
Rohrbough, Lynn.  "Playparty Kit." 1940. Delaware, Ohio: Cooperative Recrea-
    tion Service.
Sets in Order A.S.D.S.  "Youth in Square Dancing." 1971. Los Angeles: Sets in
    Order.
Shaw Foundation, Lloyd.  "Dance Curriculum Kits." 1976. Colorado Springs:
    Lloyd Shaw Foundation. (Four kits available: Kindergarten; Elementary;
    Secondary/Recreation Dance; Special Ed., complete with records, teachers'
    manuals, etc. These are the only ones available.)

## Collections of Fiddle Tunes

This list is fairly comprehensive but not complete. Many tunes remain uncol-
lected, not written down, or lost. What's listed here are the major collections
available today. Most of the tunes in these books are appropriate for any type of
country dancing. (Please note that this part of the bibliography is arranged according to the title of the book rather than the author's names.)

*Allan's Irish Fiddler*.  One hundred twenty reels, jigs, hornpipes, and set dances.
    Collected by Hugh McDermott. Glasgow: Mozart Allan.
*American Tunes*.  Eighteen reels and jigs for square and country dance. Collected
    from the *Benacre Notebooks* by K. Bliss. English Folk Dance and Song Soci-
    ety. 1959.
*The Athole Collection of the Dance Music of Scotland*.  Composed and arranged by
    James Stewart Robertson. Edinburgh and London: Oliver and Boyd. 1961.
    (A great collection reprinted from 1884, unfortunately very rare.)
*Bob's Notebook*.  Two volumes of original jigs, reels, and other tunes by Bob
    McQuillen, Dublin, New Hampshire 03444. 1976. (70 tunes in each vol-
    ume. Great dance tunes by a prolific, soulful composer, who is at work on a
    third volume.)
*Clawhammer Banjo*.  By Miles Krassen. New York: Oak Publications. (Instruc-
    tional book with tunes as played on the banjo for dancing.)
*Country Dance Tunes*.  Collected from *The English Dancing Master* by John
    Playford. Arranged by A. W. Foster. London: Novello & Co. 1929. Re-
    printed by E.F.D.S.S. (These tunes accompany the Kennedys' books.)

*Country Dance Tunes.* Collected by Cecil Sharp to go along with his "Country Dance Book" series. London: Novello & Co. 1924.

*Favorite Jigs and Reels for the Violin.* Boston, Massachusetts: Ditson & Co.

*The Fiddle Book.* By Marion Thede. New York: Oak Publications. 1967. (An instructional book with 150 tunes.)

*The Fiddler's Tunebook.* Edited by Peter Kennedy. Hargail Music Press, 28 W. 38th St., New York 10018. (100 tunes: jigs, reels, hornpipes, waltzes and polkas. A classic collection with tunes for many standard contra dances. Also includes an interesting list of other collections of tunes.)

*How to Play the 5 String Banjo.* By Pete Seeger. New York: Beacon. 1962. (Probably the best book of its kind for teaching a banjo style appropriate for dancing.)

*Irish Traditional Fiddle Music.* Collected and transcribed by Jack Perron and Randy Miller. Three volumes of jigs, reels, hornpipes, waltzes, and airs combined in one fiddle case edition (4¼"×5½"). 221 tunes in all. Available from: Jack Perron, Harrisville, New Hampshire 03450. $4.95 postpaid.

*Kerr's Caledonian Collection.* A collection of 109 airs, hornpipes, reels, jigs, strathspeys, and country dances. Glasgow. (Hard to get in America.)

*Nathaniel Gow's Complete Repository.* A wonderful, rare collection of tunes published around 1800.

*The Nelson Music Collection.* Collected and transcribed by Newton F. Tolman and Kay Gilbert. 1969. Nelson, New Hampshire. (A collection of tunes especially suited for the contra dance. Mostly traditional, some original.)

*Okay, Let's Try a Contra . . .* by Dudley Laufman. New York: Country Dance and Song Society. 1973. (Traditional and original tunes to go along with dances.)

*Old Time Fiddle Tunes for Banjo.* By John Burke. New York: Oak Pulications. (Instructional book, especially good for southern dances.)

*Old Time Fiddle Tunes for the Guitar.* By Richard Lieberson. New York: Oak Publications. (Instructional book good for southern music and dance.)

*The Old Time Fiddler's Repertory.* By R. P. Christenson. Columbia, Missouri. 1973. (Interesting collection of tunes from a selection of fiddlers from the Midwest and Southwest.)

*Old Time Jigs, and Reels for the Violin.* Boston, Massachusetts: Ditson & Co.

*O'Neill's Music of Ireland.* Reprint of 1903 edition by Dan Michael Collins. New York. (Over a thousand jigs, reels, airs, waltzes, and hornpipes.)

*One Thousand Fiddle Tunes.* Chicago: M. M. Cole Publishing Company. 1940, 1967. (The most common, easily obtainable collection of tunes. By far the best overall book.)

*The Ralph Page Book of Contras.* By Ralph Page. London: E.F.D.S.S. 1969. (Many original tunes, as well as traditional ones, to go along with the dances.)

*Riley's Flute Melodies.* Edward Riley. New York: Country Dance and Song Society. (Reprint of tunes from 1814–1820.)

*The Robbins Collection.* Two hundred jigs, reels, and country dances for violin, flute, or mandolin. New York: Robbins Music Corp. 1933, 1961.

*Scottish Fiddle Music.*    Composed by William Marshall. A complete collection of the published works of the 18th century Scottish composer. Over 200 dance tunes, slow airs, etc. Available from: Caledonia Press, Box 151, Harrisville, New Hampshire 03450. $5.95 postpaid.

*The Scottish Violinist.*    By J. Scott Skinner. Glasgow: Bayley & Ferguson, Ltd. (Skinner composed in the traditional idiom during the beginning of the twentieth century.)

*Square Dance Chord Book.*    By Jack Sloanaker. Available from Andy's Front Hall, Voorheesville, New York. (Chords for 150 commonly played square and contra dance tunes.)

*Traditional Music of America.*    Fiddle tunes. Hatboro, Pennsylvania: The Folklore Association. 1965. Reprint from 1940 edition.

*200 Jigs, Reels, etc.*    Collected by Frank Harding. New York: Paul Pioneer Music Co. 1928.

*Welling's Hartford Tunebook.*    Collected by William B. Welling. Hartford, Connecticut. 1974. (55 fiddle tunes from the United States and Canada.)

## Book Sources

This section lists commercial distributors who will supply some of the books mentioned in the bibliography, including the books of fiddle tunes. Libraries and archives are listed in the following section.

Andy's Front Hall.
RD 1 Wormer Road,
Voorheesville, New York 12186.
   Primarily a distributor of records, Andy Spence also offers many fine books on contra dancing, especially collections of tunes.

Council of the Southern Mountains Bookstore.
Berea, Kentucky 40403.
   This bookstore offers a large selection of written material on dance in the southern mountains, as well as the best selection of general material on this area of America. Write to them for a catalogue which costs $1 and is well worth it.

Country Dance and Song Society of America, Inc. (C.D.S.S.).
55 Christopher Street,
New York, New York 10014.
   Essentially, the American branch of the E.F.D.S.S., C.D.S.S. carries everything the parent organization carries. It also sponsors dances and operates a special dance camp. Catalogue available on request.

English Folk Dance and Song Society (E.F.D.S.S.).
Cecil Sharp House,
2 Regents Park Road,
London, NW 1, England.

> The society publishes many books of its own and keeps a good sized inventory of other materials available. They sponsor dances all over Great Britain through branches of the society. Catalogue is available on request.

Legacy Books.
Box 494, Hatboro, Pennsylvania
19040.

> This company has the largest listing of books available pertaining to country dance and music, as well as other folk related topics. Write to them for a catalogue. Free.

Ralph Page.
*Northern Junket,*
117 Washington Street,
Keene, New Hampshire 03431.

> Through his magazine *Northern Junket,* Mr. Page offers a limited list of fine books you can't get anywhere else. Write to him for any back issue with the list for 50 cents, or subscribe to *Northern Junket* for $4.50 for 10 issues.

Sets in Order American Square Dance Society.
462 N. Robertson Boulevard,
Los Angeles, California 90048.

> Sets in Order distributes Caller/Teacher manuals and handbooks on Western square dance and related topics. List available on request.

Lloyd Shaw Foundation.
1890 Darlee Court,
Lakewood, Colorado 80215.

> The Foundation offers a large selection of written material, films, and recordings including Shaw's own *Cowboy Dances.* Write to them for a catalogue.

## Libraries and Archives

This section lists the major libraries and archives, holding materials on country dancing in America. These collections are the most comprehensive ones that are available to the general public. Books that are out of print can be found in them, as well as specialized unpublished papers on country dance. I have also found that most other libraries (i.e. college and public libraries) carry a decent selection of books on country dancing. Libraries are often confused about how to catalogue country dance material, so be sure to check "Country Dance," "Folk Dance," and "Square Dance," when looking for a title.

American Antiquarian Society. Worcester, Massachusetts. This specialized library has a large collection of rare dance material available for the researcher. An appointment must be made to gain access to the material.

Berea College Library. Berea, Kentucky. A fine collection of dance material, some of it rare, specializing in material on the South.

Country Dance and Song Society of America, Inc. 55 Christopher Street, New York 10014. This small collection is generally available for members only.

The Library of Congress. Washington, D.C. A surprisingly limited collection, but respectable.

New York Public Library. "The Dance Collection," housed at Lincoln Center in New York, is indisputably the most comprehensive collection of common and rare dance and dance music materials.

Sets in Order American Square Dance Society. 463 N. Robertson Boulevard, Los Angeles, California 90048. The library here is loosely organized but very good. Better organized is the archive of area publications. Call or write for permission to research.

The Lloyd Shaw Foundation. The Foundation offers two services: a library in Colorado Springs, which is indexed, and a new Archives Division headed by W. M. Litchman at 1620 Los Alamos, S. W. Albuquerque, New Mexico.

Smithsonian Institution. Washington, D.C. Some good materials, especially recordings and other ephemera, such as costume.

State libraries, historical societies, local colleges, and city and town libraries. These are the best sources for localized materials which you will not find in larger collections. Some items typically found are: local callers' publications, musicians' preferred music, descriptions of dances from old newspapers on microfilm.

## Recordings

This section lists mainly recordings which are used to teach country dancing and records fiddlers use to learn tunes. I have selected a few recordings of Irish, English, Scottish, American, French Canadian, and Nova Scotian origin that contain tunes popular today and, in some cases, for hundreds of years. It should be noted that not every tune on these records is a dance tune, although most are. Also, there are many, many more recordings of this type of traditional music available than what is listed here and I have not even listed any of the hundreds of records used by Western square dance callers. Major distributers of western recordings, as well as distributors of traditional dance music are listed in the next section, and these distributors will usually supply catalogues of records upon request.

Bannerman, Glenn. "Appalachian Clogging and Big Circle Mountain Square Dancing." "Big Circle Mountain Square Dancing." (Both records are instructional, with music by the Blackhawk Bluegrass Band.) Available from Council of the Southern Moutains Bookstore, Berea, Kentucky.

The Boys of the Lough. "The Boys of the Lough." Leader LER 2086. "The Boys of the Lough 2." Rounder 3006. "Live at Passim." Philo 1026. "Lochaber No More." Philo 1031.

Carignan, Jean. "Old Time Fiddle Tunes," Folkways 3531. "Jean Carignan." Philo 2001.

The Cheviot Ranters. "The Sound of the Cheviots" Topic 12T214. "The Cheviot Hills." Topic 12T222. "Cheviot Barn Dance." Topic 12T245.

The Chieftains. "The Chieftains 1." Claddagh CC2. "The Chieftains 2." Claddagh CC7. "The Chieftains 3." Claddagh CC10. "The Chieftains 4." Claddagh CC14. "The Chieftains 5." Island ILPS 93.

"The Complete Dancing Master." An anthology of English Dance music, with interspersed readings from literature. Island records. HELP 17.

F & W String Band. "F & W String Band." F & W 1. "F & W String Band, Vol. 2," F & W 2.

Fitzgerald, Winston "Scotty." Fitzgerald, a master fiddler from Canada, has a number of albums on Celtic Records, the Canadian equivalent of London.

Fraley, J. P. "Wild Rose on the Mountain." Rounder 0037. (Fine southern fiddler.)

Ganella, Ron. "Fiddler's Fancy." Lismor LILP 5017. "The Gow Collection." Lismor. (A virtuoso Scottish fiddler.)

Highwoods String Band. "Dance All Night." Rounder 0045.

J'Etais Au Bal. An anthology of Cajun dance music. Swallow 6020.

Laufman, Dudley, and The Canterbury Orchestra. "The Canterbury Orchestra." F & W 3. "The Canterbury Orchestra Meets the F & W String Band." "Mistwold." F & W 5. "Itinerant Musicians License." F & W. "Swinging on a Gate." Front Hall FH 03.

Miller, Rodney and Randy. "Castles in the Air." Fretless (Philo) 119.

Na Fili. "Farewell to Connaught." Outlet SOLP 1010. "Na Fili 3." Outlet SOLP 1017.

Perron, Jack with Miller, Randy, and Yeats, Caitriona. "Irish Tunes." Pear Tree PT 101. 45 rpm.

Sets in Order American Square Dance Society. "Basic Fundamentals of Square Dancing." 4 albums available: LP 6001, 6002, 6003, 6501.

Shetland Fiddlers. "Da Forty Fiddlers." Leader LED 2052.

Spence, Bill with Fennig's All Star String Band. "The Hammered Dulcimer." Front Hall FH 01. "Saturday Night in the Provinces." Front Hall 05.

"Square Dance with Soul." With Rev. F.D. Kirkpatrick and the Hearts/Asch. (Available from Council of the Southern Mountains Bookstore, Berea, Kentucky.)

Tolman, Newton F., and Gilbert, Kay. "The Nelson Music Collection." (Tunes to accompany their book, available from N. F. Tolman, Nelson, New Hampshire.)

# Record Sources

This section of the catalogue lists major distributors of records for all kinds of country dance in America: southern, contra, and Western square dancing. I should first say that there are well over fifty recording companies involved in producing Western square dance music, and I have only listed a few. A complete list can be obtained through LEGACY, the organization that ties together all the components of the world of the Western square dance. Unless otherwise noted, a catalogue is available free from these companies.

Andy's Front Hall.   RD 1 Wormer Road, Voorheesville, New York 12186.
> Andy's offers a very wide selection of music appropriate for contra dance and southern mountain dance.

Council of the Southern Mountains Bookstore.   Berea, Kentucky 40403.
> The CSM Bookstore offers many records for southern mountain dance. The catalogue costs $1.

Country Dance and Song Society.   55 Christopher Street, New York 10014.
> A mimeographed list of records is available.

English Folk Dance and Song Society.   Cecil Sharp House, 2 Regents Park Road, London, NW 1, England.

Folk Dancer Record Service.   P.O. Box 201, Flushing, New York.

Folkways Records.   43 West 61 Street, New York, New York 10023.

Grenn, Inc.   P.O. Box 216, Bath, Ohio 44210.
> (Western square dance records.)

June Appal Records.   Box 743, Whitesburg, Kentucky 42858.
> (Southern music.)

Kalox Record Co.   2822 Live Oak Drive, Mesquite, Texas 75149.
> (Western square dance records.)

Philo Records, Inc.   The Barn, North Ferrisburg, Vermont 05473.
> (Fine selection of American, French Canadian, and Irish artists.)

Red Boot Records.   Route 8, College Hills, Greeneville, Tennessee 37743.
> (Western square dance records.)

Rounder Records.   186 Willow Avenue, Somerville, Massachusetts 02114.
> (Wide selection of artists from the South, New England, and foreign lands.)

Sets in Order American Square Dance Society.   462 N. Robertson Boulevard, Los Angeles, California 90048.
> (Wide selection of Western square dance records, instructional records, and Callers' Supplies: microphones, etc.)

Lloyd Shaw Foundation.   1890 Darlee Court, Lakewood, Colorado 80215.
> (Good selection of square, contra, and round dance records. Instructional materials on records for children.)

Wagon Wheel Records.   P.O. Box 364, Arvada, Colorado 80002.
> (Western square dance records.)

## Films

Few documentary films on country dancing have been made, but the following list does not include film footage that may exist in an unedited state in some archives.

"American Dance."   10 minutes. Color. Film on the Lloyd Shaw Foundation. Available in 8mm. and 16mm. from the Foundation, 1890 Darlee Court, Lakewood, Colorado 80215.

"Country Corners."   The tradition of the contra dance in New England. 26½ minutes. Color. 16 mm. Produced by Robert Fiore and Richard Nevell. Available from Phoenix Films, 470 Park Avenue South, New York 10016.

"Tomorrow's People."   25 Minutes. Color. Film by Appalshop, Whitesburg, Kentucky, with a brief scene of a southern mountain dance at the end. 16mm.

"The Visible Anthem."   30 minutes. Color. Film about the Lloyd Shaw Foundation. 16mm. Available from the Foundation.

## Periodicals and Newsletters

This list of periodicals and newsletters that deal with country dance and music does not include magazines such as *Dance Perspectives,* which deal primarily with classical and modern dance, though these magazines occasionally do publish an article on country dance. It is worth checking back issues in a library that receives these magazines. Most of the magazines listed below are available through subscription only and not on newsstands; they are sometimes available in libraries. I have not included area publications that list Western square dance activities, since they are so numerous. Every August *Square Dancing* magazine publishes a list of all such square-dance publications, along with lists of club associations, callers associations, and information volunteers throughout the world—and you can write to Sets in Order specifically requesting that issue.

*American Old Time Fiddlers' News.*
6141 Morrill Avenue,
Lincoln, Nebraska 68507.
Ed., Delores De Ryke.

*American Square Dance.*
Box 788,
Sandusky, Ohio 44870.
Ed., Stan Burdick.

*Banjo Newsletter.*
1310 Hawkins Lane,
Annapolis, Maryland 21401.

*Council of the Southern Mountains Bookstore Catalogue.*
Berea, Kentucky 40403.

*Country Dance and Song.*
55 Christopher Street, New York, New York 10014.
Magazine of the society, comes
with membership dues.

*Devil's Box.*
Clarksville, Tennessee.
(For Fiddlers.)

*Dulcimer Players News.*
P.O. Box 157,
Front Royal, Virginia 22630.
Ed., Phil Mason.

*English Dance and Song*
Cecil Sharp House, 2 Regents Park Road,
London, NW1, England. (The magazine of
the E.F.D.D.S. society.)

*Fiddlers' News.*
Northeast Fiddlers' Association,
Stowe, Vermont.

*Folk Scene.*
P.O. Box 64545.
Los Angeles, California 90064.

*Foxfire Magazine.*
Rabun Gap,
Georgia 30568. (The magazine that became three
bestselling books.)

*The Intercom.*
A directory of single square dancers
in the U.S.A. Write to J.D. Bell,
P.O. Box 408,
Bromfield, Texas. 79316.

*Journal of American Folklore.*
Library of Congress,
Archive of American Folklore,
Washington, D.C.

*Mugwumps.*
12704 Barbara Road,
Silver Spring, Maryland 20906.
(Good marketplace for instruments.)

*The New England Caller.*
Box NC,
Norwell, Massachusetts 02061.
Ed., Charlie Baldwin (also publishes a New England
Callers' Directory).

*Northern Junket.*
117 Washington Street,
Keene, New Hampshire 03431.
Ed., Ralph Page. (Straight talk editorials, articles, etc.)

*Square Dancing.*
462 N. Robertson Boulevard,
Los Angeles, California 90048.
Ed., Bob Osgood.

## Organizations and Folklife Centers

Here is a list of the major organizations and folk-life centers in the United States, Canada, and Great Britain dedicated to the survival of country dancing. These resource centers and the people who run them can help you gain access to dancing just about anywhere anytime, for free!

The John C. Campbell Folklife Center. Brasstown, North Carolina.
    (Sponsors workshops in country dancing of different types.)
Canadian Folk Dance Society.   Toronto, Canada.
    (Provides information on dance activities in Canada.)
Chelsea House Folklore Center. Route 9, West Brattleboro, Vermont 05301
    (Contra dances every Sunday night; Contra dance weekends twice a year.)
The Country Dance and Song Society of America, Inc.
    55 Christopher Street,
    New York 10014.
C.R.O.W.D.   Central Registry of World Dancers,
    213 Winn Avenue,
    Universal City, Texas 78148.
    (Keeps Western square dancers in touch.)
Eastern District Square and Round Dance Association.
    Box 78,
    Norwell, Massachusetts.
    (Publishes caller, dancer, club directory.)
The English Folk Dance and Song Society.
    Cecil Sharp House,
    2 Regents Road,
    London, NW1, England.
    (Parent organization of C.D.S.S. of America. Provides the same services overseas.)
The Highlander Center.   New Market, Tennessee.
    (The people at Highlander know what's happening in the mountains.)

International Folk Dance Clubs and Societies.
    Check local college catalogues, adult-education programs, and ethnic folk-life centers where they exist—check your phone book.
Legacy.   Dedicated to square dance coordination.
    Write to Bob Osgood, Secretary, 462 N. Robertson Boulevard, Los Angeles 90048.
Library of Congress, Folklore Archive.   Washington, D.C.
    Publishes a calendar of folk-life events in the United States annually.
The Mountain Folklife Center.   Hendersonville, North Carolina.
    Sponsors folk-life activities: dance, music, and clogging, in particular.
New England Folk Festival Association.
    57 Roseland Street,
    Somerville, Massachusetts 02143.
    Sponsor weekly dances in Cambridge at YMCA, and annual festival in Natic, Massachusetts.
Overseas Dancers Association.
    151 Dryden Drive,
    San Antonio, Texas 78213.
    Keeps Western square dancers overseas aware of what's happening back home.
The Sets in Order American Square Dance Society.
    462 N. Robertson Boulevard,
    Los Angeles, California 90048.
The Lloyd Shaw Foundation.
    P.O. Box 203,
    Colorado Springs, Colorado 80901.
Smoky Mountain Folklife Center.
    c/o Jean and Lee Schilling, Cosby, Tennessee.
    Sponsors annual Festival of the Smokies and educational activities in schools.

## Major Events in Country Dance in the U.S.A.

While there are hundreds of events all over the country where dancing takes place, the events listed here are ones where dance is or is becoming a major part of the activities. Some of them, of course, are dedicated totally to dance. The events listed here have a long history of success. Exact dates can be obtained from the sources listed in the section of the catalogue entitled "Organizations and Folk-life Centers."

Asilomar Weekends.   Sponsored by Sets in Order, these are intense sessions for western-style dancers, with top name callers and teachers. They take place intermittently throughout the year in California.

Berea College Christmas Country Dance School.  A week-long workshop in country dance. Not for the casual dancer. Usually between Christmas and New Years. Write Berea College, Berea, Kentucky 40403.

Dance Weekends at East Hill Farm, Troy, New Hampshire.  With Ralph Page and others; 3 or 4 of these a year. Write to Ralph Page about them.

Fox Hollow Festival.  Petersburg, New York. A festival of folk music at which country dancing has become increasingly popular in the last few years. Usually in the beginning of August. Write Don Burnstine, Petersburg, New York.

Mountain Dance and Folk Festival.  Asheville, North Carolina. Started by Bascom Lamar Lunsford, this festival features clogging and smooth dance team competitions. The "World Series" of clogging. Usually in August. Write to the Asheville Chamber of Commerce.

National Folk Festival.  Wolftrap Farm, Virginia. Outside of D.C. Dance is becoming popular here. Late summer. Write to the Smithsonian Institute, Folk Archives Division, Washington, D.C.

National Square Dance Convention.  Over thirty thousand Western square dancers gather in a major city every year in the summer. Write Sets in Order, 462 N. Robertson Boulevard, Los Angeles, California 90048.

Pinewoods Camp.  Sponsored by C.D.S.S. every summer, this camp features English country and ritual dancing.

Smithsonian Festival of American Folklife.  Every summer on the mall in D.C., there is some dancing, which is occasionally participatory.

Tunbridge Vermont "World's Fair."  This country fair features dancing by and with the Ed Larkin Dancers. Usually in September. Write to the town Selectmen, Tunbridge, Vermont.